HEROES

and

GIANTS

HEROES
and
GIANTS

We do all we can, and it has to be enough.

DOUGLAS B. ASHBY

TATE PUBLISHING
AND ENTERPRISES, LLC

Published by Tate Publishing & Enterprises, LLC
127 E. Trade Center Terrace | Mustang, Oklahoma 73064 USA
1.888.361.9473 | www.tatepublishing.com

Tate Publishing is committed to excellence in the publishing industry. The company reflects the philosophy established by the founders, based on Psalm 68:11,
"The Lord gave the word and great was the company of those who published it."

Book design copyright © 2014 by Tate Publishing, LLC. All rights reserved.
Cover design by Allen Jomoc
Interior design by Jake Muelle

Published in the United States of America

ISBN: 978-1-62902-553-7
1. Biography & Autobiography / Personal Memoirs
2. Biography & Autobiography / General
13.12.13

AUTHOR'S NOTE

Firefighters in small and large communities alike are willing to sacrifice everything for those they serve. They lead exciting lives. Telling their stories was easy, there was no need to embellish or exaggerate.

These memoirs are written from my heart, and the incidents are true. Due to the sensitive nature of some of the narratives, I have taken the liberty to change some names, dates and locations to protect privacy.

"THE STRENUOUS LIFE"

"I wish to preach, not the doctrine of ignoble ease, but the doctrine of the strenuous life, the life of toil and effort, of labor and strife; to preach that highest form of success which comes, not to the man who desires mere easy peace, but to the man who does not shrink from danger, from hardship, or from bitter toil, and who out of these wins the splendid ultimate triumph."

—Theodore Roosevelt, April 10, 1897.

PROLOGUE

ALL WE CAN

I t was quite a sight.

Some little guy, not much more than five feet tall, pointing a garden hose at the side of the house as orange flames flapped out of the top of the windows like windblown curtains.

I distinctly remember thinking, *what does that idiot think he's doing?*

We were the second fire engine to arrive. The distance from Station 163 wasn't far; however, when you can see that amount of smoke in the early-morning air, you know you are going to have something. It was cold that morning in February, right around fifty degrees. It's the type of listless gray morning for which the snooze button was created.

Of course, firefighters do not get to enjoy the benefits of such things. We never come to work late; we always arrive after things have gotten started.

The call had come in right around the time of our ten-to-seven wake-up call. It was never called a wake-up call; it was an alarm test. Why we had to wake up at ten minutes to seven as opposed to seven was a question no one could ever answer.

The fire was in the tiny city of Cudahy, located in southeastern Los Angeles County. Cudahy is about twenty-five thousand people squeezed into little more than a single square mile, making it one of most densely populated cities in the entire state of California.

This is ironic, considering the Irish meat packer who lent the city its name back in the early part of the century had subdivided the land into one-acre parcels that were often only fifty feet wide. That meant the original "Cudahy lots," as they were called, were also up to eight hundred feet deep. That is the equivalent of having a backyard the length of three football fields, minus a first down or two.

By 1975 the lots had been subdivided again and again, the stucco apartment buildings had gone up, and the tiny city was packed with hardworking, blue-collar residents who still tried to put out their neighbor's burning house with a garden hose.

The lot was still good-sized, dating back to those early agricultural days, but the house itself was not. It was a typical single-family home for the neighborhood, two bedrooms and probably no more than a thousand square feet. It wouldn't take long for such a house to be completely destroyed, and the large head of smoke we could see from several blocks away wasn't a good sign.

My friend Jerry from Station 39 was first in since it was his district. He'd arrived with an engine and a rescue squad with two paramedics. We arrived a couple of minutes later, if that. Station 164, from still another district, sent a truck company right on our heels.

Jerry's crew from 39 started working on a hose line to the front, which I figured would do a lot more than someone with a garden hose.

As it turned out, I was a little off the mark.

Before I walked around the side of that burning house to experience one of the single most emotional moments of my career as a firefighter, I first noticed, as we all did, the screaming woman in the front yard.

Even amid the noise of the sirens and the smoke and the flames and the neighbors and the rest of the usual chaos and confusion that exists when a structure catches fire in a densely populated area, this woman would have drawn your attention.

She looked to have about thirty years and three hundred pounds on her, and she was dressed in a bright pink muumuu that billowed in the wind like a tent with a broken pole. Aside from that, it was the look on her face that stood out. It was like a neon sign at midnight.

As you respond to a scene, you've been given as much information by the dispatcher as is available at the time; nonetheless you still never know exactly what will be waiting for you when you arrive. There is always a wealth of information just from seeing the person waiting for you outside. Sometimes there is no one there at all, which is also telling. When no one is there, it gives you a real uneasy feeling.

The fire department does not bring victims to the scene, so the time to be cautious usually starts a couple blocks away.

The woman in pink had a look on her face that spoke volumes. It was a horrible sight to see. It was a look, unfortunately, that is familiar to firefighters and first responders of all kinds.

Shock, fear, pain, and loss were all etched across that poor woman's face as she screamed at the top of her lungs that her babies were inside that burning house.

A person screams a particular way when she is truly terrified, a sound I can never forget and one I never want to hear again. I have never heard that sound duplicated on stage or screen with any real authenticity. No actor has ever been able to truly convey a scream of real terror. Not like it sounds in real life.

Can you imagine the sound you would make knowing your children were in a burning building and you could do nothing to save them? You would be reduced to just standing by and waiting for others to help.

I couldn't imagine that sound or that feeling, until I became a firefighter.

It's funny, one of the reasons I became a firefighter in the first place was for the excitement. It was the thought that each and every day was a new adventure, never boring. I never knew when I woke up in the morning what I would be doing later that day.

Sure, we have our routines. Firefighting is borne of military men, men of precision and planning. It is also a profession that deals with the unknown, the unexpected, where anything could happen, and often does. Every day holds the possibility that something entirely outside my realm of experience will get my adrenaline pumping. As much as firefighting is about planning and predictability, it is also frequently chaotic.

Our job is to control the chaos.

As a matter of fact, when a civilian comes upon a fire scene, I'm sure his first reaction is that everything is out of control. Lights, sirens, people running every which way, crisscrossed hoses, radios, shouting, smoke, and fire. If it gets our adrenaline pumping, I can only imagine what it is like for passersby.

There's always a method to the madness.

"My babies! My babies are inside!" the woman screamed.

Jerry jumped out, quickly donned an air mask, and ran to the front door. He went in the house much too early; the fire was raging inside and the heat had to be intense. The smoke was thick, so thick you couldn't see through it. It's much cooler lower on the floor, so Jerry crawled on his hands and knees to search the house room by room. That was Jerry. He never hesitated, never waited for his crew to get the hose in place; he just barreled inside the front door in search of those children. Jerry could not possibly hear a scream like that and fail to act immediately.

That is what separates movie screams from real life, firefighters from average people, and Jerry from your average firefighter.

After he went inside, I went around the side of the house to make sure the nut with the garden hose wasn't in any danger. As I approached him, I could see he was aiming the water into a bedroom window just below the flames that were obviously spreading across the ceiling. I was about to tell him to stay back when, out of the smoke, a baby appeared.

Jerry was handing a child out the window.

I took the baby in my arms. It amazes me how tiny they are. After two children and four grandchildren, I am still in awe every time I hold a child. They are God's perfect little creatures, so pure and beautiful, so much the embodiment of everything we were put on this earth to be. Each and every one of them has the potential of all humanity in their tiny little bodies. With all our flaws and imperfections, our destructive nature and tendencies, it is the children who make everything worthwhile.

As I looked into the face of that child, I could see my own children. My precious boys were two and five at the time.

The baby was in diapers and a T-shirt, and his little face was black with soot and dust. He was barely breathing. The morning was cold, and as Jerry handed the baby out the window, steam started rising from that tiny wet body. No sooner had I cuddled the baby to my chest than another child appeared through the smoke. Neither of the two appeared to be more than a year old.

The second one was in diapers too, dressed in a little nightshirt to cover his upper body. The type of shirt that has little bunnies and horses on it. He appeared just as lifeless as the first one. Appearing dead is definitely not the same thing as actually being dead.

I quickly shifted the first child in one arm and took the second from Jerry. I'm sure a mother would have handled the children more gently and with complete ease. I was more like a baker with two loaves of bread, looking for a place to set them down.

Only a few minutes ago, we had pulled up to the scene, and now I had two lifeless little babies in my arms. That is how quickly it all happened.

For the briefest moment, I wondered what to do; such thoughts are fleeting until instinct kicks in. When you look for that file in your memory banks regarding how to respond, the file is empty. Life just doesn't supply you with answers about how to save cold, wet, lifeless babies. This is why firefighters train so strenuously, because we need to react quickly in both mind and body, even if they don't always sync up exactly right.

Within seconds, I was surrounded by firefighters. I handed one of the babies to a paramedic who came up and was standing right next to me. We spread a blanket out on the hard ground and placed the babies there side by side. The poor little guys were just lying there, clothes and faces smeared with dirt and ash, their bodies still steaming. Now we began to try to save their lives.

Nothing hits us like children in jeopardy. It leaves a mark.

Incidents like this happen at light speed; you no longer get one problem solved, and another one occurs.

Jerry was still inside the house, searching.

I rushed back around to the front of the house just as Jerry burst out the front door and off the porch with a five-year-old boy in his arms. They were both covered in soot and debris that had fallen on the child in the center of the house.

This little guy had severe burns on his body.

It turned out he had been playing with matches, as some children his age like to do, and had started the fire.

Most people who die in a fire succumb to smoke inhalation. It's rare for a person to burn to death. The only thing more painful than burning to death might just be surviving the fire. The scraping of charred skin, the grafts, the operations. The healing process is excruciating. As I watched the paramedics load him into the ambulance, I knew that boy would suffer terribly if he lived.

He was about the same age as my oldest son, Colton.

As human beings we make choices every day from the moment we're able to respond to our environment. Regardless of intent, we endure or enjoy the consequences, both of our own actions and the actions of others.

Who can blame a five-year-old child for a decision to strike a match? Who can blame the mother for not having been watching him at that moment? Had she been momentarily distracted, or was she negligent? Even the best parents make mistakes. Life isn't always fair.

As a firefighter, you learn quickly that all you can do is the best you can do.

We are who we are, and we do all we can. Sometimes it's enough, and sometimes it's not. You accept it and move on. A firefighter learns that pretty fast as well.

When we pulled up to the scene, I saw the man standing in front of a burning house, with billowing fire and smoke coming from a window. I thought, *how preposterous, what fool believes he could put out a fire with a garden hose?*

Nevertheless, the water from that hose had landed directly on the two babies just inside the window, perhaps providing just enough moisture to keep them alive for a few moments until we could arrive on the scene. As a firefighter looking at his weapon of choice, I found it lacking, but it did just enough, and that's all it needed to do.

A pebble in the hands of David slew a giant. That day, that hose, in the hands of that man, had done the job. The neighbor did all he could with what he had at hand.

Perhaps he wasn't so different from all of us, after all.

Jerry ran inside that burning house even though some would have waited. He took the baton from the good neighbor outside and passed the babies to me. He did what he could.

Two little lives were saved that day, and yet, the five-year-old still perished.

Jerry did all that he could. Sometimes you win, sometimes you lose. Life is not always fair.

My friend Jerry received a commendation from the city for his bravery that day. I guess, as human nature will have it, he focused his attention on the child that was lost, not the two that were saved. Memories of those little ones and the hysterical screams of the mother will stay with all of us for a lifetime.

As firefighters we always suffer the losses much more than we savor the victories. At the end of the day, we accept what we do. A man who does all he can is a fortunate man, regardless of the consequences. We, more than most, understand life is not fair, because we live it every day of our lives. The lessons I have learned as a firefighter will stay with me always.

As I write this, my old friend Jerry has just completed a painful round of chemotherapy for a tumor in his leg and cancer of the lymph nodes. His condition may well be related to his service as a firefighter.

We have equipment and protective gear, but nothing is 100 percent. We all made a choice to fight fires, and we live with the consequences.

We do all we can, and it has to be enough, even when we fall short. This is true for everyone, not just those in my profession. Just like the good neighbor with his garden hose and Jerry with his breathing mask, everyone uses what tools he has available to the best of his ability.

We are all the same.

As firefighters, we see every imaginable type of tragedy, some that no one can possibly fathom. In order to move past some things, we have to separate ourselves from what we have experienced. It is not that we forget; we never do. It's more like we somehow find a separate place for those things that affect us most deeply, and we only go there if we have to.

I think of this as my special filing cabinet, a place where I put all the terrible things I've seen that would otherwise scar my soul. That is how we all endure the consequences.

I have been a blessed man in that I have a beautiful wife and family who were with me all the way. Not all are so lucky.

Until now, I have kept that day in my special filing cabinet.

Looking into the faces of those babies and thinking of my own boys, Chris and Colton, so close in age to children in that house, still brings me to tears. I'm older now, and more sentimental. I guess age has a tendency to do that.

I have never forgotten how I felt that day, knowing I had my sons and the mother of those children lost one of hers. The sights and sounds are with me still, as fresh as the morning after.

I went home and hugged my boys. Sometimes you feel that if you hold them just a little bit longer, they will be protected from life's tragedies. I wish it were that easy.

Even after all these years, it is a reminder to me how truly fragile we are as human beings, and how difficult it is to emerge from the flames unscathed.

We do all we can, and it has to be enough.

CHAPTER ONE

I WAS BORN AT A VERY EARLY AGE

How many people can say they lived in a community named after a big rock?

I spent most of my childhood in an area known as Eagle Rock, a nice, middle-class community known for, you guessed it, a big rock that looks like an eagle. Actually, it's an enormous boulder with an indentation visible from the west that casts a shadow that looks like an eagle in flight at certain times of the day.

Eagle Rock is a small community, the furthest part north in the city of Los Angeles as you can get. It's tucked away between Glendale and Pasadena.

My parents and my older sister, Sharon, lived in Burbank until I was about five, when we picked up and moved a few miles east to Eagle Rock.

It was a great place to grow up. I came of age after the war, when times were simpler than today. The soldiers were home, industry was booming, and Eisenhower was busy building our interstate highway system. Good old Ike liked his experiences on the German Autobahn during the war, I guess, and decided the highways were necessary to our national security.

Eagle Rock was well known for its hot rod culture, which sprang up in the late fifties and early sixties, right around the time I was old enough to drive.

We lived on a small cul-de-sac named Arbor Dell Road. The homes were all custom built in an area that was once an old lemon grove. We were within walking distance of Pasadena and the Rose Bowl.

It was an all-white community. I didn't meet my first black person until I was in college. Television shows such as *Ozzie and Harriet, Leave it to Beaver,* and *Father Knows Best* resembled life in Eagle Rock—although to have an accurate portrayal regarding our town, you would have to throw in several Archie Bunkers!

The majority of the homes on our block were constructed between 1948 to 1953, and once you moved in, you stayed there until, well, forever. My dad built our house in 1949 and lived there until 2002. That is stability; it was the norm. Most of the neighbors looked out for each other, so as a kid you had more than one set of parents to whom you were accountable. I remember my childhood fondly.

I suppose I am painting a pretty rosy picture of my upbringing. I did have my ups and downs just like everyone. As Will Rogers said, *"Things ain't what they used to be and probably never was."*

As much I would like to characterize Eagle Rock as the perfect community, like all others, it had its hardships. Misfortune, it would seem, would always befall the house next door. They were the family I grew up with, and the ones I came to love. They were second parents to me, and they would help mold my character; they were who influenced my interest in the fire department. Their story started a legacy no family should have to endure.

Between Christmas and New Year's in 1970, the mother of the house came home to find life for her nineteen-year-old son was just too much; he committed suicide in his bedroom. She lived for several more years with this heartbreak in every waking moment until her death from cancer in 1973. The idyllic nature of the neighborhood would continue to attract young couples with all the same dreams. The residents of that ill-fated house would change, but the tragedies would not. On September 11, 2001, the newly married husband, returning home to Eagle Rock from a business trip to Washington, DC, was aboard American Airlines

Flight 77, along with fifty-five other souls who died when their airplane crashed into the Pentagon.

Our home was quite different. My father worked for the phone company, which back then was Pacific Telephone & Telegraph. It was a large company, and he had a well-paying and high-pressure job as an upper-level manager. My dad was a conscientious, hardworking man. I get most of my work ethic from him.

Dad got five weeks paid vacation every year, but most years he would only take three. When I asked him why he didn't take all of it, he just grunted and said, "There's work to do," and that was the end of the conversation.

That's how many of our conversations went. My father was a warm man, but he wasn't what I'd call a scintillating conversationalist. He was a man of few words. In many ways he was like speaking to a toll booth operator; if he could get his point across in a single sentence, or even a single word, what was the point in wasting time?

He was very much a man of his time, an introverted and nose-to-the-grindstone kind of person. What they used to call the strong, silent type. His mother died when he was six and his father two years later, so by the time he was eight he was orphaned, which had a lot to do with his personality and independence. I guess when you're passed around from relative to relative as frequently as he was at such a formative age, you become self-reliant. I also inherited some of those traits, however for entirely different reasons.

Dad worked six days a week, and didn't ever leave the house after seven in the morning or return before six. He always ate dinner with his family, and he was a good provider. "Good provider" is a phrase you just don't hear as often as you used to.

My sister, Sharon, and I had a good relationship and still do today. By the time I was eighteen, she was married and living in Lake Tahoe, where she remains today.

As quiet as my father was, my mother was garrulous. She was a beautician—that's what you'd call them back then. Today they are hairstylists. She had to be a chatterbox, since in a beauty shop, everyone shares the latest gossip, and she needed to be well versed in the art of conversation, something she came by naturally.

 ⁎

When I was eighteen, my mom died. The official cause of death was pancreatitis, but it was alcoholism, and we all understood that. She was only forty-nine years old.

Her drinking was obviously harmful, but it was never a demonstrative problem. She was a quiet drinker, as was my dad. That was just the way things were back then. Everybody drank.

Everyone also smoked. Mom smoked, but Dad didn't. So the way it shakes out, I was brought up in a hard-drinking, smoking family. Life was great.

My wife, Debbie, was brought up in a Mormon environment. One tenant of that religion, which perhaps is the one they are most known for, is the Word of Wisdom. Mormons believe drinking coffee, tea, or alcohol, smoking and doing anything to excess is harmful, so it is not advised.

Not being a member of the church, I was free to imbibe with no spiritual consequence. Hey, like I said, life is good! For a short time I abused that freedom, and those days are now in the distant past.

Looking back, seeing how alcohol shortened my mom's life, and seeing other tragedies it caused, I fully understand why it is called the word of wisdom.

I find it amusing that I came from a small family of drinkers who married into a large family of Mormons; whether that says anything about me psychologically, I couldn't say.

Another component of Mormonism, which is also notable, is their support for the family. Firefighters have a life unlike any other and I have never seen a truly happy firefighter who did not have a loving spouse and family for support.

Growing up in Eagle Rock, life was simple; all you wanted was a job and a car. If a guy had those things, he could get what he wanted, which of course was a girlfriend. I suppose it is the same today, although I think maybe you need an iPad and a Facebook account too. Maybe a little more money than I had back then. Actually, in Southern California nowadays, you probably need an agent.

In the fifties and sixties, the corner stone of our social life in Eagle Rock was the Boy Scouts of America program. Most of my lifetime family friends I have today, I met in the scouts.

Its premise is simple; teach youth personal responsibility, self-reliance, and family unity.

Early teachings for young men in the Mormon Church are through the scouting program. I was familiar with the scouting agenda and was excited to bring up my boys in the same program that taught me so much about life. I had the honor of becoming an Eagle Scout.

Both of my sons were also active in the scouting program. Through hard work and tenacity, they also achieved Eagle, something of which we all are extremely proud.

Scouting also added to the independence I inherited from my father. It made me even more self-reliant. I was a very independent kid.

I firmly believe if more parents today understood the value of the Boy and Girl Scouts of America, this country would be a much better place to live.

On my sixteenth birthday, at eight o'clock in the morning, I was first in line at the Glendale Department of Motor Vehicles office to get my driver's license. You truly could not be independent if you didn't have a driver's license.

I had worked ever since I could remember with the intent of saving enough money for my first car. I worked hard for that distant reward.

One of my first jobs was washing dishes at the local pizzeria. I was tired of mowing lawns for the neighbors. It's hard to believe dishwashing is a step up from lawn mowing, but that was the hierarchy of things back then.

At sixteen, I finally left dishwashing behind, and got my dream job at the time at Dave's Richfield Service Station. Back when there was service to go with your gasoline.

I was making the big bucks. When I got a fifteen-cent raise from $1.50 an hour, that was something. My dad insisted I pay for my car up-front, with no payments. He thought it was unacceptable for a high school student to be plagued with monthly expenses, so I paid $650 in hard-earned cash as a senior for my first car.

Like your first love, you always remember your first car, and mine was a '57 Ford. I thought I'd died and gone to heaven.

At Eagle Rock High School, there were several groups—hoodlums, jocks, college bound, and the car guys. I didn't aspire to the first groups, and I wasn't all that interested in academics, so that group was out as well. Since my major achievements thus far in life were a set of wheels, I handily fit the requirements of the car guy category.

I was definitely a car guy.

There weren't any major problems among the groups; we all pretty much got along. There was your occasional crossover. For example, a car guy's parents could press him to study harder to get into a good college after graduation, which pushed him toward the preppies. Still, we all got along.

One thing everybody had in general was we all wanted a car. Having a good ride greatly increased your chances of having a girlfriend, which was universal. I worked on that car all the time. I was constantly tinkering. There was always something to polish, clean, fix, tweak, or replace. First cars are like that, at least for me. Throughout my life that never changed. Maybe today, since the kids are all buried in their computers or iPods or texting, or probably all three (and *all* while they're driving), it's different. Especially with the computerized engines the newer cars boast today, which require an advanced degree or an advanced computer, or both, to diagnose.

Life was as simple as the cars were back then.

When you got your first car, you had to work on it. A car was every bit as big a commitment as a girlfriend. I don't remember which was higher maintenance. Not a day went by during my senior year of high school when I wasn't fiddling with something on that Ford. I loved every minute of it!

Now that I had the job and the car, all I needed to complete my life's desires to that point was the girlfriend. I had dated since I was sixteen, but nothing too serious. It was hard to get serious with a girl when your parents were driving you to the dance and picking you up afterward.

As much as a job and a car were status symbols back in high school, so was the girlfriend. Since I was a nice-looking kid with a nice-looking car, I wanted a nice-looking girlfriend too.

Well, I'm happy to say I hit the trifecta.

Andrea was absolutely gorgeous. She was everything I had been dreaming of, or so I thought at the time.

In spite of all my independence, I had all the typical insecurities of a high school kid. I was worried about my appearance, my status, but not much at all about my future. Having a girlfriend started me thinking about those things. Andi was college prep and would definitely be attending college.

I was a shop kid, someone who didn't think about the future; after all, that was a long time off. That's why they call it the future.

I knew my dad wanted me to go to work for the phone company, and I also knew I would be starting at the bottom, just as he had done. My father had worked his way up, of course, and that was certainly to be expected of me as well, but the business was also changing. There were no guarantees the same would be open to me in the coming years.

With all these things on my mind, I would have to say my senior year was particularly stressful in spite of what I had achieved. That's just the way life is. The more you accomplish, the more you pressure yourself to achieve. It is all part of the game.

It wasn't that Andi's parents disapproved of me; we got along. Her dad was a Los Angeles City police officer and didn't talk all that much, kind of like my dad. Her mom was a great lady, whom Andi confided in a lot, sometimes to my dismay. They had high expectations for Andi, and equally low expectations for me.

Andi was a year younger than I was. We started dating in my senior year, when she was a junior.

Eagle Rock High School had an overabundance of senior activities. There was sweater night, for when you received your senior class sweater, pin night, ring night, prom night, home coming night, and of course graduation night. Hey, we attended them all. After I graduated, we could have attended all of Andi's special nights, but we were a little burnt out, so we only attended the big ones.

While Andi was in her senior year, I attended Glendale City College; don't ask why. That's just where you went when you were non-directional. It didn't take long to figure out college wasn't for me; after all, I was a car guy.

The dilemmas of life; if not college, then what?

Life is challenging, especially for a young, non-directional male. My parents were always supportive; nevertheless there are some questions that a well-intending parent cannot answer, such as what am I going to do for the rest of my life.

My father suggested the phone company, and seeing no other alternative, it appeared a great one.

So once again, life dictated my path. I was, after all, a simple guy.

I now once again had a job, my car, and my first love, so for all intents and purpose, I had everything I needed. Then the unexpected: Andi dropped me like the proverbial hot rock!

CHAPTER TWO

TRAINING WHEELS FOR LIFE

I was crushed when Andi and her folks moved to Huntington Beach. It was only an hour's drive, but it meant a long-distance relationship, and those usually don't work out well.

Andi's folks were kind and gracious people, and seeing two kids in love, they did not want to stand in front of old Cupid. They decided Andi could finish her senior year at Eagle Rock High School, and so she went to live with her grandmother in Highland Park. It was as if our relationship got its second wind, at least from a geographical prospective.

Her grandmother was a wonderful woman, advanced in years and stone deaf. She lost her hearing at an early age, so she was adept at reading lips. It was somewhat slow to communicate with her, but she never let her handicap stand in her way. If we came home late and she had already locked the front door for the night, Andi would stomp on the wooden front porch so her grandmother could feel the vibrations and let her in. Once she was inside and Granny was satisfied her charge was safe and sound, I could knock as loud as I wanted, and Andi would let me in. Grandma was none the wiser, as long as we didn't stomp around.

Andi and I were always respectful of the arrangement we had with her grandmother—more Andi than me, but it did allow for some latitude with visiting hours. Some nights Andi and I would still be visiting long after her grandmother's curfew had passed. To keep from being discovered, I would be forced to hide under the bed or in the closet, but that's an entirely different story...

Time weakens all recollections, but nonetheless the lifelong memory I have of this elderly woman is that she would never let you leave the house without a warm hug, a positive word, and a smile; that was the rule.

I didn't realize it at the time, but this was a benchmark in time, a gate that all youth must pass through on their way to maturity. This wonderful woman was the start of many pivotal individuals that guided and mentored me for many years to come. There is a rather sad conclusion to my memory of Andi's grandmother. Years later, still independent, she walked to the local market, and upon her return trip home, was killed by a train she obviously never heard.

In a real sense, it still reminds me how precious life is and how lucky we are to possess it. We are constantly being reminded of how short life can be and how temporary we all are.

Andi and I lasted about a year and a half all told, the most formative ones growing up. First loves serve as training wheels for life. They are a template for things to come.

Life was great between us until she graduated. We had two different visions for our future, one she thought about constantly, and one I never gave any thought.

When I graduated from high school, I was in the middle of my class of about three hundred and sixty students. I was a perfectly average student. I would not have been at all surprised had I been the exact median. I had a motto that got me through most of my school days: *C's get degrees.*

I hated graduation day; it was a historic mark in time, when I was catapulted into the cold hard world. I had just lost the security of a high school student's structured life.

I was finding that life is a tapestry of memories and events, some good, some not so good. I wish I could say everything I have learned in life was from positive experiences, but that is not the case. The lessons that taught me the most were from the more painful episodes.

When Andrea graduated, things changed; boy, did they ever.

Andi was always a good student; she was bright, mostly because she applied herself. It was a given she would go on to college. I wasn't a good student, mostly because with so many distractions, college was way down the list. I didn't have that mindset. I had never thought about college; after all, it was way off into the future. I was a day-to-day guy. That's one thing about the future; it does have the habit of showing up in the present, and sure enough, here it was.

Being idealistic, I was hoping against hope we would find a way to make things work, but it wasn't in the cards, and finally the day came when I heard those words every guy hates.

"We should start seeing other people?" I repeated. "What do you mean?"

She just looked at me for a moment, which of course made me feel even smaller.

Of course I knew what she meant. I guess it could have been worse. She could have said, "I've come to think of you as a brother."

She said, "It's just time."

Everyone has a heartbreak in their past. It's part of the growing process, one of those painful ones you learn from, or at least you hope you have learned. You have to look into your own heart and find the best way to handle passionate issues like these. Everyone's tactic is different. There is an old proverb regarding the cat that jumps on a hot stove; he will only jump there once. I fit into this category. My approach was simple, maybe because I was stubborn or just wired that way. After a few words not chosen wisely, I said, "If that is what you want, so be it." I left and we didn't speak for another year.

Significant emotional events come in all forms. They are created by your own hand or regretfully at the hands of another. I learned at a very early age the only things you can control are your own actions. You can hope and wish with all of your might, but nevertheless you cannot control the feelings of others.

Life usually works out for the positive if you allow it. I cared for her and our closeness, but once it was clear we had different ideas about our relationship and what life held in store for us, I made the only choice I could. I needed to be with someone who was on the same page. Andi was not that person.

It helped make me even more independent.

During high school, both of my boys suffered similar experiences. I would tell them how I had solved my situation, which closely paralleled theirs, and they would always ask, "How'd that work out, Dad?" I would pause and say, "Not well. Didn't talk to her for another year." They would look at me and say, "That's supposed to make me feel better?"

I would then look at them and say, "You just have to follow your heart; there is no one single approach that will fit in every circumstance." Trust me, it will work out for the best if you allow it, and it did in both of their cases.

It is funny how life does work out. Andi went on to California State University, Long Beach, and graduated as a special education teacher. (Maybe she received her calling from dealing with me!) It takes an exceptional person to teach special needs kids, and I would imagine she found her passion. She did find the love of her life in college. He is also a teacher.

In a way, I saw that early heartbreak as a stepping-stone to my marriage, and so I have to be grateful it happened. I suppose all relationships by nature are precursors to the ones that follow, and the first love lost is always tough for anyone. I know many people out there haven't been as fortunate. Several years and many different relationships later, I would meet my wife Debbie.

I would like to think everything happens for a reason, even if we do not always understand what that reason is at the time. It's arrogant to presume to know the mind of our Creator, and yet people will always try. It is human nature, I suppose.

Most emergency workers would go mad if they had to find a reason for all the heartache they witness, so we deal with it, sometimes with the mind's old filing cabinet.

If you are lucky, you find someone to keep you company in the darkness.

Maybe that broken heart I suffered so long ago happened so I would offer it up to the *right* woman. Both Andi and I eventually rose to that occasions of our lives by finding the person we were meant to spend our lives with, I know I sure did. Recently Debbie and I celebrated our forty-fourth wedding anniversary.

CHAPTER THREE

STUMBLING UPON
THE RIGHT CHOICE

In Lewis Carroll's *Alice in Wonderland*,[1] Alice was confronted with a dilemma when she came to a fork in the road and saw a Cheshire cat sitting in a tree.

"Which road do I take?" she asked.

"That depends a good deal on where you want to get to," said the cat.

"I don't know," Alice answered.

"Then," said the cat, "it doesn't matter which way you go."

That is exactly where I found myself in life, so I followed my good old dad's advice and applied for employment with the phone company.

The Pacific Telephone & Telegraph Company was an excellent career choice for my father. It provided what Depression children sought, which was security and an opportunity for advancement. It didn't take me long to understand my father's dedication to the phone company. It was filled with hardworking, optimistic people.

One year after graduation from high school, I found myself working as an installer for the phone company in Glendale. I was one of those guys who would come to your house and install your telephone, or put in a phone jack wherever you wanted, and then climb the telephone pole out back to hook it up.

That job was a real turning point in my life. I worked there for only two years, and that time had an enormous impact on me. I loved the work and the people, it was a good job, and it filled a critical time in my life.

I was out in the fresh air much of the time, and it was the kind of job where you accomplished something every day. Lastly, and maybe the most important, was the variety. Something new was always going on. I was never bored. The job was filled with good people, and it gave me a career path. I decided any future occupation I held would require those things.

You never know how sheltered in your early life you are until you go out in the world and meet other people.

My job as an installer allowed me not only to meet a variety of people, but it also allowed me to go into their homes. Most were good people who were just trying to make it in life and wanted to get along. Every day you were inside their homes, what an eye-opener. I thought I was brought up in a Middle America home, one that was normal. The older I get, the more I realize there is no such thing as normal.

I enjoyed meeting people because I found them interesting; each had his own story to tell. Both my sons would tell you I could talk the ears off a cornstalk. Every now and then, I do like to listen.

For a while, the phone company was a great fit.

You never know exactly when or where, or even how life-changing events occur, but gradually my life was changing. Perhaps it was nothing more than maturing that comes with age, but at last I was getting some direction. Most think that direction is the correct path to take; however, in my case lifetime goals appeared in the form of which roads not to negotiate.

Call it an epiphany, or just a blinding glimpse of the obvious, but I knew the present road would not take me to what I felt were my lifetime ambitions.

I have always had a loving and supportive family, so when I made the decision to leave the phone company and give college another try; I had my father's blessings, with the most important ingredient, financial support.

Major decisions like this aren't easy; they are based on a multitude of factors. No small factor thrown into the mix was the conflict in Vietnam. The military draft hung over every young man's head. In 1965 the Vietnam War was starting to escalate, and if you were in college, you had the possibility of a college draft deferment. To any young kid, that was a biggie!

Right after high school, I tried my hand at upper education. Most of the car guys I ran around with went to Glendale Junior College. No one asked why, it was just what you did. Back then it was called a junior college; now it is a community college. The new name has a ring to it. I took twelve units and failed miserably. I did not have the right mindset; after all, my life was complicated. I was too involved with my car, girlfriend, and job. All my time and effort was reserved for them, so there wasn't much time left for anything else.

I didn't have the maturity for school. I had no direction and no focus, and college was a waste of time. It doesn't matter what it is, when you do not enjoy something, the chances are good you will not excel at it either.

I firmly believe it's better to take the time to find what you love to do than to waste time doing what you don't. I didn't like it, and so I failed.

I enrolled in a paleontology class. Before I signed up for it, I didn't have a clue what paleontology was, let alone why I was there. The instructor was friendly, understanding, and easy to talk with. When I discussed my difficulties with his class, he just said, "Maybe college isn't for you. Perhaps you should try the military." I couldn't believe my ears; that was the last advice I wanted to hear. What was this guy thinking?

It wasn't much longer before I flunked out and went to work for the phone company. I figured I just wasn't college material.

It's funny how a single person can affect our lives, even one as inconsequential as an instructor I barely knew or remember. At the right time, under the right circumstances, a well-placed compliment or criticism can make all the difference in the world. It is all about recognizing things for what they are.

Fortunately, the paleontology instructor's advice didn't carry the day and two years later, I had matured. Getting out in the world and working will do that. A little experience gives us confidence to go further. I was ready to try school again.

You can bet I wasn't going to take paleontology. I wasn't even going back to Glendale College. Pasadena City College was just a few miles down the road, in the opposite direction, in more ways than one. I was ready for a fresh start.

It wasn't that I did not want to learn; on the contrary, being non-directional, I had not found anything I enjoyed yet. While I was working, I took night classes, still searching for something I enjoyed. It was never about hating school. It fell more into the dislike category.

Before I could enroll in any classes at PCC, I had to take a battery of exams to determine which classes I should take. I was assigned to a guidance counselor. After I had completed all the tests, I went to see him.

That five-minute meeting changed my life.

He spent the first two minutes just looking over my test scores and shaking his head, and uttering sounds like *hmmm*, and *oh…* Finally, he looked up and said, "Some people just aren't cut out for college. Maybe you should try something else." In the back of my mind, I was thinking, *damn, I'll bet he is going to recommend the military.*

Being the astute chap that I am, I could tell the meeting was not going well.

He was taking his place in a long line of people who had low expectations of me. I had been exposed to this attitude for so long, I was starting to believe it myself.

I was having one of those pivotal times in my life again, another significant emotional event. I used my anger as motivation to do exactly the opposite of what he was suggesting. Maybe I was just sensitive because of what had come before, yet it turned out to be the best thing he could have said to me.

I took a leave of absence from the phone company and enrolled full-time at Pasadena City College, finishing my associate in arts degree in eighteen months. That included all the remedial classes I had to take before I could attend classes that were transferable to other colleges.

I realized those two advisors, one a professor, the other a counselor, had both inadvertently taught me valuable lessons: never give up on yourself, and always question authority.

One of my favorite movies is Mr. Magorium's Wonder Emporium. At the end of his life, the titular character (played by Dustin Hoffman), tries to impart the lessons he learned over a very long life. His advice was very simple, and yet poignant admonition:

"Your life is an occasion. Rise to it."[2]

Lessons you learn early in life are the ones that leave a major mark. They remain as the origin of my propensity to always ask why.

I am amazed at how many times the direction in my life was in the hands of another. When I first enrolled at Pasadena City College, my educational plans were to receive an associate's degree, nothing more. After all, I had been convinced I couldn't do it, so I had no further scholastic ambitions.

It is almost embarrassing to admit that I had been told, and so believed, that to advance any further would require taking two years of a foreign language, something for which I thought I had absolutely no aptitude. In my mind, a four-year degree required a foreign language, and that was that.

During my last semester at PCC, while on a break from one of my classes, a group of car guys were sitting around discussing the prospects of transferring to a four year college. Trust me, this was unusual; our thoughts were generally on subjects that were much more important.

They were all headed for California State College at Los Angeles. I was surprised. How could all of them pass the language requirement? After all, they were car guys too. I told them I probably wouldn't be going there because I was linguistically challenged when it came to English. I would never be able to master a foreign language.

They were as shocked as I was; they said LA State had no such requirement. In one single moment, things changed. The seeds of further education had just been planted.

What was said next was even more mind-blowing. Someone in the group said he was going to major in industrial arts education.

Boy, had I been stupid; this was the real revelation. Shop classes were what got me through high school. I was brought up with a do-it-yourself mentality. If something needed to be repaired, built, or improved, my dad would do it. Even if he had never done it before, he'd tackle the job. He was a jack-of-all-trades, whether it was electrical, plumbing, roofing, or anything else. Maybe it was one of those things children learn living through the Depression. He could figure out how to repair anything by just looking at it. He loved a challenge, and he would never take no for an answer. He never gave up. Early in my life, he taught me ten two-letter words that I was pummeled into believing: "If it is to be, it is up to me."

Maybe I could handle a four-year degree in industrial arts.

Good fortune was smiling upon me again. At the same time I was applying for admission to LA State, they were converting from a semester to the quarterly system. Updating all of the records and transcripts was an enormous task. When I submitted my records, every class was accepted, even the dumbbell classes I was forced to take. I would be entering as a junior, with a few extra units thrown in.

Good fortune sometimes strikes twice; I didn't have another counseling session with a naysayer!

Suddenly everything started going my way. Maybe I had finally reached an age where I could recognize opportunities. The two years I spent working at the phone company had changed me. I entered California State College at Los Angeles as a junior in spring quarter of 1967, a feat that still amazes me.

∴

When you are younger, blinding glimpses of the obvious tend to hammer you. In order to continue my college education, I needed a job. Go figure. Pure luck led me to the Pasadena Fire Department.

It took a mere nine years, and in June 1972 I finally graduated from California State University, Los Angeles, with a bachelor's degree in industrial arts education.

It had been years since I graduated from high school, and perhaps the most important concept I learned was that I am more of a disciplinarian than I ever thought. The fire department taught me I did not have the patience needed to be a high school instructor.

When I graduated from college, I was well invested in my fire department career, and I was yet again at another crossroad in life. Did I continue with the fire department or start a new career as a high school teacher in industrial arts?

Sometimes the best decision is no decision at all. I continued to procrastinate, and the question became moot. Like the proverb says, *At night, if you think about the sun long enough, it will eventually dawn on you!* I had finally realized teaching high school was not what I enjoyed, nor had a propensity for. The fire service was.

I did, however, continue college; I think it became a habit. It is kind of like sipping from a spittoon; once you start, you just can't quit. It's all connected.

In August 1978, I graduated from Pepperdine University with a master's degree, from the School of Education.

Both of my sons have completed college; however, the paths they chose afterward differed. As I watched them grow up, I could see in them some of my traits, both good and bad.

One followed in my footsteps; the other did not. Both are successful in their own chosen fields, and I am equally proud of them both. They also have beautiful wives and children.

It is said nothing happens by chance, there is a reason for everything. Sometimes opportunity knocks, and it takes a keen ear to hear it, or a large hammer to thump it in. Other times you have to create the opportunities yourself. Life is not always fair, and we do not all get the same chances.

Over a several-year period, a counselor told me something I didn't want to hear, and a student told me something I didn't know, all leading me in a direction I hadn't thought of. Much to my amazement, each of those tiny events turned out to be an opportunity.

CHAPTER FOUR

THAT'LL LEAVE A MARK

I didn't realize at the time what the impact would be seeing the recruitment flyer posted at the courthouse. The Pasadena Fire Department was hiring. Many serendipitous events helped to change my life.

It was a monthly event, going to the courthouse to pay your parking tickets. They are the bane of any college student. Parking in an unauthorized area would get you a ticket from a meter maid, whose calling in life was to make college students miserable. On rainy days the closest you could park to your classes was blocks away, so five dollars for all-day parking seemed reasonable.

It's striking how many random occurrences all worked together to lead me in the right direction, exactly where I wanted to be, where I needed to be. Some might say there is nothing random about it at all, because everything works together in some way to make sure we have all the possibilities in front of us when we need them.

I believe we always have choices; the right path is always there among them. The key is choosing well, and having the courage of your convictions. Sometimes the right path is easy, and sometimes it's difficult. However, it's always there.

Hindsight is always perfect, and it is plain to see where I chose wisely and where I made mistakes.

Applying for a firefighters position with the Pasadena Fire Department was one of the times I chose well, even if my two years there were ultimately to show me my ideal path lay elsewhere, with Los Angeles County.

In the sixties fire department entrance exams were all much the same. They consisted of a written, oral board, and a physical agility exam.

From the beginning of the exam process to the time you receive the postcard that states your position on the list took about six months.

Between five and six hundred applicants took Pasadena's written exam.

If you pass the written, you continued on to the next portion, the physical fitness exam. Then hopefully to the oral board. After this agonizing process, all the results were calculated, and you were numerically ranked and placed on a list for new hires. That's when all the waiting started.

I was number sixteen. Sounds pretty good, huh?

Pasadena is the seventh-largest city in Los Angeles County. It has a population of 143,000 today. The fire department has about 180 employees, so depending on attrition, a guy could get stuck on a list until it expired, and then you would have to go through the process all over again.

It all worked out well for me because I was able to go back to the phone company while I waited. By the time I was hired, I was old enough to be hired.

Twenty-one was the youngest age you could be hired, and thirty was the oldest, which was pretty much country wide until age discrimination laws were enacted years later, giving the older guys a fighting chance. Gender discrimination laws also changed and allowed women to become firefighters.

The last step in the exam process is probably the most stressful. Before you would be hired, there was the fire chief's interview. If you passed that, you would become a firefighter recruit, the lowest position in the fire department hierarchy.

At long last, I passed the final interview. It took a little over a year from the time I first took the exam until I became one of four that would make up the second training class from our list.

Jeff, Art, and I were all twenty-one and the oldest was Jim, at twenty-seven. When you are young, everything is relative, and twenty-seven appeared old.

Fire departments are extremely regimented and have a military-like command structure, so basic training is equivalent to training in the military. Everything was new and extremely physical. After all, why give book training to someone who wasn't going to be able to handle the physical requirements of the job?

We trained behind Station 3 on North Lake Avenue, which had a six- story drill tower built just for that purpose. It was eight weeks of hose lays and ladder evolutions.

The instructor for recruit training was a battalion chief. He would stand over us, bark orders, and make sure we did everything exactly to department specifications. He taught manipulative skill precisely how it was to be performed, whether it was a ladder evolution or hose lay. Your hand is placed here, and your foot goes there, that kind of stuff. Talk about micro managing. God help you if you didn't put your hand or foot in the right place.

If you have ever stood along the curb and watched firefighters battle a structure fire, it sure looks confusing. Hose lines lying on the ground randomly, and firefighters applying water in every direction. Ladders appear to be put up in windows and on roofs haphazardly. It looks disorganized. With a little luck, and through all that confusion, there is a method and a plan.

The first day at recruit training, you are exposed to hose lays and ladder evolutions, and your last day on the job you will probably be doing some type of training regarding—you guessed it—hose lays and ladder evolutions. It's that important; it is the backbone of firefighting. There are precise ways to pick up an extension ladder, ways to carry it, and ways to climb it. There is a way to run a hose line from a hydrant to an engine. There is even a certain way to hold a hose line so you are not blown over by the pressure. Each circumstance calls for a specific tactic. It can all change depending on the situation, which is why it is so important to drum the basics into recruits from the first day. At the core of these evolutions is *teamwork*. Hose lays and ladder evolutions might be the staple of firefighting, but teamwork is the catalyst that makes it all come together.

Fighting fires is a lot like fighting any battle. We are trying to bring control to chaos. Hopefully training and experience teaches you what you need to do in any given set of circumstances.

Jim excelled in training, and was as physically capable as anyone among us. I guess it was because he was older. We all thought he was the sharpest; he breezed through everything.

He did everything just right. He was quite impressive, but he couldn't quite get the hang of describing what he'd been taught in writing.

At the end of the each day, we would write a description, with great specificity, about the evolutions we had learned during the day. If you had been the hydrant man, for example, you would describe how you had stepped off the back of the rig with hose in hand and attached it to the fire hydrant. You would describe it in the smallest detail. They were called write-ups and you turned them in the following morning.

Jim performed well on the drill field but got behind in his write-ups.

He would tell the battalion chief how tired he was at night, and no worries, he would make it up the next day. Several days after Jim hadn't completed all of his nightly assignments, and as we were about to leave for the day, he was called into the training office. The battalion chief looked at him with no expression on his face and said, "Clean out your locker. We will not be needing you any longer.

That was intimidating. We had just witnessed twenty-five percent of our recruit class being shown the door.

We were shocked beyond belief.

The chief came out and explained to us that while Jim may have been good at drills, we were expected to write the reports.

It was about being able to follow orders. As someone that always had distrusted authority, that made quite an impression.

After two months of nothing but physical, backbreaking repetition, I was ready for six weeks in the classroom, which was funny, since I never liked formal schooling all that much.

The book training took place at the old civil defense training center with forty other firefighters from a consortium of other smaller local fire departments.

I finished *first* in the class. Boy, was that a shock. I had found my calling!

During my entire training period, no matter how physically challenging the days were, or how long the nights became doing those rudimentary write-ups, I could see I was starting to live a young kid's dream. The older I get, the more I realize this was the beginning of a long and satisfying career. One that would be more exciting than I could have ever envisioned.

After training, you served a year probation period, which included test after test just to make sure you were keeping up on your fire department studies. It was mostly busy work.

My first permanent assignment was Fire Station 6 on Raymond Avenue, which happened to be the neighborhood where Sirhan Sirhan lived before he assassinated Robert Kennedy.

Fire departments are like any business; they try to utilize their equipment to the fullest. Fire engines are like any commercial truck; they wear out, but they are unique in that they look as good their last day of service as they did the first.

The components of a fire engine are a different story. The engines are so clean on the outside they sparkle; however, internally they are worn out.

Most metropolitan fire departments try to receive twenty years of service from their first line fire equipment, and then another ten years in reserve service. Some departments keep them much longer due to budget restraints. The fire engines in the Pasadena Fire Department, when I was hired in 1967, were mid-fifties and sixties era. That puts the reserve rigs dating back to World War II and earlier.

The first line fire engine at Station 6 broke down and was replaced temporarily with a reserve rig, an early1940s Seagrave 1000 GPM pumper. Luckily, the repairs were only going to take a few days.

Seagrave fire engines were the best money could buy during the forties. Their motors were as dependable as the day was long. They only had a top speed of about sixty mph, though, maybe a little faster going downhill!

From the early 1900s to just before World War II, fire engines didn't change much. The captain and driver rode in the front seat, and the firefighters hung on anywhere they could, usually on the back. The fire pumps got bigger, the ladders got a little longer, but not much else changed. On the right side of the vehicle, just outside the captain's door, was a big brass bell. One of the older rigs in Pasadena's reserve fleet even had a hand-cranked siren. The wheels of progress grind slowly in the fire service.

We received a fire call north of the station and headed up Raymond Avenue. It was up a small hill, but uphill nonetheless. With the weight of the fire engine, and the five hundred gallons of water on board, we could travel no more than two or three miles an hour going up the small incline.

Responding to a fire with red lights and siren is exciting, but not when you are moving at a snail's pace. If traveling that slow wasn't bad enough, a kid rode up on his bicycle and kept pace right alongside, talking to me on the tailboard while we made our way up the hill.

It reminded me of the old W.C. Fields quote to Baby Leroy; "Go away kid, ya bother me."

"Where ya goin'?" the little smart aleck asked.

"To a fire!" I answered, half embarrassed and half annoyed. Didn't this kid hear our captain clanging that brass bell, and using the siren?

We finally got a little head of steam (a steam engine probably would have been an improvement, come to think of it), and we pulled away. I bet if the kid had wanted to, he could have beaten us to that fire.

I have to laugh when I think back to the poor little engine that could, bell clanging, chugging its way up that hill toward the San Gabriel Mountains at the speed of Schwinn.

The fire service today, after being in the doldrums for many years, has finally kept pace with most of the automotive improvements. You no longer see firefighters, with their coattails blowing in the wind, clutching the rear tailboard of a fire engine, nor hear the clanging bell!

※

A year after I completed recruit training, I finished probation and became a regular firefighter...sort of. I don't know exactly when they stopped calling me a dumb new kid, but it sure took a while.

By October of 1968, I had several fires and rescues under my belt, and was feeling comfortable. Everyone on the crew at Station 6 got along; it was fun going to work.

Your mind is a mosaic of memories. You try to push them into the recesses of your brain, but more often than not, they come roaring back in vivid color to haunt you at the most inappropriate times.

We were staying busy by responding to a plethora (good word, huh?) of different incidents, but nothing had prepared me for what was to come. As we arrived at the scene, you could tell this was not going to be just another run.

The home was small, well kept, and was set back several feet from the street. Most of the houses on the block were constructed in the 1920s. The neighboring homes were dilapidated and were showing their age.

Several police cars were randomly parked as if they had skidded to a stop. Pandemonium existed everywhere you looked.

The rig scarcely came to a stop before the captain started running for the front door. As soon as we gathered the first aid equipment and resuscitator, we were hot on his heels.

The rooms were small, and immediately off the kitchen was a screened service porch.

In the middle of the kitchen floor was the lifeless body of a little five-year-old who had just been pulled from a disconnected chest freezer. Lying next to her on the time worn and faded linoleum floor, was the body of her twin brother. In the adjoining bedroom, in the center of the unkempt bed, was the body of a seven-year-old, also not breathing.

All the rooms were crowded with firefighters and police officers, all doing their best to revive these poor little souls.

I looked around the room, and heartbreak was everywhere. The police were doing mouth- to-mouth on one child, and a firefighter was doing chest compressions on another. There were so many people in the tiny little room, I was reduced to just monitoring the oxygen flow from the resuscitator.

As if the sight was not traumatic enough, there were the sounds. I can still hear the voices of the police officers as they blew air into their tiny little lungs. After each breath, they begged them to breathe on their own.

It is not easy to purge those images from your mind.

The parents of two of the children were pushed into the corner, the mother with tears running down her face. Wanting to help, but not knowing how. Crying aloud, not believing what she was witnessing. The father had his arms around his wife and tried to console her. He stood there stone-faced, also weeping.

As soon as the ambulance arrived, the twins were placed in the back, still cradled in the arms of the police officers, and rushed to the hospital. The third child, also in the arms of an officer, sat in the back seat of a patrol car and followed the ambulance.

As we were returning our equipment to the rig, the neighbors gathered out front. None had dry eyes.

The next day the newspaper reported the children were left unattended, and had managed to climb into the freezer, the lid closing behind them. All three passed away.

When I started my career, I gave little thought to the psychological effects of how troubling incidents bombarded you. Being young and naive, I thought nothing could ever affect me. The late Chris Farley had a classic line in the movie *Tommy Boy*.[3] He captured my feelings when he said, *"Boy, that's going to leave a mark!"* Firefighters suffer from a different kind of mark—not the physical ones that everyone sees, but the troubling ones that are hidden. Every contact writes a new line in the journal of your mind. In order to survive haunting memories, the ones you chose to forget, you need to have a special hiding place.

Your mind is a photo slide tray filled with the knowledge of past experiences and significant emotional events. A reservoir that helps manage future incidents. When confronted with a new situation, your mind flashes back to the old carousel for ideas on how to deal with new situations.

In younger and more formative years, memories of prominent people make the most lasting impressions. Images range from when your mom first hugged you as a toddler, to when a gym coach gave you your first swat for speaking some badly chosen words. Painful episodes, both physical and mental, make up the most vivid feelings. The imagery stays forever in those trays. The process continues over a lifetime and never stops. Unfortunately, some memories, usually the troubling ones, can occupy more space than they deserve. It is a constant battle to push them down and replace them with positive ones.

Keeping with the times, the mega computer has replaced the slide tray. The terminology has changed, but the result is the same. Most of those files are needed to guide you through new experiences.

The ironies of life are what compose the nucleus of our personality. We become the sum total of those memories and the not-so-pleasant episodes.

The Nobel Prize-winning French philosopher Henri Bergson said it best: *"The eye sees only what the mind is prepared to comprehend."* I seriously doubt if he had firefighters in mind when he wrote that, but in order to make prudent decisions during emergency work, the template in that reservoir needs to be easily accessible when called upon.

It is one of the paradoxes of life; sometimes you need quick access to prior knowledge, while hoping at the same time that other troubling memories stay locked away in a safe place never to be visited again.

My son Colton would not be born for another two years, but this incident would shape my attitude for years to come. Boy, did it ever leave a mark!

I learned to hold and hug both my boys. Hold them as tight as I could, as if by doing so, it would protect them from life's tragedies.

If it were only that easy!

CHAPTER FIVE

I LOVED MY JOB.
BOY, WAS IT HARD TO LEAVE

Rumors run wild in the fire service community about when the next exam will be posted for the Los Angeles County Fire Department. Everyone I ran into for a solid week either told me about the test or asked me if I was going to take it, and probably both. Every firefighter dreams of working for a large department.

The County of Los Angeles has a population of almost ten million, making it the most populous county in the United States. It is a patchwork of eighty-eight incorporated cities and many unincorporated areas. It is home to over a quarter of all California residents.

Its population and geography is incredibly diverse. The county fire department is the hometown fire department for fifty-eight cities, including La Habra, which is in Orange County. It also serves all of the unincorporated areas.

The firefighters in Pasadena were no different; they were all talking about how they were "going to the county." I kept mum. I didn't want to burn any bridges. One of my strong suits has always been a keen understanding of my weaknesses, probably because there were many.

While the others were all talking about carpooling to the exam, I just kept my mouth shut, something my friends tell me is difficult for me.

Pasadena is an excellent department, so if I spent my entire career there, I would have been completely content.

Sometimes I felt as if I were in a stampede, caught up with the masses, running in an unknown direction regarding career paths. I knew a few county firefighters and they were as happy as I was, so what was the rush to switch departments? I was taking the whole issue of moving to the county fire department and bettering myself on unsubstantiated rumors. Not the best of reasons on which to base career decisions. I guess you could say I was young and stupid. After all, I was young and stupid. At least I was smart enough to know when to keep my mouth shut.

When the day of the county test finally arrived, I drove by myself to the exam, I didn't see a single firefighter from Pasadena, which was a shock to me. There is safety in numbers, and if I were to leave Pasadena, it would have been a tad more comfortable if I had done it with some friends. It was okay no one else showed up since I could continue to fly under the radar until the time came for me to leave.

Granted, in my naïveté, I didn't realize until later how hard it was to leave. I was secure in Pasadena, and going to the county meant I would be starting from scratch. The training, the probation, everything I had gone through would have to be revisited. They were just too comfortable.

Looking for new experiences would turn out to be a hallmark of my career as a firefighter and my life in general. I like to be comfortable, but maybe *not too* comfortable. I loved change and a new challenge. The challenges overrule the comfort.

I never matured until my thirties or forties, which is ironic, considering I was a respectable family man working in an admired profession from a young age.

After thirty-plus years in the fire service, and with kids and grandkids, I guess there's still that little boy inside who wonders how it all happened, and whether or not he'll be found out.

I was with the Pasadena Fire Department for a little over two years. It was a great place to start my career. The larger fire departments were the places to be back in the late sixties, if you were a firefighter. Bigger was better, and better always meant a more exciting career.

Another reason for keeping a tight lip about test taking, and probably the most important, is that the first time I took the county's exam, I flunked it. Of course, the next time I passed with flying colors. I guess you could say the second time was a charm!

The written portion of the test, and the physical agility, all took place over a two-month period. The exam was unique in that it did not have an oral review board, something all previous exams had.

I was on the list at number 167 out of about four thousand who had originally taken the exam. Not the best position, but at least in the running for a job.

Just as before, waiting on the list felt like an eternity, but I was finally hired.

I never told a soul until I knew I had the new job. It was difficult to leave Pasadena, but like so many other decisions in my life, once it was made, I moved forward and never looked back.

※

The county's training tower was at the top of a hill in East Los Angeles. The entire area is like a county compound, with the sheriff's department, county warehouses, the women's jail, a juvenile court, and other county facilities located close by.

Our buildings were ugly, utilitarian bunker-like structures and the oldest on the hill. The entire complex could not have been simpler.

The entrance to headquarters was through two double aluminum doors in the center of the building. The concrete walls were painted light brown, and the floors were highly buffed linoleum tiles. In an effort to make the building a little warmer, pictures of old fire scenes and past fire chiefs adorned the walls. The old photographs were hung way too high on the walls. The administration offices were to the left, and to the right, at the opposite end, was the fire chief's office. In the basement, known as the dungeon, was the communications center.

When I started my career, the entire complex was too small and antiquated.

The only multistory building was the training tower, which stands at the top of the plateau, surrounded by acres of concrete they called "the grinder."

The official name of the training center is the Cecil R. Gehr Fire and Combat Training Center.

Cecil Gehr was the fire chief from 1952 to 1953, and he was tragically killed in a vehicle accident while responding to a fire in July 1953. There has to be a better way to get a facility named after you!

At one end of the grinder is the training building. I like to think that when the structure was built it was state of the art. However, from the looks of it, that is hard to believe. The apparatus floor was just big enough to fit two fire engines, and the dorm, offices and kitchen made a bachelorette apartment look big. Two classrooms are located to the rear of the building.

I wish I could say I always placed within the top tier when I took an exam, but that is not the case. History has taught me however, that being promoted as the last candidate on a present list is far better than being the first candidate on some future list!

My recruit class was the last to be hired just before the list was thrown out. Our training officers would never let us forget that fact. Thirty-five of us started training on September 2, 1969, eighteen on one shift, and seventeen on the other.

The work schedule was long. The days started at promptly at eight o'clock, although we were expected to be there at seven. That was just one of those things that was understood. I don't know what would have happened had someone shown up at eight. No one ever did.

We would train until ten o'clock at night, and then stay overnight in the dorm. We would be up at six the next morning to clear out for the next shift. The only day off the schedule was Sunday. It was the start of a fifty-six hour workweek, a schedule that would last my entire career.

Even though I had been through training with Pasadena, it was not any easier from a physical standpoint. The physical training was just as tough the second time around.

The equipment used at the training center was hand-me-downs from the field. The fire engines were Crown reserve rigs. Not good enough for first line service, but excellent for training. They were sparsely equipped. As with most of the fire vehicles of the day, they were convertibles.

The classroom was just as you would imagine it, much like all others, with chairs in the center and a small stage up front. The area that surrounded the classroom had every type of fire appliance known to man, mostly antiques by today's standards.

The first day of training, you were promptly ushered into the classroom, and given a litany of rules and regulations that were to be scrupulously followed for the next eight weeks.

Training in September meant the weather would be hot, and sure enough, the days were sweltering. The training was geared toward making all the physical requirements of the job second nature.

The day started with a lineup on the apparatus floor, in alphabetical order of course. All of your personal protection equipment was placed in front of you, ready for inspection, and there were plenty of those. As always I was first in line, having a name starting with *A*.

A long bell would ring, and the day's activities would start with a lineup. The day's activities would end with a lineup. Every time you turned around, there was a lineup for something.

Everyone was assembled into groups of four, again alphabetical. I was always the first to do whatever was being taught, and to make the first errors, I might add. There were plenty of those.

The training staff consisted of six captains, three for each shift. The ratio of instructor to student was a lot better here than it was with Pasadena.

The captains were godlike figures who observed your every move.

You established a special bond with your fellow classmates, one that lasts your entire career. I guess misery loves company. Once you were in the field, you develop close friendships, but none like the camaraderie you had in training. After recruit graduation, the training captains would also take rank in that fellowship.

Mike Cook was one of the four of our small training group, who is a quick-witted individual and made training bearable. Our friendship and the bantering between us didn't go without notice among the training captains.

At the end of each week, you had an office conference with the training captains. This meeting was stressful, to say the least. Talk about the ratio of instructor to student—this was three captains versus one recruit, not enjoyable to say the least. Almost all of us were issued an "Improvement Needed" notice in the interview; to make sure enough pressure was applied, if you did not improve, you would be terminated.

I suffer from a malady that has *not* always served me well over the years. When I am stressed and nervous, I tend to smile. Perhaps it's a defense mechanism, but trust me, this doesn't bode well in many circumstances.

Mike's name would come up in my interview more than my own name. The captains would look at me and say, "You and Cook are having way too much fun here!" Being stressed to the max, I would smile and further exasperate the situation.

"Do you think this is funny, Mr. Ashby?"

"No, sir, I don't." Talk about a downward spiral.

After we completed our first month of training, the pressure was noticeably reduced. The impression was most of us would survive and graduate.

During the hot dry weather, several multi-alarm fires broke out. The best training is firsthand experience, so the entire class was loaded onto the training engines, and we would respond to the incident. Recruits were lying in the hose beds, stuffed into seats, and hanging on wherever we could. I don't think that would have met with California's OSHA regulations.

The county fire department has grown over the years, but the training center has stayed much the same. Space was maximized by converting the dorms into classrooms, and thus eliminating recruits from spending the night. Recruits work and were paid for fifty-six hours a week during training, so the powers that be decided to utilize every one of those hours, and eliminated the overnight stay. Most of us were pretty good at sleeping, and consequently didn't require any special training for that.

Our recruit class graduated on the last day of October 1969. At the conclusion of the ceremonies, visitors and their families were invited to walk through the entire headquarters building. We were finally able to go all the way down the end of the hall to the fire chief's office, which was like pulling back the curtain on the Wizard of Oz.

It was just an ordinary office, the same as the rest of the building. Plans were in the works for a new facility. It is said that the fire service is "One hundred years of tradition, completely unhampered by progress." Many big plans stay on the drawing board for years, even decades. Now, over forty years later, the fire chief's office is exactly where it was back then, except for the addition of a couple of doors. I guess that keeps the riffraff from accidentally stumbling into the forbidden territory. The office has been re-carpeted, though, I think!

The department is in the preliminary planning stages of completely redoing the entire facility, but with all the budget cuts and turmoil in the state of California, who knows when it will happen.

I became a Pasadena firefighter in July 24, 1967, and on September 2, 1969, I finally became a Los Angeles County firefighter. Those dates are burned into my memory. It was a long road, but at last my feet were in the starting blocks of the world's finest fire department. Opportunities abounded, and I could achieve anything I chose.

CHAPTER SIX

NOT ONE CLOSE FAMILY, BUT TWO

In the spring of 1969, everything was looking up. I had two years of college under my belt, and a great job as a firefighter. I even had a little extra money in my pocket. Life was good. What could possibly be better?

My friend Tim Murphy and I were going to meet for breakfast in Glendale. The restaurant was along North Brand Boulevard, where many of the old clothing stores had been converted into offices. Just before I was about to walk into the cafe, I noticed a cute young woman, about nineteen or twenty, sitting behind a large plate glass window. Young guys tend to notice things like that. She was actually moving, so I knew she wasn't a mannequin.

Debbie was a secretary, and because of the size of the office, her desk was placed close to the entrance of the old store and near the front window. There was a great view, both from inside and out, and she could do typing or filing or whatever secretaries do for Young Americans for Freedom, or YAF, as they called it back then. I can clearly remember, I couldn't believe how lucky I was to see her sitting there. I just had to meet her.

Not wanting to be rude to Tim, I went back to the restaurant and said, "Stop the presses, I have to go next door and meet someone."

"You mean the girl in the window?"

Tim had noticed her too.

"That's the one," I said, silently thanking my lucky stars Tim had blown his chance to be the first one in to talk to her.

We both ate our breakfasts quickly. My thoughts were on what I was going to say when I finally got to meet her. I couldn't concentrate or remember a thing Tim was saying!

As we walked into the office, I was so nervous I could barely speak, but we finally introduced ourselves.

She was even more beautiful up close.

I asked her about YAF, and she answered all my questions, even gave me some literature about the organization.

The others remained in their offices the entire time, another plus, and so the three of us shared a conversation for the better part of a half hour.

My mouth was dry, and I was running out of things to say, and I am sure her boss preferred her to be doing other things. I finally showed my true intentions, something I am sure she had figured out from the start. I asked for her phone number.

That night I read the handouts she had given me so I could carry on an intelligent conversation when I saw her again, which I was hoping would be soon. She told me later that hadn't been necessary, as she hadn't read all the literature herself.

I did my homework and she didn't!

We had a good laugh over that, which is one of the reasons we're so good together. Debbie and I laugh together all the time, and that has been true since the day we first met.

When I telephoned Debbie at home on the evening we had met, I asked her out for the following night.

She told me she was busy because the cousin of her brother-in-law Rodney was visiting from Idaho. Oh man, there is an excuse if I ever heard one.

She must have heard the skepticism in my voice.

"No, really. His cousin is visiting. Could we make it another night?"

When I picked her up for our first date, I met her family. I was nervous and didn't remember a single name. It was one of my first exposures to a big family.

Our first date went well, or at least I thought it did. Guys don't remember the particulars of first dates; women do. Debbie could tell you everything we did and where we went. What I remembered was we had a great time, and I was hoping we could do it again.

Do it again we did. During the next several months, we were constantly together, and I began to learn more about her and her family.

* * *

The entire time we were dating, Debbie continued working for YAF and I got to know everyone in her office quite well. Debbie served many masters, each interesting in his own right. Several would go on to become prominent figures in California politics, some even infamous!

Lessons in life come from all avenues, and I was learning at a young age those lessons come from the strangest places.

In 1978 Pat Nolan was elected to the California State Assembly. His district included Glendale. He held the position of Assembly Republican Leader for four years.

Pat is one of the most thoughtful, intelligent, and honest people you would ever want to meet.

There is no such thing as fair in life, and it is certainly true in politics. His final days in California government belie the true character of the man. Pat was prosecuted as part of an FBI sting operation called Shrimpscam. It targeted elected officials who accepted illegal campaign contributions.

Guilt or innocence does not matter in politics and to avoid the protracted mudslinging of a public trial, and the inevitable embarrassment to the family, he entered a guilty plea on one count of racketeering.

Pat resigned his assembly seat and spent the next twenty-five months in federal prison.

He had worked for political campaigns ranging from Goldwater to Reagan to Nixon, and after he went into politics himself had even been considered a possible candidate for governor. His conviction on racketeering charges ended all that in an instant, of course.

When he left prison he went to work for a branch of Chuck Colson's Prison Fellowship Ministries focusing on prison reform, and is the president of that arm today. You have to admire someone who learns from his mistakes and becomes such a positive influence as a result. We have stayed in touch over the years, and I consider him a good friend who helped establish my life long values.

I am amazed at the number of people who have had a pivotal role in my life. You don't realize it at the time, but as you look back, people from all walks of life form your ethics, character, and personality. Pat ranks right up there at the top. He is a true giant. If I have learned a fraction of how to overcome personal obstacles as well as he did, I will have done well.

When you are young, life holds many intrigues. Marrying and starting a family is certainly one of the big ones. Little thought is given to the melding of families, or how they will have an influence on you. What the heck, the good thing about being young is you don't have to think about things like that. After all, not too many months before, I was completely non-directional. Life was beginning to change at a rapid pace.

I was about to increased the size of my extended family many fold, and coming from a small family, that was a big shock. As in all large families, some members are a little more, colorful than others.

Debbie was one of four children born to Ron and May, an even split of boys and girls.

Debbie's older brother, Royce, who was star of the family in many ways, was a lad who looked a little like Tom Selleck, with or without all the Hawaiian shirts. Being the firstborn, much of the family activity centered around him.

Next in line is Sunny, two years younger than Royce and five years older than Debbie. Sunny filled the role of nemesis for Debbie perfectly. Sunny and Royce split all the attention of the family for five years before Debbie arrived, and now with the little one, Sunny felt put upon. That never changed over the years.

Debbie's younger brother, Kevin, is two years younger and was the baby of the family.

The communities Debbie and I were brought up in were almost identical. Burbank and Eagle Rock were much like the other areas of Los Angeles where returning GI's settled in during the early fifties.

Debbie's dad was what I would call a natural-born salesman. He was almost a traveling salesman, given that his territory was so large, but he managed to get home each night to be with his family. He sold industrial hardware and tools, but he could've sold almost anything. He was easy to get to know, personable and genuine.

He was a huge baseball fan, and coached the church fast-pitch softball team for years, as well as both his sons. When they were not at the park for a baseball game, they were at home, in the backyard, practicing pitching. Kevin became an All-League pitcher, which as it turned out, was one, if not the only highlight of his life.

Debbie's childhood and mine were similar, with social activities outside our home lives. Just as I was brought up in the scouting program and all the events and social gatherings that entailed,

Deb was brought up around the Mormon Church softball league and all of their various games and activities. Most weekends when I was scouting, her family was in the park playing softball.

Debbie's mom, May, was a stay-at-home mom. The kids never came home to an empty house. That is one of those blessings of the fifties and sixties that has been left behind.

With a large family the house was never unoccupied. It was always filled with family members or friends. Being new to this big family thing, I thought it was great always having friends around. Debbie thought it was the pits; you never had any time alone.

The home they were brought up in could not have been more Middle America. Perhaps the first bond between Debbie and me was that we came from identical backgrounds. Burbank and Eagle Rock might have been separated by several miles, but the communities were identical, both in looks and values.

CHAPTER SEVEN

I'D SAY IT WAS A BUSY YEAR

I had been out of high school for six years, and life had been treating me well. Changes were coming at an astoundingly rapid rate. Little did I know at the time that life would continue at an even quicker pace.

Boy, was life changing.

I was unemployed on the day I got married.

Obviously, that is not the most ideal circumstance in which to take such an important step, but as it happened, another job was just around the corner.

Sometimes I take solace in the fact that I was young and naive. Never did I realize when I proposed to Debbie there would be so much preparation for a wedding. Thank goodness she comes from a large family, one used to planning weddings. Her family did a fantastic job preparing for the wedding.

We were married on August 9, 1969.

My father and those close to me were scratching their heads and wondering why I would quit an excellent job just before I was going to be married. I guess they didn't see the big picture. That's what is so great about youth; you don't worry about the small stuff, like having a job! The thought of twenty-five percent of my training class at Pasadena Fire department flunking out did not deter me. Failure in county training was never an option.

I left the Pasadena Fire Department with fond memories and no regrets a month before I started with the county, so I had all of August to prepare for my training and to take care of a few minor things like the wedding and honeymoon.

A wedding between members in good standing of the Mormon Church is held at the Mormon Temple. I, however, am not a member of the church, but I like to think I am in good standing—somewhere—so our ceremony was held at a Mormon church in Burbank. A Temple marriage is a sacred ceremony, where couples are sealed together for all time and eternity, unlike our marriage, where like most, you are married "until death do you part." That distinction didn't mean a great deal when I was twenty-four, but now that I am older, it holds a much more weight.

I never saw the invitations before they went in the mail, so I had no clue regarding who was going to attend. Of the three hundred and fifty or so people that attended, about ten were from my side of the family. The ushers stopped asking if they were there for the bride or groom, so everyone was free to sit anywhere they wanted. If they had separated our families, it would have looked rather overwhelming for my "team."

After the ceremony, the reception was held at Debbie's folk's home. It was somewhat disappointing to my friends, especially my dad, that no alcohol was served, but everyone still had a good time.

Debbie's dad was the coach of the church's fast-pitch softball team, and that year they were in the finals, so many of the team's players showed up in their uniforms. Deb's dad was chomping at the bit to leave so he could get the team on the field.

They would go on and come in second in the Salt Lake City championship finals. It's nice to know where you stand in the family right off the bat (no pun intended).

Since I was between jobs, Debbie took a short vacation from YAF. We took an extended honeymoon driving up the coast of California and back down again, something I highly recommend. Both the honeymoon and the drive.

We were young and in love and we had all the time in the world to enjoy our honeymoon. Time was a lot more plentiful than money back then, but that didn't matter at all. I was back to my simple desires, and in my mind, I had it all. The girl, a car, and pretty soon, I would have the job once again.

We got back to our little apartment in South Pasadena, and the next day I started recruit training. The job I would have for the next thirty-four years, and the girl was forever.

Training was tough on everyone, especially newlyweds. The schedule included long hours and nights apart, but we got through it. It was quite a change from the leisurely pace of our honeymoon, when we were together constantly and set our own agenda.

Debbie was a little surprised just how regimented my time was to become, but she was, and always has been, a real source of support for whatever task I have undertaken.

∵∵

After I completed the training tower, and was in my first station assignment for a few months, we moved to the southernmost tip of Mission Viejo. The entire Saddleback Valley in Orange County was sparsely populated in the late sixties; it was mostly grazing land until it was developed into one of the largest master-planned residential communities in the United States.

Living in Mission Viejo wasn't our first choice; driving sixty miles one way to work didn't seem prudent at the time. It was difficult to find a home in Los Angeles County that was affordable.

Our timing was just about perfect, because property values would eventually skyrocket. We paid $27,500 for our first brand-new, 1,600-square-foot home in a new subdivision, with four small bedrooms and two bathrooms, and a monthly payment of $256.

The entire area had not caught on yet, so in order to entice homebuyers, we were given twenty books of Blue Chip Stamps.

Having a mortgage payment that was two hundred and fifty dollars a month is like a fairy tale today, but my monthly income was only five hundred dollars. I guess everything is relative. This is one of those tales every generation gets to tell their children: "Why, I remember when…" That also includes the story about Blue Chip Stamps.

I had finally joined the ranks of most firefighters and had to have a second job to make ends meet.

Debbie and I settled in as newly married, newly hired, and newly moved.

Both of our sons lived in that house. Colton was born in late March of 1970, about three months before we moved in, and our son Chris was born in 1973, just months before we moved out.

Coronado Homes was a community filled with children. Most of our neighbors were much like us, young couples just starting out in their first home, looking to raise a family. It was one of those idyllic neighborhoods where the air was filled with the sounds of children playing. It was an attractive community for kids. Everyone in the neighborhood was about our age, and had at least one child.

It wasn't until after we moved that I realized how brave Debbie was. Coronado Homes was a development at the far end of Mission Viejo, many miles from the closest store or any of the conveniences that surrounded her while she lived in Burbank.

In our tract only half of the homes were occupied due to the slow real estate market. Debbie had just turned twenty-one three months before we moved in. She would tell me how frightened she was at night, being alone with a new baby and having all the surrounding homes vacant. The comforting reassurance of her mother and family was at least seventy-five miles away. She never protested; she accepted the challenge.

The downside of being firefighters is you work a schedule devoid of special occasions. Thanksgiving, Christmas, and birthdays are just another day on the fire department schedule. It is part of life, missing birthday parties. Colton's first birthday was especially difficult.

Colton was our firstborn. Debbie, being a kid herself—she was only nineteen when we were married—was terribly excited to have all the neighborhood children over with their mothers on that beautiful spring day.

Colton's first birthday was in March 1971. I felt terrible I had to miss the party; I was working and so my recollections would have to be through the pictures she took. Looking at them has always been a bittersweet experience.

After the party we could tell Colton just was not feeling well. At first we thought maybe he was just tired from all the excitement of his birthday party. After several days, when he did not feel any better, we took him to the doctor.

Looking at the pictures from that day is still painful. The poor little guy is obviously suffering. There is something about the face of a child when he is sick that strikes fear in the heart of any parent.

Colton was sick.

All new parents have panicky feelings when they bring their first baby home, especially parents who are young themselves. There is nothing more terrifying than the thought of something happening to your child. How will I know if something is wrong? Will I know what to do? Will I be able to protect my baby?

Those pictures, even today, remind me of everything that's wonderful and frightening about having children. They are so tiny, fragile, and resilient. The thought of your life without them is absolutely excruciating.

Until you have a child, it is almost impossible to know the meaning of unconditional love. Just the look in Colton's eyes in a single picture brings all that back in an instant.

He was lethargic, with an intermittently high fever, which he just couldn't shake. The poor little kid was miserable, and Debbie and I both felt every bit of it. He could barely hold his head up at times, and he had a pink rash all over his chest and stomach that lingered as well.

He would stay for several days in the hospital and then be released; test after test could find nothing. This cycle went on for the next month. We tried everything and he was not getting any better. There wasn't anything we could do. It was terrifying.

We just felt helpless. He was so small and vulnerable, and when he looked up at us with pleading eyes as if to ask why this was happening, it just broke our hearts. The doctors couldn't figure out why he was so sick.

For two weeks his temperature was hovering at 105, and when he was admitted to the hospital once again, he was finally diagnosed.

Juvenile rheumatoid arthritis.

We were stunned. Neither of us had heard of such a thing in a child so young, although apparently it is not all that uncommon. We went to specialist after specialist, and there was little good news. The disease could lead to everything from total disability to blindness or even death.

Debbie has always had a strong faith, so she and I discussed having the elders of the LDS church come into our home and give Colton a blessing. This was all new to me, and of course, anything that might help our poor sick little guy, I was for.

The elders came and gave a church blessing. They treated Colton as if he were one of their own children. Inside a couple of days, he started to improve, and within months, he was fine, and has never shown any signs of the disease in the forty years since. I have never shared that story with anyone until now. It's strange; I suppose in some primitive corner of my superstitious mind, I didn't want to jinx our good fortune.

After that experience, I could never dismiss the power of prayer and the healing powers of the good Lord. I truly believe it was a miracle that visited our home that day, and I am eternally grateful.

Looking at my tiny son in the hospital was truly one of the scariest moments of my life.

It wasn't long before we were feeling a little cramped and wanted a larger home, so three short years later we moved out of Mission Viejo into Lake Forest, another new community just ten miles to the north. I never thought leaving your first house and small community would be difficult, but it was. Everywhere you looked, there was a memory. Colton's first birthday party and the events that followed, and bringing our next son, Chris, home from the hospital were just a few.

Life is always exciting, especially when you are young. Having a stable job, one with an excellent career path, marks the start of life's possibilities. Graduation day was becoming a distant memory. Just like your wedding day, or the birth of your first child, graduating from recruit training opens the door for all that lies ahead.

CHAPTER EIGHT

I GOT DEBBIE, HER FAMILY, AND HER RELIGION TOO!

L iving on a shift schedule is quite different from the normal Monday to Friday routine. On a shift schedule, you might walk out the door in the morning, and not return for several days, maybe even longer. It became easy for me to forget what a strong woman it took to keep the family running smoothly while I was gone.

Debbie never complained and took all of the ups and downs in stride. Life had changed dramatically for her over the past few years, something I too easily forgot.

Her courage and faith came from the close family bond instilled in her by her parents. Most of Debbie's determination comes from her early childhood upbringing, and religion was a big part of it. Debbie's mother brought the family into the Mormon Church. My father-in-law went to church faithfully for eighteen years before he was baptized, or as they say within the Church, "dunked." The family was such a fixture that everyone just naturally assumed he was a baptized member; it just took him awhile to get around to doing it. Debbie and I would laugh at the thought that I had an eighteen-year buffer regarding religion, if I followed in her dad's footsteps. The family now wonders why I have passed that benchmark by years.

I wasn't raised in any particular church, which left me free to investigate all religions. The only thing I knew about Mormonism was they didn't drink coffee or alcohol, nor did they smoke. They reserved Sundays for church, and they were extremely family oriented. I would also hear they were a cult. Later in life, after I knew a little more about the religion, whenever I would hear that interpretation, I would ask, "Just exactly what is a cult?" No one could fully answer.

At first I thought Mormonism was a little unusual; after all, I was raised in a hard drinking and smoking family, and had a unique and somewhat varied religious background. I was baptized as an Episcopalian when I was young, and attended the Presbyterian Church when I was in grade school. My sister became a Jehovah's Witness, and my best friend Tim is a Roman Catholic. My mom in later years attended the Christian Science Church, and my aunt was married for years to a nice Jewish man. I pretty much have all the bases covered.

Rumors abound regarding Mormonism; you either believe in their theology or you don't, but one thing that has never been in question is their commitment to the family.

My family categorizes me as a dry Mormon, because I am still diligently studying religion, and I have not taken the plunge, so to speak. Both of my sons were baptized as members of the Mormon Church. I cannot think of a better environment in which to raise them.

As Debbie's family grew older, family interests became more varied, and as the natural course of things, her brothers and sister all married and started families of their own. The family is stretched out from Orange County to Burbank, Sacramento to Utah, and it's probably a good thing, due to the difference in personalities that were emerging. It has always amazed me how children brought up in the same family, with the same parents, can be so different. Maybe it's their birth order, or perhaps being beaned on the head by too many fast pitches.

Kevin was the youngest of Debbie's siblings. He was the last of the bunch and nine years Royce's junior. Perhaps because of the age difference, or just because Royce was such a good big brother, Kevin idolized him. It didn't take long before he decided to move to Sacramento to be near his big brother.

Soon after moving to Sacramento, Kevin met, fell in love with, and married Belinda. They moved into a home on an acre of land not far from Royce's ranch, and soon had a little girl named Janice. Kevin was a journeyman carpenter and general repairman. He was a good old boy, and did not need all that much from life. He was a dollar in, dollar out kind of guy. Everybody saw Kevin as a hard worker, but when quitting time came, he was off to the bar, and the rest of the world was put on hold. He didn't have Royce's ambition or his intelligence; he would always remain in Royce's shadow.

∴

May and Ron had become empty nesters. Debbie's dad was approaching retirement age, their children had been scattered to different areas, and the drive to visit them was getting tiresome. Burbank was just geographically undesirable.

After they retired and said good-bye to the area that had been home for the past forty years, they started anew in St. George, Utah. It was a bittersweet parting. The area that held fond memories of their children growing up and now it was being left behind for the great unknown.

The many years of hard work paid off, and finally they had the financial means to build their dream home. California real estate was much more lucrative than that of St George, so it allowed them to build a house and have a little money in savings.

Debbie's family was changing at a rapid pace and being scattered to the four winds, but they were still family.

CHAPTER NINE

BOY, DID I CHOOSE WELL

L ife is nothing more than a series of decisions. Wouldn't it be great to say every decision you made was a positive one? It might be nice, but it is not reality. The road most traveled is fraught with difficult decisions.

I don't know if maturity and self-approval are equal; what I do know is that it has taken me a lifetime to become content in my own skin.

Perhaps Mark Twain said it best: *"A man cannot be comfortable without his own approval."*

After I graduated from college, I was faced with a difficult choice: do I continue my career with the fire service, or quit and start a new profession in teaching? I had already quit one fire department to jump to another, so starting at the bottom again wasn't all that appealing.

Thirty years ago, the difference between the fire service and teaching was stark. In the late sixties firefighting was considered just another labor-intensive blue-collar job, with long hours and minimal pay. Teaching was a highly sought-after job. It had an excellent working schedule and benefits package.

Leaving Pasadena for the Los Angeles County Fire Department was a relatively easy decision; after all, the choice only involved me. Now my circumstances had changed dramatically. I had been well established as a firefighter with several years and two fire departments under my belt. The decision would affect not only me, but also my new and growing family.

Procrastination makes way to poor decision making, but in my case not making a decision was the best decision I have ever made.

Growing older, and hopefully wiser, changed me in ways I had never expected. It took me nine years to receive my bachelors degree as an industrial arts education instructor, and in those intervening years, I discovered I was not cut out to be cooped up all day with a gaggle of prepubescent teenagers. I didn't have the patience it takes to deal with today's youth. Coming from a strong disciplinarian family and maintaining that spanking does have a place in discipline, doesn't look good on a high school teacher's résumé, and it certainly isn't politically correct.

It is difficult to say why you choose a particular career; fate plays a large role.

It is the burden every high school senior endures; you must choose an occupation at which you will toil for the rest of your life. It is truly a lucky person who chooses well in those formative years.

Staying in the fire service was the best choice I could have made. Perhaps it was my early childhood upbringing that steered me in the right direction. I can't say for sure. I had more adult mentors from the fire service than any other vocation.

From a young man's perspective, a career in emergency services appears incredibly exciting, but the choice wasn't limited to just the fire service. The other natural choice was law enforcement, so I gave a career as a police officer some deep thought. It didn't take long before I discovered the two occupations attracted completely different types of personalities. Fortunately, I discovered early that I didn't have the frame of mind for law enforcement.

Political correctness has run amok. The professions affected the most are education and law enforcement.

I was beginning to feel like Goldilocks, but finally I did find the "one that was just right." Just as I found out I didn't have the qualities to become a high school teacher, I had a blinding glimpse of the obvious: law enforcement didn't fit well with my personality either. I didn't find out until many years later just how different police officers and firefighters are. Each day in the news, the stories bear out that difference.

Fire departments have traditionally provided lifesaving services in the form of fire protection. They have changed over the years and are no longer just fire departments. They now include emergency medical services, which in most cases include paramedics and emergency medical technicians, urban search and rescue, hazardous materials incidents, confined space, swift water and high angle rescues, and a multitude of other dangerous tasks brought on by the onslaught of terrorist threats. The firefighter's toolbox has changed, and has kept pace with today's new challenges.

The most critical ingredient in protecting the public is prevention, especially with terrorist threats. This formidable task falls squarely on the shoulders of law enforcement.

Police have the obligation to keep the public safe through the enforcement of laws; they keep a civil society civil. As terrible as it is to say, and as difficult as it is to hear, the enforcement of law often requires force, intimidation, and fear. One needs to look no further than the police officer's uniform to completely understand his role.

Displayed prominently on a law enforcement officer's head is a hat with a badge, the symbol of authority. The hat increases the height of the wearer and elevates the insignia above the crowd so all can see. The badge is also worn on the chest and is usually larger. It immediately identifies the wearer as a person of power and authority.

The belt around their waist supports implements of domination. Handcuffs, mace, spare bullets, a baton, and of course, a gun, the ultimate symbol of power. Just in case that's not enough intimidation, farther down on their leg is usually a Taser gun. In today's dangerous society, if these tools were removed, there would be no law enforcement. Unfortunately, when the only tool you have is a hammer, all of your problems start looking like nails!

The backbone of any relationship, especially emergency services, is confidence in your partner. Fire and police have to develop a relationship based upon mutual respect and trust. Firefighters learn from the beginning that teamwork and a high regard for your coworkers are essential, because we literally hold one another's lives in our hands.

Law enforcement starts with the same formula: teamwork and trust of fellow officers. However, one of the primary elements of law enforcement is skepticism and distrust of the public. You cannot let your guard down or take anything for granted. If you do, it could have devastating consequences. Due to this simple premise, the line between friend and foe often becomes blurred.

Firefighters are heroes in the public eye, and receive gratitude and respect from the inception of a call to the conclusion. They are always welcome. Rarely do they receive complaints.

Law enforcement receives a different mind-set from the community. To maintain peace someone must be held accountable. I don't believe a highway patrol officer will ever convince a motorist the citation that was just issued was a good thing.

The police constantly receive complaints for just doing their job. As unfortunate as it might be, they are often thought of as the villain, and after years of constant criticism from the public, the community becomes the enemy. As a result, police may become more distrustful of those they serve.

Despite the differences between emergency responders, we do get along quite well. Police are always welcome in the fire station for a cup of coffee and some friendly banter. We all recognize protecting the public is extremely dangerous. Police officers appreciate the fact that when they are injured or shot, in the vast majority of cases, the face they see coming to their rescue will be that of a firefighter.

There is, however, an occasional bump in the road to peace and understanding between the two services. The following incident occurred on February 15, 2010, on Highway 101 in Montecito, California:

In the center divider of the northbound 101 Freeway, a traffic collision occurred involving two vehicles and six injured people. The responding fire engine blocked the fast lane, the number one lane, for police officers reading this. This provides a safe working area for firefighters and paramedics, which is standard operating procedure for most departments. It would be ludicrous to expect emergency workers to stand in the middle of a highway without some form of protection. The big red fire engines with flashing lights serve as a notice to oncoming traffic there is an emergency ahead.

The Montecito Fire Department normally has an excellent relationship with the California Highway Patrol and area law enforcement officers. This was an isolated and rare incident, I hope.

A California Highway Patrol motor officer, apparently a recent transfer from the Bakersfield area, told the newly arriving battalion chief to have the truck moved because the apparatus was causing too much traffic backup.

"Move those rigs!" I can imagine him saying in his most cop-like, arrogant voice.

The battalion chief had been at the scene a little less than a minute, and the firefighters had not made contact with the victims yet, so the battalion chief respectfully said, "I have to protect my crew from oncoming traffic."

The exchange between the battalion chief and CHP motor officer must have gotten a little heated, because the following events became ridiculous.

The chief was not about to jeopardize the safety of his men, so he requested a CHP supervisor to come to the scene. To the astonishment of everyone, the next thing the firefighters saw was the CHP manhandling the battalion chief, putting him in handcuffs and placing him under arrest. According to newspaper and witness accounts, the officer threatened to arrest the engineer and have the apparatus towed away.

The battalion chief gave in and ordered the engine moved, but within a few minutes, a CHP supervisor showed up and un-cuffed him. I would have thought the sergeant would have been so embarrassed, he would order an apology, but instead the motor officer wrote the chief a citation for "obstructing a police officer during an investigation," proving once again, you can't fix stupid.

When common sense breaks down, we all have a tendency to retreat to our area of comfort. The officer fell back on brute force. Remember the uniform he was wearing.

Fortunately, this is an isolated case. Police are the same as firefighters; they want to do their job correctly and safely, and then go home. However, incidents like this travel through the emergency service grapevine at lightning speed.

Embarrassed by the whole situation and hoping to keep the relationship between the sheriff and fire department at the high level it had been in the past, a pair of Santa Barbara County Sheriff's deputies stopped by the fire station right after the incident with a peace offering: two freshly baked cakes.

In typical sheriff's department humor, one of the cakes had a file in it!

The California Highway patrol does have many common-sense folks. The night watch sergeant also came to the fire station and couldn't apologize enough.

You might think that would be the end of the story, but it's not.

Five days later, the front page of a Bakersfield Sunday newspaper carried the story: "CHP Officer Who Arrested Firefighter Beat Unconscious by Bar Patrons."

As tragic as it was, I'll bet it put a smile on your face too! You can't make this stuff up.

The officer got his ass kicked in a small bar in the Bakersfield area.

According to the news article, police responded to reports of a man down at a bar and grill in the northwest section of Bakersfield, where they found the off-duty CHP officer in need of medical assistance.

Police said witness accounts alternated between the officer attempting to break up a fight between two women, and the officer being jumped by three men, one of which broke a beer bottle over his head. I suspect the former. It's just more satisfying to think he got knocked out by a couple of girls.

I hope as he was lying on the barroom floor waiting for the little birdies in his head to clear, the first face he saw when he regained consciousness was that of a firefighter.

As I said, you just can't make this stuff up!

Bakersfield Police said he was transported to the hospital and was released and returned to active duty.

The CHP officer's captain said, "When a person gets hit on the head, they don't remember much. He remembers going out to dinner, that's it. He doesn't remember anything else."

That would pretty much be my story too!

Even with the memory loss, the officer is "still healthy enough to be on active duty." No word on whether he meant physically or mentally.

I know this will come as a real shocker, but no arrests have been made in the case.

My distrust for authority started many years ago, only to be heightened by a lifetime of experiences.

In a later chapter, I will discuss my arrest by the California Highway Patrol when I was a battalion chief.

CHAPTER TEN

NEVER REGRET GROWING OLDER. IT'S A PRIVILEGE DENIED TO MANY

My Dad was never chatty, but he was a positive person, and I never saw him down or depressed. If he ever was, he never showed it. When he spoke, it was always with confidence, and he didn't worry about the things he had no control over. It is like the Alcoholics Anonymous creed about changing what you can and accepting what you can't. He would always say, "Just take it a day at a time." Another favorite saying he had if you were worried about something was, "This too shall pass."

He was a shy and introverted man, but loved to dance. Those two genes were not passed along to me. Being introverted is one of the last words that would be used in describing me; at six foot two and 220 pounds, when I tried to dance, it looked as if I were having a seizure. Debbie and I make the perfect pair, though; she has two left feet and neither of us have rhythm, so we learned early on not to include shuffling around the dance floor when it comes to an evening out.

Dad was approaching ninety when he had his gallbladder removed. In preparation for the surgery, we discussed the process with his doctor. They would be doing laparoscopic surgery, which has little recovery time. The whole operation wasn't supposed to take longer than an hour.

I sat nervously in the waiting room, and after three hours the surgeon came out and told me Dad was fine. He asked if my dad had been a drinker.

I just looked at the doctor and smiled.

"My father enjoyed a drink or two, mostly two."

The doctor said he thought so, because his liver was in bad shape.

Wherever Dad went, he took a small attaché case that opened up into a little mini-bar. It had a flask and the various mixers and drink-making utensils. Both of my sons were in awe when they saw it.

That attaché case is now a family heirloom, but as a father, I hope it doesn't get the use it once had.

Dad soon recovered and decided he could no longer live in the house he had called home for the past fifty-three years. He moved to a nursing home in Glendora. The move was only twenty-five miles in distance, but a lifetime in change.

One of the routine emergency responses for a firefighter is to nursing homes. The facilities range from unsurpassed care for the elderly, to horrible conditions to which no one should be subjected. Treatment of the elderly is a subject not a soul wishes to discuss. As the baby boomers grow older, we will all eventually be at the mercy of others, and could well end up in one of these facilities.

Firefighters at one time or another have remarked, "I hope I never end up in a place like this!" I have always tried to keep a wise and old Indian proverb in mind: *"Never regret growing older. It's a privilege denied to many."*

My father spent the last eighteen months of his life in a nursing home. He was always positive; I never once heard him say anything negative about his living conditions. He accepted things as they were without complaint.

Time was finally catching up with him and he was becoming lethargic, wouldn't eat, and was much weaker. He was gradually going downhill.

I finally had transferred him back to the hospital.

After getting comfortable in his hospital bed, he looked at me for the longest time, and then slowly in a raspy voice said, "Why aren't I getting any better?"

My dad and I never spoke of death; it was always the furthest thing from his mind. Death, so imminent in his case, was simply not an option.

I spent the next couple of hours with him. We had a nice conversation regarding…just about everything. Not feeling well, he tired easily, so I thought I would let him get some sleep.

As I walked out of the room, I looked back and said good-bye, but I didn't say, *I love you, Dad,* and for that, I am truly remorseful.

He passed away that evening.

That is one of those things you play over and over in your mind, and cannot reverse.

Maybe it is one of those macho things—not showing your feelings. I don't know, but I am learning.

"I love you, Dad," was the way I felt, but for some unexplained reason, as I walked out of the room the last time I saw him alive, I didn't utter those words. That memory now lives with all the other troubling thoughts I try not to remember.

I was privileged to have my father for as long as I did. If I inherited just a modicum of his confidence, wisdom, and values, and pass them along to my sons, I will consider myself a fortunate man.

CHAPTER ELEVEN

SO QUICKLY LOST
AND FORGOTTEN

Nineteen sixty-nine was indeed a busy year. Leaving the Pasadena Fire Department behind was not easy; after all, it was the first time I realized that in the fire service, you establish friendships that are akin to a second family. Getting married that year was the easy part.

In the closing days of the county's recruit training, the beginning of my career finally was coming together. After weeks of hot weather, long days, endless drills on the grinder, and a never-ending stream of exams, there was finally light at the end of the tunnel. Graduation day and my first assignment were within sight.

Where you are assigned is a mystery to everyone. If you dare to ask, the training officers will give you a lengthy explanation regarding the process, but in reality they try to get you as close to home as possible. Other than that, no one knows.

My first assignment was the truck company at Station 42, Battalion 10, in the city of Rosemead.

Veteran firefighters can move around the county from station to station on a yearly basis if they choose. The only requirement is that you stay in that assignment for at least one year. At the beginning of each month, the vacancies are published, and if you wish to transfer, you submit a request. At the end of the month, the person with the lowest seniority number is awarded the position. This process is used throughout the ranks up to the position of chief officer. Chief officers do not have any transfer rights; they are assigned by the fire chief.

The whole process has a domino effect, and in the end, the positions left are assigned to new recruits. It is only a small stretch of the imagination to think the positions that remain are the ones no one else wants.

Station 42 had two pieces of equipment, an engine and a truck company. Each were staffed with four personnel.

As a probationary firefighter, the list of things you are forbidden to do is lengthy. It far outweighs the permissible activities.

Most of the day revolved around routine, most of which made sense. There was a lot of busy work, but as a probationer you kept a smile on your face, did as you were asked, and said absolutely nothing. There is nothing like a wife, child, and mortgage to keep you on the straight and narrow. You might say I went with the flow whether or not I agreed with the speed.

My captain was an affable individual by the name of Ed, and the engineer was Wayne Monical. Wayne and I would remain friends my entire career. The captain on the engine was Clarence "Bud" Hund. Captain Hund was approaching retirement age, so his thoughts were on other things rather than the fire department most of the time. Anytime you are within ten years of retirement, you are close enough to adopt the "I am going to retire" attitude.

The "old guys" were constantly talking about retirement. Once they became close, you couldn't shut them up. Another expression you would hear repeatedly was, "You kids just don't know what the real fire department was like, I remember when…"

In today's job environment, people cycle through several different occupations during their work life, but the fire service is one career that would suffer greatly if people didn't stick with it. Nothing beats the wisdom that comes from the actual experience of fighting fires. There is no equivalent job. It's definitely not the same as most other occupations. Firefighters deal with stress and human tragedy on a daily basis; and it's just plain hard physical work.

∴

The station was small and cramped, so you couldn't help bumping into each other all day long. Surprisingly, everyone got along quite well.

I spent most of my time in the office, pretending to be studying; there is only so much busy work you can do in a day. New recruits were not allowed to participate in any of the normal relaxing techniques of a seasoned firefighter. The attitude was, you would have an entire career to hone those skills. Your leisure time was to be used for study, and of course, doing busy work.

When I started with Pasadena, everything was regimented. Shift change was at 8:00 a.m. When the alarm test bell rang, punctually at eight o'clock, you'd find eleven guys from the off going shift standing opposite eleven guys of the oncoming shift, facing off across the apparatus floor like gunslingers at the OK Corral.

The county was a little bit looser; there was no face-off and no bell, but we did have a schedule we adhered to, unless we had an actual incident to go to.

After morning briefing, the first chore of the day was to clean the underside of the fire engine. Yep, that's right, take a kerosene-soaked rag and climb under the rig, and look for unsightly smudges of grease or road dirt that needed to be removed. At first blush, you would think this was some type of hazing for new recruits, but it was not. This ritual is preformed countywide, first thing every morning. The common answer to the question, "Why are we doing this?" was that we were looking for safety hazards, loose bolts, and the like. Nope, I didn't accept it either, nor did I ever find anything loose. The only loose nut was the guy who came up with this ritual. This custom was a carryover from the "keep them busy all day" attitude with whatever it takes.

I wish I could tell you this tradition has died a slow death, but it has not. It's still alive and well. Up to the time I retired, first thing in the morning, I would see boots sticking out from under the rigs. This routine is so permeated in the culture that during the annual inspection, the battalion and assistant chiefs would shimmy under the rigs with their dress uniforms on, flashlight in hand, and inspect the underside of the equipment. God help the engineer if the chiefs found dirt under there.

Due to the size of the station and the number of firefighters to perform cleaning duties, housework was completed within the first few minutes. Leave it to a firefighter to find the quickest and most efficient way to do rudimentary cleaning chores. Dusting and floor sweeping were a breeze, so to speak, when we used a gas-powered leaf blower.

New recruits are on probation for a year. At the end of your probation period, there is a follow-up exam back at the training center. This was an all-day exam where you had to show your proficiency in all of the hose lays and ladder evolutions. You also turned in your completed recruit notebook.

The recruit notebook was nothing more than stacks of busywork. It contained some valuable information, but most was lost because it was intertwined with twaddle. The biggest time-consuming chore was drawing a road map of the district your fire station served from memory. This included fire hydrants and the water main sizes. Training officers must all come from the same school. In Pasadena, the follow-up exam included drawing the entire city map from memory.

I always thought that was why you had maps on the rigs, but what do I know? I was just a dumb new kid! Come to think about it, I never once had a captain ask me which way to turn while responding to a fire.

There was no use fighting it; that was just the way it was. As my father told me not long before he died, "I learned early on in life, negative thoughts never get you anywhere." "Attitude is everything".

I passed my probation period and final exam. I guess the second time around made it a little easier.

∴

My captain was a low-key man who had the ability to let most things roll off his back. Captain Hund, on the other hand, was the nervous type. As they say, "He could have made coffee nervous." Their attitudes balanced out quite well.

In mid-July 1970, Station 42 responded to an automobile accident. Two cars collided in the intersection and one was pushed through the front display windows of a carpet shop. The building suffered major damage and the cars were totaled, but there were no injuries. Both of the cars were easily towed, but it took the entire crew an hour to move the carpet rolls in order to secure the store.

That evening after dinner, Captain Hund started complaining about how difficult it had been moving all the carpet, and how heavy the rolls were. We all thought he had just pulled a few muscles in his chest. Later in my career, I would learn hearing statements like his should have made bells and whistles go off, but we were naive to say the least, and did nothing more than listen to him complain.

A few days later, while off duty, I received a telephone call at home. Captain "Bud" Hund was dead. He had died of a massive coronary at his home, and never made it to the hospital. He was forty-seven years old.

Everyone went to the funeral, of course. It was a moving tribute to a well-liked man.

The image still trapped in my mind is that of Captain Hund's parents. They sat almost motionless during the entire service, grief etched into their faces and still in shock over the death of their son. No parent should ever have to bury their child!

Within two months of Captains Hund's death, another cold wave of reality swept over me. His locker was cleaned out, and his personal protective equipment sent back to the warehouse. His assignment was soon filled with another captain. Within a month, the only legacy that remained were stories friends repeated while sitting around the kitchen table. Those even came to pass.

This was my first experience with losing someone I had closely worked with, and unfortunately, it would not be the last.

Captain Hund's death had a profound effect on me. What struck me was how quickly he faded from our collective consciousness. Maybe it is like that in every profession. I am not so naive to think firefighters are all that different in terms of basic human nature. Once you leave, whether it is that big off-ramp in the sky, or just a transfer to another station, you're yesterday's news.

When old retirees returned to the fire station, they are treated respectfully, but it only takes a few minutes before the entire crew grows impatient and wants to go about their daily routine. You are just a time gone by; it is the nature of the business.

Pete Seeger wrote one of my favorite songs, and the Byrds made it famous. It comes from the Bible: *"To everything there is a season, a time for every purpose under the heaven."*

I have been retired for a number of years, and so far I've resisted any temptation to return to any of my old assignments and bore them with stories. I know they want to get out there and make their own legacies, and I am glad to let them. At the end of our careers, firefighters have two families—the brotherhood at work, and the family at home. Firefighters instinctually know which is the *most* important.

Perhaps Thomas Jefferson expresses my feelings the best when he said, *"I like dreams of the future better than history of the past."*

The greatest thing we could do is to teach the next generation the best we can, and then get out of their way.

As a new firefighter at my first station, I was introduced to many good people and realized how temporary we all are.

I thought my probationary period would never end, but in two short years, I would leave Station 42 for my next assignment. In my time there, I developed close friendships that would last me a lifetime, and met people who would change my attitudes toward life forever.

CHAPTER TWELVE

I ALMOST LOST COLTON, TWICE

My career was beginning to pick up speed, and everything was starting to fall into place. Sometimes that is a scary feeling; not that I am a fatalist, but life's lessons have taught me just how fickle life can be. I couldn't help but think of the guy that jumped off the top of a twenty-story building. Someone on the tenth floor heard him say as he went by, "So far, so good!"

Ever since Colton was diagnosed with juvenile rheumatoid arthritis—a disease he has fully recovered from, thanks to medical help and lots of prayer—my faith has gradually, but ever so surely, increased. "Today is a gift from God, that's why it's called the *present.*"

The good Lord does truly work in mysterious ways. Naysayers could dismiss the blessings Colton received as a mere coincident, or just the healing power of the body. After witnessing his truly remarkable recovery, I would be a fool if I did not give the credit where it was due.

Almost losing him was never far from my cognizant mind. Little things would pop up every now and then that would catapult me back to the days when we sat next to him while he was laying in his hospital bed.

Eighteen years later, I received a telephone call that would shake me to the core and test my faith all over again.

"Mr. Ashby?"

"Yes," I said into the phone, instantly worried. No one who knew me called me mister. It was Doug or Captain, or sometimes something worse; after all, I am a firefighter. If someone I didn't know was calling me at work late in the evening, it had to be bad news.

"Your son Colton…"

My knuckles instantly became white around the receiver.

"He's fine, don't worry, but there's been an accident."

The voice on the other end of the line was that of a fellow firefighter, someone I didn't know. Your son asked me to call you and explain what happen. He's okay, but he wants you to come up here."

I would not be convinced he was okay until I saw him.

In the summer of 1989, Colton was nineteen and heading off on a road trip with his two friends, Chad and Kevin. The three of them had been friends since grade school. They were driving to the Colorado River, where Chad's parents had a vacation home.

I wasn't keen on the trip, and told my son I had a bad feeling about it. There was nothing in particular to make me nervous, just three teenagers on a road trip to the Colorado River. What could possibility go wrong?

What would a trip to the river be without beer? However, they were in a hurry to get on the road and decided not to purchase the beer until they arrived. Will small miracles ever cease?

They were driving Chad's Toyota pickup, which had a camper shell on back. It was nicely done with carpeting, so Kevin rode in the back, and Colton rode up front with Chad. Chad had a habit of refusing to wear his seatbelt; it was a macho kid thing. Colton had gotten in the habit of wearing his, and started some good-natured ribbing for Chad to put his belt on. For some reason that day, Chad buckled up without much fanfare.

The trip was uneventful until they were on I-15 just south of Victorville.

The interstate is the main route between Los Angeles and Las Vegas, and has four to five lanes, all of which move at a pretty good clip. Have you ever noticed that when traffic is moving safely at seventy miles an hour, there is always someone who has to go faster? A sedan was approaching in the rearview mirror doing in excess of a hundred miles per hour.

The driver came up behind the group of cars, including my son's vehicle that were going much slower, and swerved to the side. He was attempting to pass the cluster of cars on the dirt shoulder. Chad's truck was in the number two lane.

Once that maniac hit the dirt, he lost control of his car, swerved ahead of Chad, and crossed the freeway toward the center divider. Suddenly there was a loud noise and the car was perpendicular to Chad, just off his left front bumper.

During an incident such as this, things often move in slow motion to the participants.

Colton heard Chad yell, "Oh shit!" and saw him frantically try to simultaneously brake, downshift, and steer into the skid to correct the truck's slide. Colton looked from Chad to the other car, which they had just hit. For a brief moment, he thought Chad was going to be able to right their vehicle and avoid careening off the guardrail.

Unfortunately, it was not to be.

Even as they hit the center divider, my son remembers thinking the impact wasn't too bad, just before being disappointed as the truck began to roll over.

After the first couple of flips, his memory suddenly ended in darkness.

Colton awoke sometime later right side up, still belted securely in place. Chad was frantically yelling and trying to force open his door. The bed of the truck was empty; the impact had thrown the camper shell off onto the roadway somewhere.

Not yet remembering that their friend Kevin had been riding in the camper, Colton tried to calm Chad down.

"It's all right! Just sit tight until help gets here!"

Then he remembered Kevin. Colton looked in the back again. Nothing was there.

Colton yelled to Chad, "Where's Kevin?"

Frantically he said, "I don't know!"

"We gotta get out and look for him!"

Colton unbuckled his seatbelt and forced open the door with his shoulder, conscious of pain for the first time. The back of his head and his face were suddenly throbbing, as if the act of moving his body reminded his brain to send the pain signals.

Colton quickly scrambled out of the truck, bleeding and unsteady.

His vision was blurred and he tried with all his might to focus. Then he saw Kevin's limp body lying a few feet in front of the vehicle.

As the cobwebs started to clear, and the limp body came into focus, he realized it wasn't Kevin. The body in front of him was a black man. It must be the other driver.

"Kevin!"

Shouting made the pain shoot through his head like a nail gun.

"Kevin!"

Colton continued to survey the crash site, which was extensive. The speed and force caused the sedan to hit several others vehicles after the initial impact with Chad's truck.

After the vehicle careened into Chad's truck, the man was ejected from his car, and the driverless vehicle continued down the freeway with his young daughter still seat belted in the front seat. It finally came to rest on the shoulder several hundred feet down the road. His daughter appeared to be unhurt.

"Kevin!"

Chad yelled, "I've found him!"

Colton whirled around, almost falling over. His eyes were still a little out of focus. He could see Chad standing near the back of the truck, ashen-faced, looking at what they thought was Kevin lying on the pavement at their feet.

"Oh, this doesn't look good."

Before my son could reply, he heard the terrified voice of a twenty-something male bystander. "There's his legs! Oh my God, it's just his legs!"

Colton turned to see the lower half of Kevin's body, his legs broken and mangled.

Except they weren't Kevin's legs. They were no one's. Chad was in the firefighter academy, and what they had seen was a pair of his firefighter turnout pants, which he kept rolled down over his boots for quick access, lying in front of them on the ground.

Colton was instantly relieved and turned from the screaming man back to Chad. Now feeling even more panicky, he said, "Where is he?"

Chad pointed to a small group of people standing over someone lying in the road under the center guardrail.

It was Kevin.

Colton rushed over to Kevin and knelt beside him, feeling some relief but shocked at his condition and said, "You're gonna be all right, Kev. You might have a broken femur and some cuts, but you're gonna be all right."

He told someone in the crowd to go and get some blankets. It was busy work to keep them from yapping about how terrible Kevin looked.

"I feel broken up inside," Kevin whispered, his voice raspy and faint. Colton knew that was a bad sign. He continued to reassure his friend.

Chad rushed over, even more upset than before. He was waving an empty liquor bottle and screaming someone had accused him of drinking. He'd shoved his accuser to the ground.

"Calm down!" Colton yelled. "We haven't been drinking... remember?"

Chad's thoughts cleared a bit, apparently remembering they had skipped the beer run. The road was littered with bottles, but they were all from the sedan.

Colton and Chad stayed sitting on the ground with Kevin until the fire department arrived on the scene, at which point my son calmly turned to Chad and said, "I'm gonna lie down. I don't feel well. I'm going into shock."

When a firefighter finally came over to Colton, he said, "Please call my dad. He's a captain with the Los Angeles County Fire Department. I need him here."

Receiving a call like that from a complete stranger is every parent's nightmare. After the cold chills stopped running up my back, I asked, "What happened? Are you sure he's okay? Where are they?"

"A drunk driver swerved in front of them. It wasn't their fault. All three boys are alive, but one is not doing well. Your son is not seriously injured. He's being taken to Victor Valley Hospital."

Debbie and I rushed to the hospital, of course, and by the time we got there, Colton had been stitched up and treated for bumps and bruises.

The gash on his head from hitting something inside the truck looked nasty.

Ironically, the doctor's name was Dr. Colton. He had just flown in from St. George, Utah. He did an excellent job with two rows of stitches in Colton's head.

When we saw him sitting alone in that waiting room, calmly holding his x-rays, Debbie and I could hardly hold back our tears.

Colton stood up, gave both of us a hug, and said how good it was to see us.

He was worried we would be angry because I'd told him I would rather he not make the trip.

Angry?

It was just the opposite. He stood there, somewhat battered, but he was still able to stand there.

The cold chills were replaced with a feeling of relief; his mother was able to give him a comforting hug, which only mothers can.

When I walked into that waiting room and saw my son's innocent look, a lifetime's worth of memories flooded through my mind.

I remembered our canoe trip through Snake River Canyon with the scouts when he was twelve, and how blasé he'd been when I marveled at the sight of lightning striking the top of the Grand Tetons. All of his childhood sporting events, graduating high school, sticking up for his little brother, picking on his little brother, all of it came back to me in an instant.

Only the valleys of your life can make you truly appreciate the mountaintops. I managed to experience them both in the same instant. Even though your children are always in your prayers, I have been twice blessed with prayers for Colton. Once when he was just a tyke, and again on that horrible evening. I don't want to push my luck a third time.

I have written portions of this chapter with the help of my son. Every firefighter has arrived at the scene of an incident with someone else's loved one lying on the ground in front of them. The true trauma doesn't have its full impact until you have been on both sides of an unpleasant incident. Colton and our family have been extremely lucky; other families have not.

Time slowed for my son, and then rushed by for me.

My son and his friends were lucky, or as I like to say, "blessed."

Kevin was in the hospital for a month and lost a kidney. He continued with his college education, graduated, and today is a forest ranger in Humboldt County.

Chad also continued his education, graduating from the fire academy, climbing the ranks of the fire department, and is now the fire chief of a fire department in Northern California.

My son Colton is a paramedic and fire captain with Orange County Fire Authority, and the proud father of two of our four grandchildren.

The erring driver, despondent over the loss of his job, went on a drinking binge, chose to get behind the wheel of his car, and almost destroyed the lives of many others. His daughter was safe, but is now fatherless.

I learned a valuable lesson many years ago from a wonderful old deaf woman. She would insist you should never part company without a loving hug, a positive word, and a smile.

Boy, am I glad I was taught that lesson!

CHAPTER THIRTEEN

NO ONE IS IMMUNE FROM CHANGE

Transferring from one fire station to another is unsettling; it is almost like moving from one fire department to another.

Arriving at your new fire station is just as nerve-racking as when you walked in the door of your first assignment as a probationary firefighter. Everything is new; all of the familiar surroundings are gone. New station and city, new boss, and new relationships. Nothing is the same. The only good part is that you are no longer a probationary firefighter.

Transfers are processed at the end of every month, and the amount of personnel transferring depends on promotions, retirements, vacancies, and unfortunately death, like Captain Hund's position.

There is no limit to the amount of transfer requests you may submit.

It wasn't that I was unhappy with my assignment on Truck 42, but there was a whole department out there waiting to be experienced. I submitted seventy-five transfer requests and received the one that was twenty-fifth on my list, in the city of Paramount, Station 31, Battalion 9.

Firefighters use different criteria before requesting a transfer. They weigh what the station's activity level is like, who is assigned there, and a multitude of other factors. Not me. I just filed transfer requests, and then let the chips fall where they might. For such a lackadaisical attitude regarding transfers, I did very well.

Debbie and I had moved from our apartment in South Pasadena to our new home in southern Orange County, so it was nice to work in an area closer to home.

The crew was one of the best, and fit that time of my life perfectly. We had one of the closest relationships of any group I ever worked with. It was a real pleasure to go to work every day. Everyone did their job, and everyone was fun to be with, which made it easy for us to get along. When you're dealing with emergencies and stressful situations, it intensifies the bond among firefighters. We had great chemistry together. The personnel were truly unforgettable. Mike Cook, whom I first met in recruit training, was there, and it was a pleasure to be working with him again. Over the course of our careers, we would work several more times together.

We had such a good rapport, I almost had to pinch myself—all of this and I was being paid too. It is a fortunate man who can say that.

The city of Paramount is a small city bordered by Compton and Lynwood to the west, Southgate and Downey to the north, and Long Beach to the south. Paramount only covers about five square miles, and is a balance of industry, commerce, and residential homes. It sounds strange that such a small city could border so many others. Los Angeles County is a patchwork of such tiny municipalities, with the city of Los Angeles in the center exerting its gravitational pull, holding things together.

Even if you're unfamiliar with some of the city names aside from Long Beach, you'll probably recognize Compton, which began to lose its tax base with the white flight of the early sixties. It was hit hard by the Watts riots of 1965, and has since been beset by corruption and cronyism within its city government for years.

There was always a lot to do because the area had a little bit of everything. It consisted of the city of Paramount and two unincorporated areas in Compton.

The fire station itself was the common two-bay, drive-through station, which is used throughout the county. It could hold up to four pieces of equipment.

The staffing was three on Engine 31—a captain, an engineer, and a firefighter. The two on the rescue squad were also firefighters.

There is typically plenty of activity in lower-income areas, which have denser populations with lots of emergencies just waiting to happen. The district was so diverse that within my first few months we responded to a second alarm fire in an industrial building, a fire in a hay storage area in one of the stockyards that was still in the area, and a fully involved over turned double gasoline tanker on the Long Beach Freeway. As if that wasn't enough, I responded to my first swift water rescue in the Los Angeles River, where a seven year old boy drowned in the swollen channel.

Fresh out of recruit training, I was equipped with a first aid certification card from the American Red Cross. CPR as we know it today barely existed, or at least it had not been widely used by firefighters yet. With several years under my belt, I now thought I was ready for anything. What I didn't realize was change was on its way, monumental change. I thought I had found a new home, a station where I would be for many years to come. However, the changes that were just over the horizon not only would change the face of the fire service, it would also alter my career.

CHAPTER FOURTEEN

IT DOESN'T MATTER
WHO GETS THE CREDIT

Eighty years ago, when Los Angeles County was just a fledgling fire department, the primary mission of the department was to combat and prevent fires. In 1960, Fire Chief Keith Klinger placed resuscitator/inhalator units on all fire equipment. The resuscitator was a portable oxygen supply system in a small suitcase that opened up like a clamshell. No one could foresee at the time how small changes would completely transform the mission of the fire service in years to come.

The fire department's response to early medical calls was more comforting to the victims than anything else. A typical rescue was for someone having trouble breathing. The fire crew would arrive and ask what the problem was, put an oxygen mask on them, and wait for the ambulance to arrive. It wasn't until after years of using the resuscitator that someone noticed that the unit cycled. It would supply positive pressure and deliver oxygen, then it cycled to negative pressure, much like breathing. If care wasn't taken when applying the oxygen mask, the unit could be in the negative position and not deliver any oxygen.

The department did not transport patients; that was left up to private ambulance companies. Across the country in the mid-sixties, 50 percent of ambulances were provided by funeral homes. The simple fact was hearses were better equipped to accommodate stretchers.

It might have been practical, but it didn't give the family any comfort seeing the firefighter administering oxygen to poor old Grandma while a hearse was waiting outside!

In the late sixties, the number one cause of death in the United States was coronary artery disease, and about seven out of every ten patients died before they got to the hospital. This simple statistic was the initial focus of early paramedic programs and the development of CPR training. There was a growing acknowledgement that lives could be saved with improved operations in the field.

Los Angeles County is often mistakenly thought to be the father of the paramedic program; it wasn't the first, but it became the most widely known.

The television show *Emergency!*[4] would eventually popularize and promote the new paramedic program, just as it did for the Los Angeles Police Department with shows like *Dragnet* and *Adam-12*. Jack Webb made Los Angeles County Fire Department and paramedics into instant heroes.

The history of paramedics in the fire service did not start with *Emergency! Rescue 8*[5] premiered in 1958 and originally ran for two seasons with syndicated reruns continuing for almost another decade. A total of seventy-three half-hour episodes were produced.

The series portrays two rescue specialists with the Los Angeles County Fire Department, Fire Station 8, whose job it was to rescue people from a variety of dangerous and life-threatening situations. The show predates *Emergency!* by at least fifteen years. The real Station 8 is located in West Hollywood, on Santa Monica Boulevard, one of the county's contract cities.

The series stared Jim Davis as fireman Wes Cameron, and Lang Jeffries as fireman Skip Johnson. The program aired long before political correctness, so the term *fireman* is correct. Jim Davis would later become Jock Ewing in the television series *Dallas*.

The image of a firefighter is that of a robust, masculine, man's man. Perhaps the roots of that image can be traced, not only to the job they performed, but also to the men that portrayed them.

Lang Jeffries was a Canadian citizen, born in Ontario in 1930. He served in the US Army during the Korean War. In the fall of 1950, General Douglas MacArthur conducted a mass landing in Inchon, South Korea, and Jeffries was among only three survivors of the 177-man unit that made the landing. It is truly an honor to have such a military hero as Jeffries portray a firefighter.

The Los Angeles County Fire Department has perfected the art of utilizing its resources in the most efficient and effective manner. In a day when making things complex tended to justify your existence, the county mastered the simplest and most efficient approach to firefighting and rescue calls by eliminating redundancy wherever possible.

When a call is received in communications, the closest resources are dispatched. That sounds rudimentary, but you would be surprised the number of fire departments that do not use this model.

The fire service was divided; many departments would stand on tradition and resist embarking into the EMS and paramedic arena. The common thought was *we fight fires, we don't treat sick people.*

The two largest fire departments on the West Coast took two different approaches to the paramedic program. One embraced the program; the other treated it like an ugly stepchild. Some established completely new divisions just for EMS within the fire department. Supervision became a nightmare, with firefighters and paramedics working and living alongside one another with entirely different job descriptions and a different chain of command.

All of the efforts put forth would have been moot if the fire chief had not given his approval. For an organization hindered by tradition, I am sure this decision was a difficult one.

As with any new programs, ideas were abundant, and the need was evident, but solving the issues was complex. A multitude of decisions had to be made before the system could be put into place. Fortunately for the public, many people were in the right place at the right time, and made the right decision.

The paramedic program was a cooperative effort of many politicians, movie producers, directors, doctors, firefighters, and actors that all came together to form a stable foundation that catapulted the paramedic program into what it is today.

The path my department took, from today's perspective, appears to be a correct one. In light of the advances made in terms of paramedic and EMT training, the treatment that grandma got back just a few short years ago, was truly the dark ages.

Today fire fighting accounts for only 4 percent of all emergency calls each year. More than 80 percent are emergency medical calls, from traffic collisions to heart attacks. The number of lives that have been saved over the forty-plus years of the paramedic program in incalculable.

※

The paramedic program was now in full swing. Fire fighters were volunteering for the new program and being trained at an unprecedented rate. Rescue squads across the county were being converted into paramedic units.

The rescue squad at Station 31 was targeted to be one of the first to become a paramedic squad, so my friend Mike Cook signed up for the training. Our close-knit crew was being broken up.

They say—whomever *they* are—that opportunity knocks but once. Perhaps I lost a chance of a lifetime by not becoming a paramedic. The first time I was exposed to the program, I turned the training down. By the time the second chance rolled around the department turned me down. I guess you could say it just wasn't in the cards.

CHAPTER FIFTEEN

COMPASSION COMES FROM THE STRANGEST PLACES

After I was displaced by the new paramedics at Station 31, I received a transfer to Fire Station 87, near the city of Industry, in an unincorporated area known as Bassett. It was also a busy station, with an extremely large area.

The city of Industry is unusual in that it is home to thousands of businesses and tens of thousands of jobs, but less than eight hundred residents. When the sun sets, they roll up the sidewalks, and it becomes a ghost town with an extremely attractive tax base. Freeways and railroad tracks crisscross the area. Small residential areas are amid light and heavy industrial tracks. Centered in the middle of town is the well-known Puente Hills Mall. Michael J. Fox and Christopher Lloyd blasted *Back to the Future* from the Puente Hills Mall parking lot.[6]

The district has the potential for just about every type of incident. It has small chicken farms and large industrial buildings. There is even a wildland area in the foothills, which causes problems during hot weather, particularly when the Santa Ana winds kick in. For firefighters, the city has a little bit of everything.

Station 87 was staffed with four people—a captain, an engineer, and two firefighters. Wayne Monical was the engineer, and Lenard was the other firefighter. Wayne I first met at Station 42, when I was a probationary firefighter. He helped to guide me over the years, and is a true friend.

My captain was a fellow by the name of Bill Wright, who was as quick-witted and sharp-tongued as anyone I have ever met.

He was definitely the type of captain the department needed; the men respected him, and he was under-utilized.

Bill was the administrations nightmare. He never took things on face value and always questioned authority. He helped foster my propensity to ask why.

He had a wonderful command of the English language, which was based in his wealth of knowledge. You didn't want to get caught in a verbal sparring match with him, because if you did, you'd lose, even if you won.

To some, Bill was a gruff captain. I say to some, because if you didn't know your job, he would take you to task. To those who knew him, he was a softy on the inside. His outward perception was he had a lackadaisical attitude toward the job, but nothing could be further from the truth. His training and experience made him an excellent fire captain.

Anyone who spent time around him came to love him.

One evening we responded to a rescue call in a single-family home. The house was shabby and not well kept in a working-class neighborhood. As we entered the home, we could see a somewhat rotund woman sitting in the middle of a dirty kitchen floor, crying and distraught. She couldn't catch her breath because of the protracted sobs. The sobbing made it uncomfortable to watch; it was the kind of thing you would normally turn away from out of respect. It was both intimate and effusive. There was no shame in it, just pure grief and pain that flowed out of her like a river. Something terrible had happened to this woman, but it was a moment or two before we could figure out exactly what, so huge was her emotion.

Bill finally calmed her enough to learn what was causing her pain.

The woman's son had just been killed in a motorcycle accident that morning, and she had literally been overcome with grief and heartache.

We helped her up into a chair and then Bill pulled up a small stool and sat directly in front of her. We all watched as Bill sat with this poor woman. He remained there for at least an hour, holding her hand and conversing quietly—in essence, talking her through her sorrow. It was a side of him I never would have expected, but then he was someone who would constantly surprise you.

It was still relatively early in my career, and up to that point, I had never seen anything like that. In later years, I would see other firefighters act much like social workers or therapists, as rescuers. I was finding this is one of the core elements of a firefighter.

Within the next several months, we had many calls, each completely different, but whatever the circumstance, Bill handled it professionally.

The fire and sheriff's departments have a close working relationship. I have worked with many good sheriff's deputies over the years. They were a cut above most policing agencies.

The Los Angeles County Sheriff's Department is one of the largest and best trained in the country. They have a mixture of disciplines within the department, as you can well imagine. One section is the arson and explosives unit.

My first exposure to the bomb squad was when we were asked to assist with an explosive device. We received the call over the telephone; the dispatcher stated the sheriff was on scene, and needed a bucket and five gallons of kerosene. I didn't know why they needed this stuff, and never found out.

Our entire first in district was chock-full of small manufacturing businesses. I would love to say this was a mom-and-pop business, but it doesn't fit with the story.

At the rear of the fire station, two blocks to the east, was one of these businesses. It was an older building with about ten or so employees. You couldn't tell what type of business it was from the street. It didn't have any markings. It was just plainly wrapped!

As soon as we arrived, the sheriff met us at the front curb. He said the scene was already secured, and he didn't need us any longer, but we could come in and see what was going on if we would like.

Bill must have seen the curiosity in my eyes, and said we would love to look around.

The deputy took us back into the storage area of the warehouse. There, stacked from floor to ceiling were thousands of boxes marked "Marital Aids and Sex Toys."

The business manufactured many unmentionables.

The manager was proud of the operation, and said they had everything imaginable, and some things that were not. Evidently a disgruntled employee, or a neighbor who wasn't as proud as he was, had placed six sticks of dynamite among the boxes. They were all wired to an alarm clock. It looked exactly the way it is portrayed in cartoons, with multi-colored wires twisted and running to an alarm clock, just sitting there and ticking away.

The deputy had already defused the bomb. As we were watching him, I couldn't help but notice his fingernails; they were chewed halfway down his fingers. I guess that goes with the territory.

When we returned to quarters, I saw what a great sense of humor Bill had; he started into a litany of things that could have happened if the bomb had not been discovered and had actually exploded. Every possible scenario was cited about the way unmentionables would rain down on the surrounding neighborhood. Of course, everyone joined in, adding their own depiction about flying marital aids. It doesn't take too much imagination to come up with your own anecdote regarding the happiness of little old widows, whose backyards would become littered with dildos, and how their prayers had been answered.

There was a lot more to Bill than met the eye. He was someone who had many interests. Whatever he chose to do, he did well, very well. His interests were wide ranging. He loved the outdoors, loved boating, and was creative too. He was always full of surprises.

∴

I spent a year at Station 87, before I was promoted to Firefighter Specialist. The rank of FFS is an umbrella title that covers many different job titles. Camp foreman, engineers, fire prevention inspectors, and tractor operators are all in this rank.

I was assigned to the fire prevention bureau. A bureau assignment was one of those left over positions after transfers were processed at the end of the month. It was not one of the most sought-after positions, mainly because you were back behind a desk, in a forty-hour-a-week, eight-hour-a-day position. Everyone preferred being in the field, driving a fire engine to fires; after all, that's why we were firefighters.

I lost touch with Bill after I left 87's, but the values and experiences I gained from him have lasted a lifetime. Over the next twenty years, you were never far from a Bill Wright story.

Bill retired and moved around awhile before settling in Cedar City, Utah. His tales of Cedar City are legendary.

As with most people and life in general, Bill suffered his own tragedies. However, being positive by nature, he took the hardships of life in stride. After his beloved wife passed away, he remarried and moved to Lake Havasu City, Arizona.

He exchanged Cedar City's cool mountain air for the desert weather of Lake Havasu City, but that was Bill, never afraid of change.

It appeared the life of a retiree was suiting Bill just fine. He had time to spend with friends and to pursue leisure activities, which until then his job would never allow.

No one knows for sure what happened, but Bill died when five of the seven bullets fired at him from a .32-caliber handgun met their mark.

It took two full years for the investigation, arrest, and trial, but finally on Thursday, August 20, 2009, Candice Lynne Wright was convicted of killing her husband. After an eight-day trial and twenty-two witnesses, the jury deliberated little more than two hours in the Mohave County Superior Court in Kingman, Arizona, and found Bill's wife guilty.

The prosecutor would later say, "It was a tough case with no murder weapon, *no* confession, no motive, and no physical evidence." He credited the Lake Havasu City Police Department, saying they did a great job on a case that was purely circumstantial.

After the sentencing of Bill's wife, another one of life's harsh realities struck me. Candice Lynne Wright would spend the rest of her life in confinement, never accepting the realities of her crime and the gravity of her deeds regarding the impact on Bill's family and friends. She will probably die without taking responsibility for her actions. Perhaps she and O.J. Simpson can exchange letters and commiserate on how the system was stacked against them.

A guest book has been set up on the Internet for friends to share their thoughts and feelings about Bill. You are literally taken aback regarding the wide range of sentiment expressed on that website. It brings tears to my eyes every time I read them.

During Bill's lifetime, he touched many people. He is dearly missed.

CHAPTER SIXTEEN

MY MENTOR IN LIFE
IS ALSO MY BEST FRIEND

Firefighters by necessity are a tight-knit bunch. We live together much of the time, and the job requires a level of trust and dependence not found in other occupations.

Getting along with us can sometimes be difficult. Citing studies or surveys regarding the divorce rate of firefighters would be almost useless; every profession has statistics of which they are not proud. I could probably quote figures to satisfy just about any conclusion. As the saying goes, there are lies, damned lies, and statistics.

We are a competitive group with a desirable job, and we spend a lot of time away from home. If that is not a recipe for divorce, I don't know what would be.

Your crew is like a second family, and sometimes they're like your in-laws. You may love 'em or you may hate 'em, sometimes both, but most of the time you're just stuck with them.

I loved moving from station to station and meeting new crews with divergent interests and personalities. It always charged my batteries. I was most uncomfortable when I started getting too comfortable.

The County Fire Department is different from most smaller and midsized departments. The most obvious difference is its size. Duh! When I started with the department, it had twelve battalions. Each battalion has eight to fifteen fire stations. The department has grown to twenty-one battalions. Each battalion is larger than most fire departments. "Bigger is better" does not always work to your advantage.

Tim Murphy is one of my closest friends and a firefighter from outside my department. I never was able to work with him on a daily basis. He worked for the San Marino Fire Department, which has one station in the affluent city with a population of fourteen thousand.

He would work with the same twenty or so firefighters over a twenty-year period. The bond they created was a strong one, one that still lasts to this day. He has been gone from San Marino for a number of years, but those ties have never diminished. I envy relationships like that. Most small departments have that camaraderie.

The county fire department is so diverse, building these types of friendships is more difficult. After changing stations, it is uncommon to go back and visit. After all, life is demanding, and you keep busy keeping busy.

I moved from assignment to assignment on regular basis, and was fortunate to develop many close relationships. I stay in touch with many, even now in retirement.

Timothy Joseph Murphy is, you guessed it, a good Irish Catholic boy. I first met him when I pledged Kappa Sigma fraternity in college; he was my big brother.

Fraternity life is somewhat like the fire service. It is a select group of guys—at least it was back then—whom you come to know well over the four years in college. In my case it was a few years longer!

In a fraternity your big brother guides you through the tumultuous days of pledging. Tim has kept the title of big brother ever since. I thought the tumultuous times would end when we graduated.

From the time we first met, we clicked as if we had known each other all our lives; given the resemblance of our paths to that point and after, we easily could have. He grew up several miles away in Monterey Park, where the communities were similar.

Our families had much the same values, and our fathers were cut from the same cloth, hardworking men of few words who took care of their families and taught by example. They were very much the epitome of the good provider so often used to describe men of their time.

My life had been on a parallel track with Tim's even before we met, with one exception. Tim attended Catholic school, Don Bosco Technical Institute, a college-preparatory high school in Rosemead. His primary education was vastly superior to mine, in every way except one. Bosco Tec was an all-boy's high school. He was not exposed to the wonders of the female form as early as I was and with the same regularity.

Even though he was thereby prevented from marrying his high school sweetheart, he managed the next best thing and married the girl next door, a lovely Irish lass by the name of Patricia. Patty grew up in a fire department family; her dad was a captain with the Monterey Park Fire Department.

I beat him to the altar by barely a month, and was proud to serve as Tim's best man.

Before we met our better halves, we were just a couple of typical young guys hanging around the fraternity house and wondering what was going to happen in life. It was a turbulent time for male college students our age. The Vietnam War was raging and the entire country was as well. Nobody knew what was going to happen next. There was a lot of uncertainty in our lives.

Tim had his early life figured out. He was sure of himself, mature and wise beyond his years.

The first day I met him, he told me about flying. He had always wanted to be a pilot, and already had been working on his pilot's license. To listen to Tim, he knew what he was going to do tomorrow and the next day; he was born to fly.

We were sitting in the cafeteria having lunch and unexpectedly he asked, "Just what is it you do? You always have money in your pocket and the time to spend it."

That is when I introduced Tim to the fire service. That day we went to the San Marino and Monterey Park Fire Departments. They were the only two in the area that were testing. San Marino just happened to have an exam coming up within the week. He took the exam and aced it, as I knew he would. Shortly thereafter he was hired as a recruit firefighter.

He always breezed through his college classes seemingly without the need to study like the rest of us mere mortals, so I knew recruit training wouldn't be difficult for him.

By the fall of 1969, we were both young, married firefighters with our lives all mapped out, or so we thought.

The San Marino Fire Department was not the best place for an upward career path. It was a one-horse outfit, with roughly twenty employees including the chief's secretary, so someone would have to retire or die if he was ever going to advance.

I should not have been surprised at what Tim did next, but I was.

"Hey, Doug, I have something to tell you. I enlisted."

I just stared at him. Was he crazy? New wife, new job, new house, and he wants to go into the military?

"In the air force, six years."

Tim had talked about this before, because back then most airline pilots began their careers in the military. Tim figured that was his ticket to becoming an airline pilot, which was what he wanted to do. He was willing to pay the price to realize his dream. I admired that; whenever we had discussed it, I couldn't help reminding him a war was going on, and a pretty nasty one at that.

I hadn't heard him speak of it for a while since he had been a firefighter and had gotten married. I thought maybe he'd changed his mind. He hadn't. His dream was burning as brightly as it ever had, and so there was nothing more to say than congratulations and Godspeed.

Life has a way of throwing us a curveball, and three months later during physical fitness training he sprained his ankle and would never fly for the military. He was looking at six years behind a desk.

Now that's a curveball!

I knew that wouldn't fly with Tim, pardon the pun, but I couldn't see how he was going to get out of his military commitment.

He has always been a friendly and affable chap, and the air force doctor treating him took a liking to him. He asked Tim if he wanted to stay in the military or go back to civilian life. Tim received an honorable discharge several months into a six-year commitment, his military requirement fulfilled. A sprained ankle changed his life. Although it was a terrible blow to his lifetime career goals, ultimately it proved a blessing in disguise.

Since he'd been in the military, San Marino hired him right back, so there he was, safe from Vietnam, while I had a brand-new 1A classification after I graduated from college.

⁂

After several years with San Marino, Tim just was not getting enough done in life, and so he attended law school and became a practicing attorney.

He set up his first law practice in Arcadia, upstairs in a spare bedroom of his home. He would remind me that just because you passed the California State Bar exam, it didn't mean a line of people were standing at your door waiting for legal advice.

He presented me with one of his new business cards. Proudly printed on the card was:

Timothy J. Murphy
Attorney at Law

The only problem with the card was through some printing error, or so I thought, the type was placed running downhill a little.

Tim had an eye for detail, so it surprised me.

"Tim, the printing, *it's crooked!*"

"Perfect card for a new attorney don't you think?"

Firefighter, pilot, attorney-at-law, and a sense of humor; he was running out of room on his business card.

The expression is "hit the ground running," and that was Tim. His feet were always moving, whether they were on the ground or not. To an outsider, he accomplished things with ease; no one ever saw the internal struggle. It is the old duck-on-a-pond theory. The waterfowl glides across the water's surface with apparent ease, while just under the surface it's paddling like hell to stay afloat.

He had a propensity to drag me along, kicking and screaming. My "type A" personality traits were there, but just below the surface. Once I got where I wanted to be, I was perfectly happy staying right where I was. Just like in high school, once I had a job and a car and a girlfriend, I was totally content.

Tim was always certain, deep down, I couldn't possibly be happy until I attacked every day and accomplished great things. I realized early on if I tried to keep up with him, I would fall short, so I learned to pace myself.

He served then, as he does now, as my motivator-in-chief, mentor, and best friend.

It is a good thing he has such a positive outlook on life, because in spite of his intelligence and spirit, he has been a victim of Murphy's Law: whatever can go wrong has probably happened to my friend Tim at one time or another. Perhaps the law was named after him.

Tim has tenacity and the ability to bounce back; no matter what was thrown at him, he would always spring back.

In 1978 California voters passed the infamous Proposition 13, or the People's Initiative to Limit Property Taxation, which enacted strict limits on property taxes and thus lowered tax revenues.

For reasons I still do not understand, San Marino's fire chief immediately panicked and laid off eight firefighters, including Tim, who had just bought a house and had a new baby.

Within days the chief had a blinding glimpse of the obvious; he had more fire equipment than men to operate them during an emergency. No one has ever said that just because you are the fire chief, you're smart.

He quickly rehired the firefighters he had just let go. Tim and I both came to the realization that nothing was certain in life, especially employment.

My general suspicion and distrust of authority was reinforced yet again.

Time heals all wounds, and the advancing years were good to Tim. From a precarious start, he would work his way through the ranks and eventually be offered San Marino's fire chief position.

The timing was not right, so he respectfully declined, preferring instead to bide his time and wait. It is truly an intelligent and fortunate man who can pick and choose his opportunities.

Another opportunity did arise a few years later. He was hired as an assistant fire chief with the Westminster Fire Department, which was a larger department and the pay was more.

Sure enough, Murphy's Law struck again. Shortly after leaving a department and friends he had worked with for over twenty years, the Westminster Fire Department was dissolved and incorporated into the Orange County Fire Authority.

Tim was back as a captain with another new department. He enjoyed his time there, but his feet were still running at a hundred miles an hour, and the call for upward movement was still ringing in his ears.

When we were in college, he placed an application for employment with the Monterey Park Fire Department. Twenty-seven years later, he was hired there as a battalion chief.

There is no keeping a good man down, so his career path would take him to the top position of that department. He served as fire chief until he retired in 2005. If anything had a hand in shaping Tim's career, it was, ironically, Murphy's Law.

⁘

One evening, I was going to meet Tim for dinner with Lynn Clark, a fellow battalion chief from our department.

Tim was late as usual; punctuality was never one of his strong suits.

One of the good things about meeting for dinner while you are on duty and in uniform is it usually gets you a good seat, and at Marie Callender's a bigger piece of pie for desert.

Firefighters for the county are a prideful group and their uniforms exemplify that pride.

The Los Angeles County Fire Department badge is impressive, and second to none. The uniform of the Monterey Park Fire Department was much less notable: black pants, white shirt, and tiny gold badge, at least an inch smaller in all directions than ours.

Lynn and I were already seated, and after several minutes, a server came over. She was a pleasant woman, and we had a nice conversation before we told her we were waiting for another person.

A few more minutes went by and she approached again. This time I said:

"Ma'am, we're waiting for an older gentleman who's mentally challenged. He always wanted to be a fireman, so we gave him a white shirt and a little badge. When you speak to him, you have to look directly at him, and speak slowly and a touch louder. He's hard of hearing. He's proud of those things we gave him, so I'd appreciate it if you made him feel special when he gets here."

"Aw, that's sweet. What's his name?"

"Timmy," I answered, inspired.

"You got it, Chief."

Monterey Park's badges and uniform fit my scenario perfectly.

As soon as Tim sat down, the waitress walked over and unrolled Tim's silverware from his napkin as if he were a child.

"You must be Timmy," she said, very deliberately.

"Uh...yeah."

"You look like a real fireman!"

"Huh?"

"That is a nice badge, Timmy."

The look on Tim's face was priceless, and we lasted about another two seconds before we burst into laughter, as did most people sitting close to us.

Tim had the last laugh. He looked up solemnly at the elderly waitress and said, "Well, you know what they say. Small badge, big ..."

As a lawyer, Tim always had a good closing argument.

Recently I attended an anniversary party for Tim and his wife. Several members of Tim's family were there. I recounted the story and received a good laugh from all his relatives.

His wife, Patty, looked at me with a serious expression and said: "That was mean. Why would you do that?"

My answer is what all firefighters know and understand: "Just because I could."

From the moment I met Tim and introduced him into the fire service, we connected. He and his accomplishments have passed me as if I were standing still; I have received much more from our friendship than I have ever given.

Nothing is more valuable than a friend who challenges you to become the best you can be. Tim has served as my mentor for many years now. My father shaped my early years and honed my values, but after college, it was Tim. His steady hand pointed the way to broader horizons and a way to achieve potential I might never have imagined.

Just being around Tim made me work harder. It's funny, because trying to keep up with him makes me feel like Sisyphus, the mythological king doomed to continuously push that boulder up the hill, only to see it roll right back down into the valley. That could have described Tim just as well, with all of the curveballs thrown his way over the years, only he managed in the end to finally get that boulder to the top.

CHAPTER SEVENTEEN

COULD I HAVE DONE MORE?

I had just lost my position at Station 31 because of the new paramedic program, and moved to the city of Industry, Fire Station 87, thirty miles to the northeast.

Change always seems to come in threes. It was starting to be a busy year. My youngest son was born, I was displaced from the crew I came to know and love, and I had a new assignment in an unfamiliar area. I still loved every minute of it.

Chris was born in March of 1973. He is three years younger than Colton. I was twenty-seven. Debbie amazes me; she rose to the occasion without complaining. My new assignment took me farther from home, her mother and family were still seventy miles away, and at the age of twenty-three, she now had a new baby to take care of, most of the time by herself, while I was at work.

As young mothers have an inclination to do, she passed me with light speed on the maturity scale. They say women develop faster during puberty, but I'd say their lead on us probably lasts a lifetime. Being a firefighter allows you to keep that little boy alive within you. Sometimes that is a blessing, but if you ask Debbie, it can be a real curse. She would often remark she thought she was raising three kids! "Won't you ever grow up?" she would say.

I was learning the hard way, *"there is a great woman behind every idiot"*.

Like all brothers, my sons definitely went through vastly different stages in their relationship. Colton was fascinated by this new little brother named Chris, who garnered so much attention in our budding household, and was protective of him as he began to walk and talk.

That doesn't mean they didn't have their differences. As any parent knows, especially in raising boys, there was plenty of conflicts and then some growing up. Generally speaking, both were good kids. They were both active Boy Scouts within the Mormon Church.

The similarities in their personalities could be counted on one hand.

Colton was always more directional, but they are both sharp kids. Sometimes too sharp for their own good!

Chris once bragged to me that he could keep the kids in his junior high school English class laughing at the teacher.

"Chris, do you think maybe that's why you got a D in that class?" I asked innocently.

Chris, who was falling behind in class, asked his mother to help with his term paper. Both mother and son slaved over that paper, writing it and rewriting it many times. You can imagine the look on his mother's face when *they both* received a D on the paper.

It is a painful lesson for a father when he learns the nut didn't fall too far from the tree. I wish the positive lessons in life would germinate as well as the negative ones do.

Life is full of little moments with your kids when a light starts to dim, if not extinguish altogether. You realize they're going to go through everything you did, and not reap a single benefit of your knowledge garnered through hard-fought experiences.

Parental advice is like a GPS. Just because you give them directions doesn't mean they won't hit a few bumps in the road along the way.

They were good kids, but like most, needed to learn things on their own. Chris especially had a real knack for learning everything the hard way. I can't remember all the times I asked Chris why he had done something in a way that ended up being harder or more painful than it needed to be.

"Why'd you do that?" I'd ask. "Why do you need to bump your head on that same old rock every time?"

"I don't know, Dad."

Chris is one of those kids who personify the phrase, *it seemed like a good idea at the time.* He was a typical second son who wanted to emulate, impress, or outdo his older brother, maybe all three.

By comparison Colton always found a way to skate through life. That is a polite way to say he didn't have as many bumps on his head!

When you are the firstborn, sometimes you're learning right along with your parents. By the time Chris came along, Debbie and I were getting better at this parenting thing, or so we thought.

Colton would always say to me, "Cut me some slack here, Dad. I have never been a kid before," and my response was, "Yeah, well, I've never been a dad before either!"

Chris always had a lot of cuts and scrapes garnered in new and unusual ways. We stopped counting the broken bones and the trips to the emergency room for stitches.

Colton and Chris are on both sides of forty, which is still hard for me to believe. Given their propensity for accidents, I know the good Lord has kept a watchful eye on them.

After bumping around in Lake Forest and Mission Viejo, we moved into the home we were building in a community named Coto de Caza in Orange County, California. We spent most of the boys' formative years there.

The guard-gated private community was originally built as a hunt club on five thousand acres of prime Southern California real estate located adjacent to the Saddleback Mountains. Some notables such as John Wayne, William Shatner, James Drury, and James Darren belonged to Coto's hunt club.

Coto de Caza is the home of Vic Braden's tennis college.

During the 1984 Summer Olympics, the community served as host to the riding, running, shooting, and fencing portions of the modern pentathlon event.

It is also known for the reality-based television show *The Real Housewives of Orange County.* I am not sure if that is progress or not.

It was a great place to bring up a family. In 1980 the area was considered rural; the total population of Coto was less than five hundred residents. Our home was on a three-acre site.

Both of the boys attended the little Trabuco School, an elementary school located close to Coto de Caza. The school dates back to the late 1890s, and had a total enrollment of one hundred kids.

It had a great animal husbandry program. The kids raised chickens, goats, rabbits, and horses as part of the course, so you might say they were in hog heaven. On Fridays, the kids could ride their horses to school—that, of course is if they had one.

Chris's best friend was a quiet boy named Michael, who was doing well to give you three words at a time, something he got from his dad, who was also not the most loquacious person you would ever meet. Our family and theirs became close. He was a good kid, with good values; we were happy to have them as family friends. Michael had an older sister, Stacie, so he suffered from being the second child, same as Chris.

Coto was a small community by today's standards, and Michael lived within an easy walking distance of us. Chris and Michael were always together.

Michael was only ten years old when his mom and dad divorced. His father moved to Contra Costa County in the bay area. Divorce is always troubling for kids; Michael didn't adjust well to not having a father at home.

The friends you make in your formative years have a huge impact on your life. It's difficult to make friends like that in later years. If Chris is one of your friends, you are truly blessed. The bond he creates lasts for a lifetime. He is truly loyal and sticks with his friends through thick and thin, and he never asks anything in return.

I don't know if it was life's experiences or just the maturing process, but Michael became more introverted. We would spend as much time with him as we could. He was always welcome in our home.

He was so withdrawn, you never knew what he was thinking. We tried to give him a loving second family, and someone to listen whenever he needed to talk. Debbie was always good at that.

He missed having a father at home, and envied the stability Chris had in his home.

The life of a firefighter takes you away from home. It is common to be gone for three or four days at a time. That is the dilemma of a firefighter's wife; she has to be both mom and dad, and the decision maker in her husband's absence. Debbie was always a hands-on mom, and when I was gone, it gave her plenty of time to spend with the kids.

Drawing Michael out from his shell was a difficult task; I wish I could have spent a little more time with him.

When Michael turned thirteen, he moved to the Bay area to live with his dad.

A new area is tough for any child, especially one who has a difficult time expressing himself.

Michael began a new chapter in his life with his father. Everything was beginning anew, from his neighborhood to a new school. All the familiar anchor points were left behind; nothing was the same.

As a new teenager he found his first girlfriend.

In summer of 1988, Michael came down to visit. This was a perfect time for Chris and Michal to renew their friendship and discuss the changes in his life, and of course share stories about his girlfriend.

As always I tried to engage Michael in dialogue at lunch one day, but it was a typical conversation.

"How's everything at your new school?"

"Okay."

"How's your dad?"

"Fine."

"I hear you broke up with your girlfriend."

"Yup."

That was the last time I had an opportunity to speak with Michael; within days he returned to his father's house, his new school, and the troubled relationship with his girlfriend.

No one could tell what was going on in Michael's mind, or why he decided to pull his dresser against the bedroom door and put his father's pistol to his head. Michael ended his short fifteen-year life in a split second.

I wish I had done more, anything that might have prevented that heartbreaking moment. I knew Michael had a difficult time expressing himself and he needed someone to share his innermost feelings. There is a lingering question in the back of my mind that if I would have listened to him just a little bit longer, and shared just the right thoughts, I could have changed the course of events.

Today our family still suffers from the frustration that Chris lost his best friend and we were powerless to do anything about it.

Debbie received the news regarding Michael and through tear-filled eyes had to tell Chris.

Chris sat silently with his head in his hands and finally said, "If he would have only waited…things get better, they always do." I couldn't help but think what insight my fifteen-year-old son had.

It broke my heart to see my son deal with such a catastrophic loss at his age.

Michael's mother was a lost soul after the divorce, and she was now dealing with the indelible memory of the loss of her son. Debbie was friends with her, and did what she could, but what could you possibly say to a parent who has just lost a child?

Michael touched many people with his quiet ways; he didn't know how many hearts he would break with his ill-fated decision.

Along with the good memories of Michael, a note in our scrapbook sadly sums up his short life:

> *Fifteen-year-old Michael of Coto de Caza, a dear friend of the family, died Tuesday.*
>
> *Memorial services Friday at St. Andrew's Presbyterian Church.*

Michael's death was the second time in my life a close, young family friend has committed suicide.

During the 1950s, families were a little closer. Wally and the Beaver's neighborhood might have been the norm.

In my childhood neighborhood, whenever I would stray off the beaten path, there was always an adult who would "cough me up to my parents." It was as if I had a couple of dozen fathers.

Our next-door neighbors, Walt and Doris, were good neighbors and good family friends. Our families were so close, we would even vacation together. It was nice having two kids living next door. Michael was one year younger than I was, and his brother Stanley, six years younger.

Walt was a Los Angeles City firefighter and introduced me to the fire service. I owe much of my direction in life to his early mentoring.

If there were any problems within their family, it certainly wasn't visible from the outside.

Michael graduated from high school, and being an excellent student, went to the University of California, Santa Barbara. Walt was proud of Michael and extremely frustrated at the same time. Their family values bordered on the redneck side of conservative, and after he graduated from college, he returned home with political, social, and economic values about 180 degrees the opposite of Walt's. It probably made for some interesting dinner conversations.

Stanley was not as driven as Michael, but had optimistic goals nonetheless. He chose the US Coast Guard as a career.

Life would change for their family shortly after Stanley's graduation from the Coast Guard academy.

It's a scenario that has been played out since the beginning of time; when Stanley returned home, he found the young love of his life had found another.

The last time I saw Stanley was just before Christmas, and he was in excellent spirits. We discussed some of the troubles he was going through, and life in general.

Several days before New Year's, I received a call from my father. He started our conversation with, "I hope you are sitting down." That opening in no way leads to good news.

My father, never one for long-winded conversations, quickly blurted out, "Stanley is dead. Doris found him lying on his bedroom floor after she returned home from a shopping trip. He put newspapers down and shot himself in the chest with the .22-caliber rifle Walt had given him during scouts."

I cannot image the pain Stanley's parents must have gone through.

Several years later, while I was working in Roland Heights at Fire Station 145, we responded to a call of a possible suicide. I thought by this time in my career I was becoming immune to heartbreaking emergency calls, but nothing can prepare you for witnessing the pain of others.

The neighborhood was Middle America through and through; everything smacked of the area from my childhood.

When we arrived, the front door was open, but no one was there to greet us. The house was a beautiful two-story home with the bedrooms upstairs. Just off the entry was a den that had been converted into another bedroom. Sitting on the floor next to the bed was a mother cradling the lifeless body of her son. He had committed suicide. She sat there, rocking back and forth, hugging his body. Again that sense of helplessness washed over me.

I sat down on the floor next to her, trying to comfort her a little. I immediately had a flashback to the time Bill Wright sat next to a grieving mother. I was hoping I could summon the comforting words Bill had spoken years before. Perhaps I could do or say something to ease the mother's pain just a little.

I do not know how long the mom sat there with her son in her lap before calling us, but he had been gone for some time.

We sat there together for what felt like an eternity before I spoke to her. I could scarcely speak myself, due to my own emotions. My son Chris was the same age as this boy.

The sheriff came to the scene and took charge of the situation. Both the sheriff's deputy and I had a difficult time leading the mom into another room; she wanted to spend as much time as she could with her son.

The role of a firefighter is one where you witness the tragedies of others, then return to quarters, never to speak of them again. You just cram the thoughts away in that filing system and with any luck never visit them again.

Emergency room physicians and nursing staff learn, as do firefighters, we have to maintain a distance from the people we assist if we want to continue to help them. The concept is easy, but the application is difficult. We are human beings after all, and we bring to our profession everything we have ever seen and heard. As much as we try to divorce ourselves from prior unpleasant experiences, they do visit more than we wish. Some memories you can't keep sealed.

CHAPTER EIGHTEEN

I ALMOST LOST CHRIS TOO

I never liked responding to traffic collisions. They happen quickly and by their nature, they are nonselective. A family can be driving down the freeway on their way to visit Grandma, and not arrive through any fault of their own. Their lives change beyond measure in the blink of an eye.

Not every firefighter is as reluctant as I am about traffic collisions. When I mentioned my reservations to a new paramedic, he looked at me as if I'd just expressed distaste for Mom and apple pie.

"Are you kidding me?" he said. "I love a good trauma! I'll finally get to use all that training and knowledge I have learned."

Who can say why someone dies in a tragic accident, while others do not? The newspaper reports accidents on a daily basis in which a driver will just walk away, while other minor accidents take lives.

Certain aspects of what we do just go with the job. I guess not liking vehicle accidents is akin to moving to the desert and complaining about the heat. You just have to adjust. I could say I got used to seeing vehicle accidents, but I never did.

Seven years after the death of Michael, Chris was involved in a serious car accident. I thought I was going to lose my son.

It is an odd thing to thank the good Lord that your child is safe, lying in the hospital, until you consider the alternative.

As a father I had always been adamant about my sons wearing seatbelts. Colton was more conscientious about it than Chris. You notice little things like that, and so it becomes almost second nature that you have to say twice to one what you say once to the other.

I always told Chris twice.

Chris attended Feather River College after he graduated high school. It was a beautiful rural area for college in Quincy, California, bordering Plumas National Forest. The population is less than 1,900.

Chris loved Quincy and stayed at the college as much as he could.

He was a typical kid who wanted to stay out from under the thumb of his parents—not as much Debbie as me. After all, as much as I tried to fight it, I was an overprotective dad.

Chris had left college for a short period and was living in Sacramento with his Uncle Kevin, Debbie's youngest brother.

In April 1995 Chris was on his way back to Quincy to see a college friend. He was driving on a rural road just outside of Sacramento when a youthful driver (he had his driver's license for just two weeks) unexpectedly turned left in front of him. Chris T-boned the other car. The momentum of the crash propelled Chris into the steering wheel and dashboard, eventually hitting the windshield. The other driver was not hurt. Chris spent ten days in the hospital with head and neck trauma, a crushed cheekbone, a broken jaw, various other lacerations to his face, and pain just about everywhere.

When I saw him, I had flashbacks to Colton's accident, and it wasn't any easier the second time around.

The one tiny comfort—if there is any comfort in an "I told you so!"—is that the last thing Chris remembered just before he hit the windshield was how many times I had told him to wear his seatbelt.

I had to smile. At least he didn't have his sense of humor knocked out of him.

Chris's jaw was wired shut for six weeks and he lost thirty-five pounds.

It was one of those times as a parent when you wish that somehow you could bear at least a small portion of your child's pain; however, you know you never can. The most frustrating feeling in the world is waiting for your child to heal.

As I said, "Chris always had to learn things the hard way."

All of his injuries were just the beginning. He lost feeling in his face and mouth, and required several surgeries in future months to fix his jaw.

He convalesced in South Lake Tahoe at my sister's house for several weeks before moving to St. George, Utah.

It's one of those good things about family; everywhere Chris went, a family member wanted to help him. He lived with Debbie's dad for several months until he got his feet on the ground.

Chris can never be accused of not having tenacity. When it comes to learning new things, he is fearless.

In St. George he worked at everything from a plumber's helper to a heavy equipment operator. He continued college there and had enough time to get his private pilot's license.

I admire his persistence.

Out of calamity comes fortune. While living in St. George, he met Jodi, the girl who would become his wife. They dated for a year before moving to Carson City, Nevada. They live in Reno, close to us, with their firstborn, Emily, and little Liam, a tenacious little lad just like his father. Liam just turned four.

Unexplained accidents grant credibility to the expression "Here but by the grace of God go I." There isn't a firefighter who walks the face of this earth who hasn't thought at one time or another, "Boy, that could have been me."

While I was at the scene of a terrible-looking traffic accident with no injuries, I made the comment to the firefighters around me, "Boy, that guy sure was lucky!" One of the firefighters looked at me and said, "Are you kidding me? If he was lucky, he'd be home right now, with a beer in his hand, watching television."

I guess everything is relative.

CHAPTER NINETEEN

THE KNIFE AND GUN CLUB

To be the proverbial first-string fire station within the county, you had to have a nickname. Fire Station 163 in Bell was known as the House of Pain.

Bell was one of a cluster of small cities, all of which contracted to Los Angeles County for fire protection. The city of Cudahy was located to the south, Maywood to the north, and Bell Gardens to the east. Most Angelinos probably didn't know where these cities were, until the recent boondoggle with the city council of Bell and its mayor.

Station 163 had two fire engines. Most stations with two engines also had two full crews, which included two captains. Station 163 was an aberration in that respect; it had only one captain of the engine, and an abbreviated crew on Engine 263. No captain, just an engineer, who acted as a driver and an abridged captain, if there was such a thing. How and why this arrangement was originally set up is a mystery. The good thing is that it worked, because of the heavy response load.

The bid system finally worked, and after two years of being in the fire prevention bureau, I received my transfer to Fire Station 163. It was quite a change from doing fire prevention inspections every day from eight to five.

To say the station had interesting calls would be an understatement. I guess when the call volume goes up, just by sheer numbers you are going to have many diverse calls.

I was learning there was no one reason for a call to stick in your mind or leave a mark. Some are so grotesque or unique, they stay in that area of your brain reserved for the calls that are just plain weird.

The city of Bell is an older city, with most of the homes being small and built when the area was first growing. The ripple effect of social migration was taking hold, and many of the homes were being used as rentals. The entire area was mostly lower-income families, which experience has taught me take advantage of social services more frequently.

One evening we responded to a call for a young man on a weekend furlough from Metropolitan State Hospital. Metro is a hospital for the mentally ill and is located in the nearby city of Norwalk. It is a city within a city. The place was huge. It covers over three hundred acres. Built in 1915, it is somewhat eerie at night, with its old buildings and their foreboding presence. I guess knowing it was an asylum had something to do with that. Today most of the old brick buildings have been condemned because of earthquake standards, so large sections make it a ghost town.

We didn't know the history of our victim until later, but as the story unfolded, we found out he had been a resident of the hospital for some time, and had convinced his doctors he was sane enough to roam free and unfettered for the weekend. That turned out to be a colossal mistake for all concerned.

Upon his release, he went to visit his girlfriend. It was a cool night in January when he went to her upstairs apartment not too far from our station. Of course, in Bell nothing was far from Station 163. The entire city is less than three square miles.

He and his girlfriend apparently got into an argument, a heated dispute, and he did something completely unexpected, at least for most of us. He pulled out a machete.

I'm not going to speculate as to where he was hiding the thing. I suppose it's possible the machete was already in the apartment, maybe left there from a former tenant. However, when the huge knife came out, the girlfriend reacted like any sane individual and made a hasty retreat for the door.

One could argue as to the sanity of allowing a mental patient to come into your apartment in the first place, but the woman suffered greatly for her actions, and as a sign of respect, I'll just call it an honest mistake.

Emotions were out of control, and as she made her run for the door, he was in hot pursuit. He brought the machete down hard, directly onto the back of her head. He then swung it twice more as she was falling, once on each shoulder blade so she had the imprint of an almost perfect X across her back. The initial blow left a wound straight down the back of her head.

His girlfriend was either faking unconsciousness or death. It doesn't matter, but she lay there on the floor for some time, listening to his rants and ravings. Assuming the girlfriend was dead, he stomped around the living room and kitchen area, rubbing his hands in the blood of his girlfriend and writing slogans on the apartment walls. When he got to the kitchen, the woman, seeing an opportunity to escape, managed to stand up and run out the door and down the stairs, finally collapsing on the porch of a neighbor. The neighbor called for help.

The Bell police and Engine 263 responded to aid the poor woman who collapsed. The police, following the bloody footsteps back up to the apartment, found the perpetrator.

Engine 163 was dispatched to the upstairs apartment.

The mental patient, realizing his girlfriend had escaped, in what can be only described as suicidal rage, swung the machete with such velocity, when it hit his neck, it nearly cut off his head.

When the girlfriend made her hasty escape, she left the front door open, and the cold night air made vapors rise from the profuse amount of warm blood on the apartment floor. The stench was unimaginable.

When we walked in the door, the place looked like a slaughterhouse. The girl's blood was all over the floor and the walls, and his body lay across the room in the kitchen.

We made our way, slipping on the blood, to the victim, who still had the machete in his hand.

I kicked the blade away and leaned down to turn him over. He felt light, and his shoulders moved easily.

His head didn't move at all.

"Oh, man," I said to no one in particular. "That's not good." Boy, if that's not an understatement I don't know what is.

The knife had cut a good three quarters of the way through his neck before he passed out, which is a pretty impressive feat. Within seconds he bled out and died. Fortunately, his girlfriend, or I guess I should say *ex*-girlfriend, lived to hopefully find a decent guy.

Heck of a way to end a relationship.

As luck would have it, the paramedic unit that responded with us had a nurse ride-a-long from their base hospital with them. We asked her if she wanted to pronounce the upstairs victim dead. She declined. I'll bet this incident resides in her memory banks too.

For whatever reason, and I don't know why, this incident didn't bother me all that much. It was one of the bloodiest, most horrific scenes I had witnessed, but it just didn't affect me in the way you might expect. I guess it was simply so outrageous that all I could do was shrug my shoulders and say, "Oh, well." I filed this incident in a place I never venture. Other incidents are in a more accessible area, ones that remind me of how strange the world is we live in, and the unpredictable nature of human beings.

Witnessing the result of suicide by machete pretty much left me unscathed. Perhaps it was the strangeness of it all; however, witnessing the results of vehicle accidents has always elevated my emotions. Anyone can be involved in an automobile accident. It happens every day. It's such a random thing, crossing all social and economic boundaries in this country. As I described in earlier chapters, I almost lost both of my sons in vehicle accidents.

Not many people you know have been killed by a machete-wielding crazy person; it is just something you cannot wrap your head around.

I have no idea if the mental hospital changed its furlough policy. I hope so.

⁙

Human nature is truly a strange and wondrous thing.

Maybe it's the cold, rainy nights of January that bring the worst out in people, I don't know, but we had our share of weird responses that month. Early in the evening, the night manager of a cheap Florence Avenue motel thought he heard a gunshot coming from the upstairs hallway and called the police. When Bell PD arrived, they found a thirty-something male slumped in the hallway, just beneath the pay phone. He was unresponsive, so they called us.

When we arrived, they had pieced together what had happened. The poor devil was arguing with his girlfriend over the phone. I guess their exchange got a little heated, and at some point, he threatened to kill himself, to which she responded, "Go ahead, hotshot!" The next sound she heard was the same gunshot that prompted the motel manager to call for help.

He was deader than a doornail, and she was now freer than a bird. Strange how those things work out.

A few days later, the days were clear, no rain, but just as gloomy for some as the inclement weather. We responded to a call of a person down in a trailer, at the rear of a home located in a residential area just west of the station.

The old and dilapidated twenty-foot travel trailer was sitting at the end of a long driveway toward the garage, which was located at the rear of the property. As soon as we opened the door, which was in the center of the trailer, we could still smell gun smoke. To the right was a small kitchen table, and to the left, an unkempt bed and the body of a young lifeless woman. Cradled next to her was a nine-month-old baby dressed in spotless blue pajamas.

No one will ever know the torment this young mother was suffering that drove her to place the barrel of a .22-caliber revolver in the nose of this precious little baby and pull the trigger. The mom was dead, but the baby was still warm and even showed faint signs of life.

We grabbed the little guy, and in the back of a police car, responded to the local hospital. All of our efforts were in vain, and the little child slipped from this life.

Some calls just don't make any sense, as hard as you try, and you just cannot dismiss them from your mind.

The lovesick man whose girlfriend provoked him into pulling the trigger was certainly easier to forget than a little baby lying next to his mother. I couldn't relate to the first incident, but the second one profoundly affected me; both of my boys were not too much older.

⁙

I was brought up in a family of hunters, so there were always guns around the house. They are kept in a safe place, and everybody in the family had been taught how to safely use them. I have always been comfortable around firearms.

Debbie's family was the same, and so we raised our boys as both Debbie and I had been raised. They were taught to use firearms safely from an early age. Both of my sons were typical boys in that regard, and we all enjoyed hunting and the outdoors. During dove season, I would take them out hunting, and it was an enjoyable family outing.

We were never intimidated by firearms, or thought they were evil. They just became a part of our lives.

When my oldest son was around eight, my attitude toward guns was gradually changing. The number of gun-related tragedies was starting to accumulate in my mind, and they were becoming harder and harder to forget and purge from those deep recesses. I was starting to bring home concerns from work and relating them to my own children.

I finally decided I no longer wanted guns in my home. The older I got, the more I worried about my family. I was more afraid of a gun accident than I was of an intruder breaking into my home. A parent with young children sees innumerable dangers, and it appeared this one could be easily eliminated.

In one fell swoop, I purged my home of firearms. I took most of the guns to my dad's house for safekeeping. The rest I sold or gave away.

My unexpected attitude change was a personal issue. Shifting my opinion about weapons was not an easy undertaking; it took years and many unpleasant sights, but nonetheless I had changed.

The number one purpose of firearms is to kill. The design and technology have improved, and we can now kill things with more efficiency. Yes, a number of sporting events use guns, but it does not negate their prime purpose.

I had always been a passionate supporter of the Second Amendment, but I was becoming more liberal in my views. Debbie was never anxious about having guns in the house, but she saw that I was, and so she supported my decision.

My long held views were in jeopardy. I was afraid I was going to awake one morning and find myself a full-blown progressive regarding the Second Amendment, and God forbid, life in general. I was scaring myself. I didn't know how far I was going to walk down this path.

I still thought individuals should take personal responsibility for their own actions, go figure, but I was learning this simple philosophy was becoming a lost art. Just because I had a personal epiphany regarding guns didn't give me the right to control others. After all, if I were to adopt a full-blown liberal attitude, I would be on the forefront of machete control.

By the time I was in the middle of my career, my attitudes were completely solidified, and I was holding fast to the notion. I never once responded to an incident in which a person used a firearm to protect himself or his family.

Boy was I mistaken; the future would prove me wrong, terribly wrong. Little did I know how much Debbie's family would come to rely upon firearms for their very survival.

My friend Tim is a hunter, and once a year he would travel to Alaska to hunt with a group of his fellow attorneys. Yup, there is another joke in there somewhere.

He was completely amazed regarding how my attitudes were changing.

Upon Tim's return from one of his hunting trips, we planned to go out to lunch. I arrived at his law office a little early, and as usual, he was late.

Tim's secretary Lori, took me into his office and showed me the trophy he had bagged in Alaska. In the corner was a black bear standing in an upright position with his paws raised and teeth growling, frozen for eternity in that position.

Lori said, "It was just delivered today. Don't you think it's a little small?"

"I don't know. I have never been this close to a black bear before."

"Don't say anything to Tim about his size; he is sensitive."

Within a few minutes, Tim finally arrived. We sat in his office for a few minutes and then he finally said, "What do you think of my bear?'

"Little small, isn't it?"

"You a—h—!"

The fire department has an abundance of outdoorsman and hunters. What would a group of macho firefighters be without tales of fishing and hunting? I would listen intently to the stories they would share about their hunting excursions.

"What a great trip. We hiked in for what seemed like forever and hadn't seen a soul for days. The setting couldn't have been more picturesque. Finally, there he stood, a huge six-point buck. The beautiful beast leisurely raised his head after drinking from the stream that flowed into a small lake. The mountains reflected off the water in a perfect image. We looked at each other and thought, *'It doesn't get any better than this.'* After we watched for a minute, taking in the good Lord's magnificent wonders, I raised my rifle, took aim, and shot. It killed the buck instantly!" (Sorry, I must have become more of a liberal than I thought.)

My sons were a little older when we moved to Coto de Caza; they were also maturing, but in the opposite direction from me. One day they came to me with serious looks on their faces.

"What's up, guys?"

"Dad, we know you don't want any guns in the house."

"You're right, I don't," I said, knowing full well what was coming.

"We want to go shooting at the hunt lodge."

Part of me had dreaded this conversation, but part of me was impressed they had made a decision to stand up to their old man on the issue.

"I'll make a deal with you," I said. "You both take and pass NRA gun safety courses, and I'll buy our licenses and some shotguns and take you hunting again."

"Yeah!" they agreed, and ran off to play or to tell their friends, and I sat back in my chair, smug with the knowledge it would never happen.

Of course, you can guess the end of the story. My sons on their own went down to Coto's hunt lodge and joined Ducks Unlimited, a hunting and gun safety advocate organization. They took the NRA hunter safety course, passed, and gleefully showed me their certificates.

"Okay, Dad. We're ready!" they exclaimed, smiling like the cat that ate the canary.

Over the next few months, we bought new shotguns for my ten-and thirteen-year-old sons, and we went hunting for the first time in years. Just as before, it was an enjoyable family outing.

My attitudes ran the spectrum from liberal to conservative, and I didn't have a clue where they were going to stop. I didn't realize until sometime later that having a handgun for my own personal protection would play another pivotal role in my life, and change my attitudes yet again.

CHAPTER TWENTY

THE FUTURE IS NOT ALWAYS PRETTY

At last I received my transfer to Station 14, Battalion 13. The waiting was killing me.

It wasn't that I didn't like it at Station 163, but to be a real firefighter you had to pay your dues in Battalion 13. At least that is what the guys in Battalion 13 thought.

Station 14 was at the southern tip of Battalion 13, surrounded by the city of Los Angeles and directly across the street from George Washington High School.

In 1977 the department was comprised of thirteen battalions. Each battalion was said to be a department within itself—thirteen battalions and a different caliber of firefighter for each. The busy battalions drew young, energetic firefighters who loved the stimulation of constant activity. The more affluent areas attracted the more seasoned firefighters. *Seasoned* is a code word for *older!*

Battalion 13 encompassed cities that were some of the oldest in Los Angeles County. Station 14's first-response area was small by county standards, but one of the busiest. Each year it would be in the top five in total responses and fires. The homes were older, per capita income lower, and the homicide rate higher. The crime rate was among the highest in the county, and nothing was sacred; the fire station had been burglarized several times.

The sheriff's deputies and the CHP used the station as an island of safety. They were always welcome. The camaraderie between the organizations was greatly appreciated; we needed and relied upon each other.

The station was a two-bay drive-through, with two engine companies, Engine 14 and Engine 214. Throughout the department an engine with a 2 as a lead-in number indicated it was the second engine at that station. As the county grew, and the fire station numbers got larger, the numbering scheme started to fall apart. Some engines with a *3* lead-in number are the second engine at that station. Go figure. The second engines supplemented the staffing for busy districts. When engines in surrounding districts were out of service due to calls, breakdowns, drills, or for any reason, resources were moved around to maintain service levels.

Each battalion had its own identity. It was if you had a secret handclasp, you talked and walked a certain way. Battalion 13 was steeped with arrogance. I felt like I was back in high school.

Soot and dirt on your turnouts and helmet was a sign of respect—the dirtier they were, the more respect you got.

Emmett Kinney was my captain on Engine 214. He was truly a unique and memorable boss. Emmett was one the toughest firefighters I ever knew.

He was a big, scrapping Irishman who everybody called the Buff, which was short for the buffalo. When Emmett walked into a room, it immediately felt crowded. You could sell advertising space across his back. He squeezed into a fifty-six long turnout coat, which was, of course, always dirty.

His older brother was captain of the other shift, and was as scrappy as Emmett was big. He was just as quick-witted, and interesting to be around too.

Emmett's brother would say when they were kids, he could remember lying in bed at night listening to Emmett grow. His calves were so big; he held his socks up with thumbtacks.

The Kinney brothers were iconic figures in Battalion 13. Everybody knew them, and everybody liked them. I never met a firefighter who thought about crossing them, or if they did, it was only once.

Everyone looked up to Emmett, some due to his size, others because he was a true leader. His demeanor was unimpeachable. I never saw him intimidated by any emergency response, or by anyone. His self-confidence allowed him to take everything in stride.

I enjoyed working with him, and I learned quickly you did things his way. He liked things done the way he liked them done, and nobody with any sense ever crossed him.

Not everything you learn is something you want to emulate; you take the good and try to learn, and if the characteristics don't fit your personality or style, you evaluate and move on.

The firefighter on Engine 214 with Emmett and me was Leland Stuart, whom Emmett nicknamed Howard Hughes. He was tall and thin, and did look a little like Howard Hughes.

Leland almost never spoke. Rarely would he say a word to anyone about anything. He was one of the least talkative people I have ever known, which was unusual at that station, because everyone had an opinion on just about everything. He was a good basketball player; boy, that put even more pressure on me. There is an assumption that if you are tall, which I am, you are a good basketball player. In my case, nothing could be further from the truth. I was so bad at basketball, I was a source of great entertainment for the rest of the crew.

Leland and I were about the same age, both in our late twenties. He never spoke about his personal life; he didn't have a girlfriend or wife that he spoke of, and lived either with his parents or close to them. He came from a close-knit family—just how close I wouldn't find out until years later.

The captain on Engine 14 was Mark Fieldstone. Mark and I graduated from the same recruit class. He was on the other shift during training, so I didn't know him that well. There is a bond between guys that came on the job together; it lasts your entire career.

Mark's engineer was Bill. Billy was everyone's friend. He never had a bad word to say about anyone. The firefighter was Wayne. Emmett nicknamed him the Weird Dude or WD for short. Emmett had a moniker for everyone. You couldn't become a real Battalion 13 guy unless you had a nickname.

Everything at the station was a contest; the rivalry was palpable. Competition was on every front, whether a friendly game of basketball across the street at the high school, or a game of cards after the evening meal, the loser having to do dishes. It didn't have as much to do with winning as it did with losing. You just didn't want to suffer that indignity.

The days were always busy and time passed quickly. Everyone got along, or at least I thought we did. Sometimes I marvel at my own naivety.

The management style of the fifties and sixties was quite different from today. The feelings of "I know what is best, and I will pummel you into my way of thinking" might have worked well for its time, but as attitudes have changed, so has the philosophy of motivating.

Older chief officers would belittle firefighters as a way of motivation, feeling they had accomplished their job when they had completely humiliated you in front of peers. Thankfully, that attitude was somewhat rare, and the officers who utilize this technique have long since retired.

Attitudes were changing, partly due to the views of the Vietnam War and partly because the younger generation was starting to distrust authority.

Styles and people adjust gradually. I have a propensity to blame the fire service for being slow and resisting any new ideas, but many large organizations suffer from the same lethargic feelings. Organizations that truly lead are those that shed the mantle of archaic thinking.

Mark and I had a lot in common; we were about the same age, came on the department at the same time, and were brought up in the same type of neighborhood. That is where the similarities ended. Mark had all the attributes you would want, not only as a firefighter, but also as a human being. He was intelligent, handsome, and a natural athlete. He had once appeared on a firefighter calendar. However, his arrogance made it difficult to be around him. He was raised in a fire department family. His dad was a battalion chief, and from his management style, I can only assume old school managers taught him.

Promotions are sporadic; it depends on the amount of retirements each month, and only happens two or three times a year. When the rumor of promotions is in the air, there is a constant buzz about who will get the nod and who won't.

When the promotional list is published, and if you are one of the fortunate ones, you start receiving calls from well-wishers. Everyone is happy for you. Well, almost everyone.

I was working the day I received the news about my promotion to captain.

Mark asked me to come in the office; he wanted to speak to me for a minute. What he said is still as fresh in my mind as the day the words were spoken.

He walked into the office first and sat down behind the desk. I pulled up a chair and sat directly in front of him. I had been getting calls all day, and was hearing plenty about how I was becoming one of "them" now, so I pretty much thought Mark was going to say the same. But I hadn't a clue about why we were being so formal, sitting in the office and all. He looked at me and without any type of preamble, he said, "You're a shitty engineer, and you'll be a shitty captain." He then got up, turned, and walked out.

I sat there for a few minutes completely bewildered. I could not believe what I had just heard. We had just spent the better part of a year working side by side, and had a good time doing it.

With a few words, Mark single-handedly turned the joy of a promotion into uncertainty and self-doubt. Where in the hell did that attitude come from? The statement hurt on a multiple of fronts; first and foremost, I thought we were friends.

Not quite knowing how to digest what I just heard, I walked into the next room and spoke with Emmett. I relayed the conversation Mark and I just had.

Emmett gave me a pep talk, and said that was just the way Mark was, which of course I knew, but it still felt good to hear encouraging words.

"You'll make a good captain," he told me. "Fires are fires, and you've seen plenty of those, so all you have to worry about are the people issues. If you ever have any trouble with anyone, just do what I do."

"What's that?" I asked.

"Take 'em out back of the fire station and kick the shit out of 'em."

That was Emmett's style, a tough message from a tough guy, who also had a soft heart.

Years later, when I was a battalion chief teaching a leadership class, I'd often tell stories about Emmett, although without using his name. I would relate something he did or said that made an impression on me. That was Emmett, someone who made an impression on you. Anyone who ever met him never forgot him. That was also Mark. I could never forget him, but for entirely different reasons.

After a class, a firefighter came up to me with a familiar glint in his eye and said, "You were talking about my dad, weren't you?"

I looked at his nametag, and sure enough, he was a Kinney.

We talked for a while about his father, and you could tell he was going to do well in his career. He was a good firefighter and a nice young kid. Emmett would be proud. The Kinney legacy is intact and is living on. If I made a fraction of the impact on him as an instructor as his father made on me, I will have done something right.

∗∗∗

It is a tradition in our fire department that on your last shift before you leave for your new assignment, you prepare a feast for the entire crew. I cooked a prime roast dinner with all the trimmings. It was a banquet to behold. You try to outdo the last person who was promoted; it's the competitive spirit that surfaces at every opportunity.

I had received news my new assignment was going to be in La Canada, Fire Station 19, Battalion 4. It was in an affluent area, and activity was slow, the opposite end of the response spectrum.

We sat around the table, lethargy setting in with full stomachs, and I received a lengthy diatribe regarding the "worthless firefighters" that were in my new assignment. Everyone had a good laugh, completely at my expense.

We had just finished dessert when Emmett looked at me and said, "Close your eyes; I have something for you."

Wow, what was this?

I scooted my chair back from the table, sat upright, and closed my eyes. Normally I am a little more astute, but I guess my brain wasn't up to full speed after an enormous meal.

The first drop of ice-cold water, and the startling realization how stupid I had been, hit me at the same time. I sat there for what felt like an eternity waiting for the water to stop cascading off my head, and listened to the laughter of those sitting around the table. I slowly opened my eyes and there was Emmett, grinning from ear to ear, waiting to present me with a new white captain's hat.

Anyone can be presented a white hat, but it took the cold-water drenching to solidify the memory not only in my mind, but also in my heart.

Years later, I had the opportunity to present that same hat to my oldest son when he was promoted to captain with the Orange County Fire Authority.

※

After I left station 14, I didn't have much of a chance to see Mark. It's a good thing, because when I did, it only dredged up unpleasant memories of my last conversation with him.

I had been a battalion chief for a number of years when I ran into Mark at Station 34 in Cerritos. He was a captain there, and my boss, Skip Bennett, had his office upstairs.

I would run into Mark on occasion, and we would exchange a few words (pleasant words…really). We never spoke at length; the exchanges were always brief.

Mark had some personal problems since the last time we worked together, including a devastating injury he suffered at an industrial fire. A thirty-five-foot extension ladder, which weighs nearly two hundred pounds and takes three men to lift, slid off the side of a building, and with its full force struck him. It hit his helmet, literally driving him into the ground. He spent many days in the hospital. Anyone who knew him said the accident made him a changed man.

I was walking toward Skip's office, deep in thought, when I almost ran into Mark. I was about to continue on my way, but something in his eyes slowed me down. He uttered a few words that stopped me in my tracks, just as they did many years ago.

"Doug, I would like to speak with you for a minute, if I could?"

Boy, was this a flashback. I didn't know if I should listen to him, or go on my way. I didn't know if I wanted to expose myself to another round of his criticism. After all, the last time we spoke privately, the words he uttered crushed me for a long time.

I could see he was serious, so we stepped into an empty office, and I waited for him to speak first.

He cleared his throat and sluggishly started to speak.

"Do you remember the day you made captain?"

I had to smile at that. Whenever I saw him or heard his name mentioned, that was all I could think about; the memory was burnt into my mind. Very few times in your life do you hear words that hurtful.

"Yes, I do, Mark."

"I've always felt terrible about what I said that day, and I just wanted to say I'm sorry."

For a brief moment, I could still feel the pain.

I had heard he had changed since his accident. I guess it was true.

I could have given him an egotistical response, me being a battalion chief and him a captain, but I had learned many years ago, the mark of a good man is how he accepts an apology, so I thanked him and left.

Everybody makes mistakes, and even though the apology was a long time in coming, it was welcomed.

Mark was excellent at whatever he chose, and was an excellent engineer. I was just so-so.

There is an old saying, *"In the sting of any rebuke, there is usually a kernel of truth."* Mark and I learned a little about human relations that day. We both grew.

Mark was promoted to battalion chief several years later and eventually became an assistant chief. In his last years with the department, his health took a turn for the worse and his speech became slow and labored.

It was painful to watch, because through it all, we did start out as friends, and after some detours, remain friends. In retrospect, I learned from having Mark in my life; we learn from all avenues, and hopefully change for the better.

✳

Emmett also left Station 14, and jumped from the frying pan into the fire. He transferred to Fire Station 9, one of the busiest in the county.

He was reunited with Jim Howe, the Tasmanian Devil, Taz for short. As the nickname would imply, Howe was a ball of energy, and a firefighter's firefighter. He was legendary. The fire chief would later described him as the "the epitome of the fire service professional."

The bond between Emmett and Jim could not have been tighter.

Jim Howe was a fearless firefighter and emerged from burning buildings covered head to toe with ash and dirt. He loved the action; the dirtier he was, the happier he was.

Fighting fires is dangerous work; no two incidents are ever the same. The best you can wish for is to learn what to do from your last fire, and to not repeat any mistakes. Expecting the unexpected is the only certainty.

In early January 1991, Emmett and Jim Howe, now engineer of Engine 9, responded to a fire in a commercial building. After life safety issues, cutting off the spread of fire is one of the first concerns. The building was two stories with businesses on both floors. Ladders were put into place to check for extension of fire on the upper floor.

Six firefighters were advancing hose lines on the second-story walkway when the unexpected happened. A massive eighty-foot section of ceiling facade overhead collapsed and trapped the firefighters. Emmett was pushed against the building and pinned to the floor along with another fire captain. The hose line they were using was still charged and allowed them to protect themselves from the heat of the fire. A couple of feet away, other firefighters were also trapped. They were so close to the fire that heat melted their helmets before they could be freed.

Jim Howe was not so fortunate; he was trapped underneath the rubble.

Time started to move in slow motion. Extinguishing the fire became secondary to saving the trapped firefighters. All of the available resources were used in the rescue operation. It seemed like it took forever to rescue Jim, but it couldn't have happened any quicker. Everyone at the scene was trying their best to save his life.

In all, six were injured, Jim the most serious.

At the hospital, Jim's diagnosis was grim; he was unconscious and unresponsive. Chief Freeman ordered a hospital room vigil, so he was never alone.

He had the best of care and was surrounded by his personal and firefighting families when he passed away. Jim Howe was only forty-seven years old.

Several days later, hundreds of firefighters and friends paid their last respects. The church was filled to capacity, and many had to stand outside.

After the eulogy, the flag-draped casket was placed on the hose bed of Engine 9 for the short journey to the gravesite.

Emmett, the family, and a few close friends walked step by step behind the engine up a small hill to Jim's final resting place.

His casket was taken from the hose bed and placed into the grave, thus closing the life of a legendary firefighter, father, husband, and friend.

As the crowd left, I saw Emmett standing alone near the tailboard of Engine 9. I was a little hesitant at first, but I finally approached him so I might have a few words in private.

We shook hands and I said, "I am so sorry, Emmett, how are you doing?"

He hesitated for a second and then slowly said, "Not well," and turned and walked away.

That was the last time I saw Emmett. Some moments, as I have said in the past, cannot be removed from your memory. I am not sure I want this one to be erased. I prefer to remember Emmett with a Cheshire cat smile, holding an empty water bucket after he had drenched me.

The fire service does not forget its fallen firefighters. In honor of Howe's ultimate sacrifice, County Supervisor Mark Ridley-Thomas and Fire Chief P. Michael Freeman officially renumbered Engine 216—the second engine at Fire Station 16—as Engine 9 at a special ceremony held in January 2009.

Jim Howe will not be forgotten.

Leland was the firefighter on Engine 214. I had never seen anyone so quiet and secretive regarding his personal life. Unknown to most of us, he had his own private pain.

Time changes all things and within a few years, Leland became an engineer. He moved away from the hectic activity of South Central Los Angeles to the more reasonable pace of the San Gabriel Valley.

After I made battalion chief, I would bump into him every now and then.

He appeared to be in a time warp. He looked the same as I remembered him, the only noticeable change was his hair was just a little grayer around the edges. He looked like a mature Howard Hughes. Same old Leland, though, never offered much, and spoke in short word bursts.

He was easy to like, but I cannot say I got to know him because he was so quiet.

Both of his folks were getting up there in age and were having health problems. He was committed to his family, and his elderly father could not take care of his convalescing mother by himself. It's just the way firefighters are wired; they want to help, and Leland was no exception. He had his hands full caring for both parents. Besides his folks, the only other relative he ever spoke of was a sister, who lived somewhere in flyover country. His parents were all he ever had.

I saw Leland for the last time just after his mother passed away; he and his father were devastated.

His Howard Hughes nickname was still fitting; still waters do run deep, and I never would have thought his internal turmoil was as troubling as it was. Perhaps because he had no one outside the family with which to share his inner feelings, he became a brewing cauldron.

Within a few months after the death of his mother, Leland's father was diagnosed with cancer. He dealt with it the best he could, but watching the slow and devastating path the disease was taking became too overwhelming.

Overcome with grief and saddened by the road that lay ahead, Leland shot and killed his dad and then took his own life.

You can learn immensely from those who surround you. The lessons are there; all you have to do is pay attention. Everyone changes you little by little, for the better, I hope. Only time will tell.

It makes me appreciate my own family even more. I realize how blessed I have been.

As we all sat around the kitchen table at Station 14 after my promotional dinner, I could never have envisioned how the next few years would unfold. I didn't realize how many memories would be attached to the white hat I was given. It has an unforgettable legacy.

CHAPTER TWENTY-ONE

PROMOTIONS ARE EXCITING, WELL, KINDA

If I would have listened to my fellow firefighters at Station 14, I should have turned down the promotion instead of going to Battalion 4. The area's response load is low, very low, at the bottom in response statistics. In the minds of Battalion 13 groupies, that part of the county didn't even receive honorable mention. They loved telling stories about a recruit who was assigned there fresh out of the training tower twenty years ago, and still has his original issue turnout gear without a speck of dirt on them!

Station 19 is in the city of La Cañada Flintridge. It is one of the most expensive areas of the country to live. Most of the homes are worth well north of the million-dollar mark.

The city is situated in the far western end of the San Gabriel Valley, nestled between the Angeles National Forest on the north and the San Rafael Hills on the south. It is a beautiful city.

Districts with little activity have the standard fallback for justification: we might be slow, but look at the potential for disasters we have in the area. The city is in an area prone to Santa Ana winds, and has suffered many devastating wildland fires in the past. The potential for another disaster always exists.

To the east is NASA's Jet Propulsion Laboratory with its cluster of high-rise buildings overflowing with mad scientists! I am just kidding about the mad scientists, but you never know what new and exotic experiments they might be working on to keep this country first in the space race.

I thought I was ready for a different environment, but I didn't realize just how different it was going to be. To transfer from one of the poorest areas of the county to one of the most affluent was a real culture shock, and adding the burden of being a new captain was even more trying.

For my first full year as a captain, I was just plain miserable. I was only thirty-one when I was promoted and had been in the fire service for ten years. I thought I was prepared, but it was one of those jobs you have to do to appreciate. That is a polite way to say I made plenty of mistakes.

Being a captain requires an entirely new set of skills; you are no longer just responsible for yourself. Decisions can have a dramatic impact on those around you.

I was comfortable with making decisions, but I was trying too hard not to change. Eventually you hear those unwelcome words from your fellow firefighters: "Boy, once you made captain, you became different." I was trying to be the same old person I had always been, not realizing that with a new position came new responsibilities, and I had to change to do my job properly.

When you are the supervisor, sometimes you just have to lay down the law. Tell 'em how the cow ate the cabbage, so to speak. It took me a while, but I finally discovered no matter what I did, or how polite I thought I was being, I was going to ruffle a few feathers. I might as well just do the job the best I could, and let the chips, or feathers, fall where they may.

I spent the minimum amount of time at Station 19; the lack of activity was killing me.

Los Angeles County is home for many Hollywood productions. Segments of the television show *CHiPs* were filmed in the La Cañada Flintridge area. It was quite a phenomenon in its day. It starred Larry Wilcox and Erik Estrada as two California Highway Patrol officers named Jon and Ponch.

In my new district, a short stretch of the Glendale Freeway had been constructed, but not yet opened. The freeway ended at Foothill Boulevard, almost directly in front of the fire station. It was perfect for filming.

One day to break the monotony, we decided to watch the filming of *CHiPs* on the closed section of the freeway.

The day's activities included using several pieces of Los Angeles County Fire Department equipment. The studio rents the equipment from the fire department. The rental agreement comes complete with a safety officer. One of my training captains was on the set doing that job.

Tom was the paramedic on my shift; he and I were in the same recruit training class. Captain Barber, who was our training captain, Tom, and I were back together again, this time under much more pleasant circumstances; it was akin to a recruit training reunion. It was the first time since we graduated that the three of us were together.

Watching the production of *CHiPs* didn't do much to break the boredom of the day. If you've ever watched filming on a Hollywood set, you know what I mean. They sometimes prepare for what feels like hours and then roll the camera for what seems like seconds, and then start all over again. It is terribly repetitive. Sometimes it takes many, many shots to make an actor look good!

When the director needed the rescue squad turned around, Tom volunteered and jumped in to move the vehicle.

Most of the county's rescue squads are the same, a pickup truck with a utility bed for all of the equipment. The county personalizes the truck by putting handrails on the rear. The back step is about eight inches wide, just barely enough room to stand.

As Tom was about to move the vehicle, Captain Barber jumped on the rear so the squad could be safely backed up.

What was in Tom's and the captain's minds couldn't have been more different.

The good old safety officer thought Tom was merely backing up to turn around in a matter of feet. Tom, on the other hand, was going to the end of the freeway and then come up on the opposite side.

It startled everyone when we saw the rescue squad flying down the empty freeway at sixty-five-plus miles per hour, with the poor captain hanging on for dear life. He was ashen-faced and white-knuckled. One hand was firmly grasping the safety rail, and the other was on the back of his head to keep his hairpiece from flying off. His precarious position only allowed him to hang onto his toupee toward the back, which made the front flap like storm shutters in the wind.

They came to a soft landing in front of the set. Everyone tried in vain not to make eye contact and to keep the smiles from their faces, but the laughter came through, and everyone had a good chuckle. Except of course, the captain.

To say he was pissed would be an understatement. It was entirely impossible for him to maintain his hard-guy training officer image with his rug blown over to one side of his head and drooping over his ear. Within seconds his embarrassment diminished, and he finally joined in the laughter.

Memories are what you make of them. No matter how hard you try to perform your duties safely, firefighting remains a dangerous occupation. The captain did not make it to retirement; he died of a job-connected ailment while he was in his mid-fifties. He was denied a well-deserved retirement. He was a good man, and I much prefer to remember him on the set of *CHiPs* that day than any other way.

THE EARLY DAYS

Los Angeles County Fire Department Recruit Training Class
B Shift
October 1969

NOTICE OF DEFICIENCIES

Date September 9, 1969

Name Ashby, Douglas B.   Assignment Recruit Training

Subject: Employee needs improvement in ladder techniques, both in command and execution. It is recommended to him that he show more "Hustle" during drill evolutions.

The purpose of this notice is to call the above deficiencies to your attention and give you an opportunity to correct them.

Employee's Signature   Instructor

Copies: 1. Employee
        2. Training Section
jst   Instructor

I almost lost both of my son's in traffic collisions
Colton

Chris

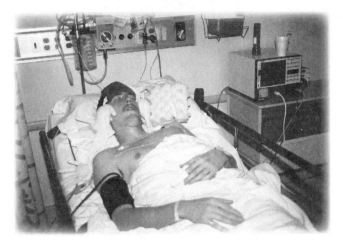

Valley Communitation Center

Dispatch floor

Valley Communitation Center

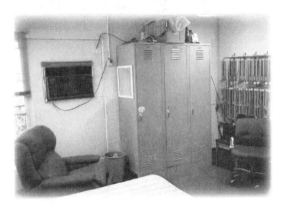

MY FRIEND ROY

In Loving Memory of
ROY ELTON CHAPMAN
November 17, 2005

St. Andrew's By-the-Sea
United Methodist Church
2001 Calle Frontera
San Clemente, CA 92678

Susanville California

Debbie, raised the camera above her head and shouted,
"Stop right there or I'll smack you with this!"
The woman, who was poised for a roundhouse,
pulled her punch and missed my intrepid photojournalist.

That poor deputy could be pummeled out here in the middle of nowhere.

Colton and Doug

Tim, Colton and Doug

Colton

Doug

Colton and Tim

This isn't one of my favorite memories

```
       IN THE MUNICIPAL COURT OF THE WHITTIER JUDICIAL DISTRICT
            COUNTY OF LOS ANGELES, STATE OF CALIFORNIA
   HON. MARGARET M. BERNAL, JUDGE            DIVISION NO. IV


   THE PEOPLE OF THE STATE OF CALIFORNIA.)
                              Plaintiff, )
                                         )
                  -vs-                   )    CASE NO. 8WH07376
                                         )
   01 DOUGLAS BOYD ASHBY,                )    REPORTER'S
                                         )    CERTIFICATE
                              Defendant. )
   _____)
```

184

CHAPTER TWENTY-TWO

ONLY THE GOOD DIE YOUNG

As soon as I was eligible to leave Station 19, I did. It wasn't that I didn't like the area or the people, but the activity was a kin to watching your ant farm when you were a kid. Not much happens.

The county is a large place. I put in enough transfer requests to cover this side of the Angeles Forest, and that's a lot. When the transfers are processed at the end of the month, you are naturally nervous. You never know where you will end up. That is one of the blessings of youth; you are flexible.

The fickle fate of the bid system landed me in the city of Glendora, Fire Station 85, Battalion 2. Which, as luck may have it, was an excellent assignment.

Fortune smiles on you in many ways. I was lucky enough to have a battalion chief at my new assignment that understood the struggles of a new captain.

John Yoder was my battalion chief for about a year, and he was a real father figure to me at a time when I needed it the most. He was one of those levelheaded, common-sense type guys who always found a way to boil a problem down to its simplest solution.

"Doug," he'd say, "you're a good captain and you're doing a good job. You can't worry about pleasing everybody. You've got a good head on your shoulders, so just use it and don't worry about the guys that criticize you; they aren't your friends anyway." It sounds so simple, but it was one of those times when I couldn't see the forest for the trees.

Chief Yoder reminded me how I was promoted in the first place. Those who were negative were not the ones I should be listening to he pointed out, and his guidance during that time steered me in the right direction. He was a great mentor.

The late seventies were a time when the old-school mentality was starting to give way to a young and enthusiastic breed that had great hopes and expectations for their future. Old traditions and archaic thinking were starting to take their proper place in history.

Very few, if any, were of the caliber of John Yoder.

Chief Yoder had been gone from the battalion for a number of years and decided to come by the station to visit. It was good to see him. It was unusual for him to drop by, because he was assigned to Battalion 12, which was quite a distance away. That was the kind of person he was, always going out of his way to make someone else feel good.

At fifty-six, and getting close to retirement, he was assigned a battalion close to his home. His office was within walking distance, a reward for a faithful employee.

The fire service is a young man's job. Most of what firefighters do is labor-intensive under the worst of conditions. Incidents don't just happen during regular office hours, or in good weather. Wildland fires are in temperatures well above a hundred degrees, in mountainous terrain and in a smoky environment. They can last for days, even weeks. That is just your summer job.

Fifty-six doesn't sound old for the vast number of professions, but for firefighters, the years have a way of taking their toll.

Two weeks after Chief Yoder came to visit us, he started feeling ill. It was the kind of malaise that keeps you from being your best. Life is busy, so you don't want to take the time to see a doctor. That's firefighters, always in denial.

Wives are always the ones who worry the most, so on his way out the door, she asked, "Are you sure you're well enough to walk to work?"

He joked and said, "If I am not, you'll find me lying alongside the roadway somewhere."

He didn't know how prophetic that statement would be. He collapsed and died of a massive heart attack about halfway to his office.

John Yoder was a beloved firefighter and is greatly missed by all who knew him. He was a good man and had a huge impact on my life. He occupies a special place in my heart, reserved for those who made a difference in my development as both a firefighter and as a person. His death, however, is in that mental file I prefer not to visit very often.

As fate would have it years later, I would transfer to Station 61 and work with the paramedics who responded that morning and treated Chief Yoder at the scene. As you can imagine, they said it was a very emotional call; they did all they could for him, and then a little bit more.

Glendora is twenty miles east of downtown Los Angeles, and has a population of nearly forty thousand. The sheriff's department protects many smaller cities, but Glendora has its own police force. I guess this gives the city leaders a little more control. It is an upscale community with a rather low crime rate and good schools.

Station 85 was a welcome change from my first captain's assignment.

It does not matter how upscale your community is, it still has problems. After all, people are people. It didn't take long before I was back in the swing of exciting calls.

Shortly after our morning wake-up call, we were dispatched to assist an assault victim.

We did the unthinkable; we arrived before the police. An assault can be many different things and take many different forms, but one thing it always is, is a crime. Crime is the responsibility of the police department.

You are caught between a rock and a hard place; you know someone is in the need of help, so you want to arrive as soon as possible. However, and this is a big however, you also do not want you or your crew to become part of the problem.

You never know what will greet you, or if the perpetrator is still there.

As we arrived, I could hear the scream of pure terror that always sent a chill up my spine. That shriek I already described as something I have never heard successfully faked, by anyone, once again filled my ears as I stepped off the rig.

A woman ran out of the house carrying a four-year-old girl in her arms and was screaming at the top of her lungs, "I knew he was going to kill her! I just knew it!"

That'll get your attention!

The house itself looked like any other on the street, giving no exterior clues as to what had just happened inside, or what was happening now. It was a typical home for the neighborhood, probably sixteen-hundred square feet with three bedrooms.

From the minute you arrive, the public expects help. You are in a uniform, and it doesn't matter to them whether you are a police officer or a firefighter, they expect you to do something.

The woman was across the street and continuing to scream, "He killed her, he killed her," at the top on her lungs.

I silently cursed the cops for being so slow and made my way into the house through the front door, which was left open by the high-pitched, ear-piercing woman.

The first thing that greeted me just inside the door, propped up against the back of an upholstered living room chair, was the body of a young woman. She was covered in stab wounds. Her arms had several defensive wounds. She had also been stabbed in the chest and head, and blood was everywhere. Her assailant had done a successful job of ending her young life.

The first thing that went through my mind was, of course, "Who could have done something like this?"

It was quickly followed by, "Are they still here?"

Most of the time someone will greet you when you arrive, and tell you what is going on, but in this case, no one was around unless you count the screaming woman who had bolted across the street. Even though I was in the house, I could still hear her screaming from across the street.

It was a creepy feeling not knowing what to expect next, but I felt better when I turned around and saw my fearless crew had caught up with me carrying all of our emergency equipment.

I hesitated, took a deep breath, then walked down the blood-soaked hallway and looked into the master bedroom. The bed and floor were also soaked with blood. I noticed a broken wine bottle on the floor, which may have accounted for the cuts on our victim's head.

The smell of blood and the wine, I believe a merlot (sorry, gallows humor), was enough to make you sick, and the stench of death filled the house.

We searched the house for more victims and of course for the person responsible for this terrible deed.

By the time we were back at the victim's side, the police started showing up like gangbusters, sliding to stop in front of the house. Even though they were late, it was good to see them.

The victim had bled out sometime during the night and had been dead for several hours, so we turned the scene over to the police, and they began their investigation.

The screaming woman was the roommate of the victim, and had just returned from her job on the night shift. The little girl had apparently awoken that morning and plopped herself down on the floor in the living room to watch television, completely unaware her mother lay dead next to the wall behind her.

I can't imagine a more horrifying way to start your day or end your night.

The roommate told me later that the child was at the center of a bitter custody dispute, and she always thought something like this might happen.

It appeared the *"ex"* had shown up the night before a scheduled custody hearing with a bottle of wine and reconciliation on his mind.

The offer was obviously not accepted.

At the custody hearing in the local court, the ex-husband showed up with his attorney and pretended to know nothing about the crime.

He was later arrested and brought to trial. I don't know if he was convicted. Incidents have a way of backing up in your mind, with the most current one taking precedence. It's not that you don't care, but life goes on, and there is always the next incident.

Had the two parents just agreed on custody issues, that poor little girl might have grown up with a mother and father instead of such a horrible memory. The mom is now dead and the father probably is in for a long stint in jail.

The term "assault victim" does cover an accumulation of incidents.

It was late in the evening when we were dispatched to a liquor store in the southwest end of our district.

Again, we arrived before the police. This time no screaming woman greeted us, just the open door of a liquor store. The front windows were large, so you could see the entire front of the store. The clerk was leaning against the counter.

I was the first inside the door; the engineer was parking the rig, and the firefighter was getting the medical aid equipment.

As I approached the dazed clerk, the most notable thing was the bullet wound in his forehead. This was something that wasn't covered in my EMT training.

He told me he had just been robbed and then shot.

Fifteen feet away, in front of the beer cooler, were two more victims. Both also had gunshot wounds in their heads. The two had come into the store to buy beer before they walked to their trailer in the park behind the store. Just as they were about to pay for their brews, three young hoodlums from Pomona came into the store to rob it.

Each man was told to kneel down in front of them, and they were shot in the back of the head. Both died instantly.

Then their attention was turned to the clerk. He did everything he was asked, and gave them all the money in the till. Before running from the store, they shot the clerk dead center in the forehead.

The .22-caliber bullet hit the clerk's noggin at a glancing angle. It penetrated the skin, but did not have enough velocity to enter his skull. It then spun around the outside of his head just under his skin. Who said a hard head couldn't be beneficial? He had just a headache, and was one lucky guy.

All were caught and tried. Two of the three were twenty years old, and tried as adults. They are now residing of California's death row. The third, a seventeen-year-old, was tried as a juvenile and now I am sure walks the streets freely.

You realize as a firefighter, that life can change in an instant.

The trailer park behind this liquor store is where we had many calls. Like many older trailer parks in Southern California during the fifties and sixties, families pulled in to the park and never left. Their homes are now fifty-plus years old.

Days later, we were dispatched to a shooting in the middle of the trailer park. A teenage couple, while smoking marijuana, entered into a suicide pact.

The nineteen-year-old boyfriend shot himself through the heart and died instantly; the girl picked up the gun and shot herself in the stomach. The gun used was a powerful one. The bullets they fired penetrated the two adjoining trailers. The neighbor in the second trailer is the one that called for help.

Even with that powerful weapon, the misguided teen managed to miss every one of her vital organs. She survived and showed up at the station weeks later to thank us.

We'd occasionally get cards, but seldom do victims come to the fire station to thank us. After we spoke for a while, I realized this woman was truly remarkable. I still didn't know much about her, but she appeared to be a wonderful person. She just briefly had a few faulty brain cells. I believe the world is a better place with her in it. Sometimes miracles do happen.

CHAPTER TWENTY-THREE

LESSONS FOR A LIFETIME

Endless opportunities and a wide variety of assignments are one of the many benefits that come from working for a large department.

Few restrictions govern transfers. The only limitation is you must have the proper qualifications for the position and be the proper rank; that is pretty much it. Your career path is yours for the choosing.

In one respect, firefighters are like most people. They become comfortable with routine, and resist change. Once someone is in his position for any length of time, in my case almost six years, transferring is unexpected. It was a shock to everyone when I left 85's for the new county fire station 32 in Azusa. Actually, sometimes I even surprised myself.

Changing assignments is challenging; you are not only leaving behind firefighters that have become good friends, but also many memories.

:':

Dwindling revenue for smaller cities dictates cost-cutting measures be made wherever possible, so to balance their budget, the entire Azusa fire department, with its full entourage of upper staffing, was disbanded. The choice was not an easy one for city officials; it took years for them to make the decision.

In the spring of 1983, the more efficient Los Angeles County Fire Department began serving the citizens of Azusa. The choice was a prudent one; city officials could offer paramedic services to the community, something that up until now was not affordable. Their new fire department would be an engine company and a paramedic rescue squad. By reducing redundant services and eliminating overhead, the department became far more cost-effective.

When an existing fire department is disbanded, their employees are well cared for and not left out in the cold; they are assigned elsewhere in the county as new firefighters. Younger firefighters embraced their new assignments; they were excited to become part of one of the most respected fire departments in the country. Change is always intimidating, so some of the older firefighters are not elated by the move.

My first year at Azusa's new fire station was hectic. Countless jobs were required to bring the station and equipment up to county standards. The days flew by, packed with activity, either emergency responses or training.

I have been fortunate to work with firefighters who are above the norm, and this assignment was no exception. They worked hard every day and never complained. That might be a little stretch; at least everyone got along and the grumbling was kept to a minimum. The new crew had a diverse background. The engineer was a captain with the Azusa fire department for a number of years, and due to his seniority was demoted during the transition. His experience with the city was valuable during the changeover. The firefighters on the crew were all experienced paramedics. The last member was a new recruit firefighter.

It wasn't that I did not like probationary firefighters, but adding a new fire station to the county system was trying enough in itself, so I had doubts that I could give a probationer the attention that was needed.

Traditions, attitudes, and training, like everything in the fire service, have evolved sluggishly. Public opinion, lawsuits, and an ever-increasing litany of responsibility were altering the face of the fire service. What was once an all-white men's club was being transformed into an organization that included women and others from all races and ethnical backgrounds. The training service section had its hands full with changes that were coming at a phenomenal rate.

A completely new system of hiring and training had been established to reflect what society was demanding. Recruits now spent months at the training center, in the classroom and on the drill field. Once the basic techniques were completed, they were sent to the field to finish their training. They spent the remainder of their probationary period in the field assignments. At the conclusion of their first year, a final exam was administered at the training center, once again by the legendary training staff.

I was sitting in my office doing the morning report when I heard a knock on the door just before it opened.

Standing there was a freshly minted recruit firefighter. He paused for a second and then calmly walked in, stuck out his hand, and said, "I'm Tim Cremins, your new firefighter."

You can tell a lot from your first exposure to someone, and this was no exception.

Tim did not have an imposing look about him. If anything, he appeared to be polite and mild mannered. In reality I'd bet he could bench press 350 pounds.

It was only a few steps from my office door to the front of the desk, but during that short walk, you could tell this man was bursting with confidence and self-assurance, and not the least bit pretentious. It was an attitude that was honest and genuine, the kind gradually attained from life's experiences.

During our short conversation, Tim mentioned a good friend of mine was one of his training officers, so I decided to give him a call. Just as I had expected, he was equally impressed with him. Our assessment was much the same; he was quiet and self-assured.

Just before we hung up the phone, he said, "Keep an eye on him."

"Whoa, back up the truck, what is that supposed to mean?"

One day, well towards the end of training, all of the recruits were practicing basic hose evolutions under the watchful eye of the training captains. Suddenly, a big, I mean really big green bug, buzzed between the recruits and landed of the chest of the drill captain.

The critter was about three inches long, with scraggly legs and resembled Jiminy the Cricket.

The intrepid captain instantly became frozen and stood motionless for the next few seconds, not quite knowing how to protect himself against the unwanted attacker. The expression on the captain's face was priceless and spoke volumes. It was as if a prehistoric monster mutant had just landed on the captain's lapel, and hordes of his friends were in close pursuit and poised for an assault.

Tim, the ever helpful recruit, quiet and nonchalant as always, leisurely walked over to the insect, and said, "Don't worry Cap, I'll protect you." Quickly Tim cupped his hands and trapped the protesting orthoptera critter, and popped it in his mouth. The first few bites probably killed the creepy-crawler, but his legs kept kicking in Tim's mustache, as yellow and green juice flowed from the corners of his mouth.

Recruits and drill captains alike started retching as Tim went back to complete the drill, proud he had just saved his captain, and completely un-phased by his afternoon snack.

⁙

Once recruits are assigned to a fire station, they begin a ritual that has not changed much over the years. They are at the bottom of the pecking order and thus are reduced to spending all of their free time by themselves studying. Tim appeared to be quiet by nature, and being in a new position as a recruit only made him more standoffish.

He was respectful of others and was reluctant to join in the banter at the kitchen table during dinnertime. He would offer little about himself, and usually spoke only when asked a direct question.

Over the next few months, little by little, I was able to learn more about him, and gradually light was being shed on the source of his self-confidence. In the ten years since he graduated from high school, he had managed to accomplish a lot. He graduated from a university with a bachelor's degree, and for the past five years was a firefighter with the Chino Fire Protection District. He might have been new to the county, but certainly not to the fire service. Tim also was a master in the martial arts. Prior to the fire department, he participated in full-contact martial arts competitions.

Every now and then, he would slip and tell a story about his wild younger days of high school. One day on a dare from a friend (nice friend), he drank an entire bottle of liquid cold medicine.

Completely amazed, I asked, "Why?"

His response was one I had heard a number of times coming from the lips of my own sons.

"I don't know, it just seemed like a good idea at the time!"

I then asked, "How'd that make you feel?"

As expected, his response was succinct "Very lethargic."

Tim was well prepared by the time he took his recruit follow-up exam and passed with flying colors.

He was now no longer a probationary firefighter; he became a vital part of our team.

After you leave a station for a new assignment, it does not take long before you become embroiled with other challenges and lose touch with your last crew.

I did not see Tim much after I left Station 32, but I would bump into him occasionally. Even if I didn't see him, the old rumor mill kept me in touch with how he was doing.

During the next few years, Tim would attend paramedic training, graduate, and become his class valedictorian.

It didn't take long before Tim was right back at Station 32, this time as a paramedic.

∗∗∗

The personnel at a station might change, but the activity level stays the same: active. The unknown is the part of a firefighter's life that makes it so exciting; you never know what the next emergency will be or what it might entail.

In the early months of 1989, the days were starting to turn warm, so the rear apparatus doors were left open to let in the fresh spring air.

After lunch the entire crew went upstairs for an afternoon siesta, and Tim was left alone in the kitchen to clean up.

Normally fire stations are secured and public access is limited, but this day was different. Somehow, a thirty-something couple managed to find their way into the rear of the fire station.

You could tell in an instant this was not your normal couple stopping by for a few tips on fire prevention. They wouldn't be making an appearance on *The Dating Game*. They were dirty, disheveled, and appeared to be under the influence of some type of drug. The medium-built boyfriend was yanking the 110-pound woman by her hair into the apparatus room with a knife at her throat.

Her bloodcurdling screams were piercing and certainly got Tim's attention.

Life-changing events occur in an instant. There is no time to think; you just act on your instincts, and that is what Tim did.

The woman continued to shriek unabatedly, "Help me, please help me, he's going to kill me!"

Tim could feel chills run up his spine as he went to investigate.

At the rear of the station, he could see the woman cowering on the apparatus floor with her boyfriend towering over her and continuing to threaten her with the knife.

When he saw Tim, he became more agitated and started shouting, "Get back, you mother f——er. Get away from me. I'll use this knife, I'll kill her!" He pointed the knife at Tim and then back to the poor trembling woman. The man continued to rant and was becoming more visibly unstable.

In a calm voice, Tim told the attacker, "No one is going to hurt you," and then quickly went back into the kitchen to dial 911.

It took only a second to inform the station captain, who had just come down from upstairs, what was going on. Tim then ran back to the apparatus floor...alone.

The terrified woman continued to scream as she was being manhandled by her assailant.

Tim remembering his fire department training, "We don't bring victims to the scene," so he slowly approached the two and started speaking in a calming and reassuring voice.

"You don't want to hurt her. Please put the knife down."

The boyfriend became even more distraught. He handed the knife to the woman and starting shouting, "Kill me, just kill me." He then rapidly grabbed the knife back and began threatening Tim again.

Tim continued to plead in a soft voice to put down the knife. "No one needs to get hurt." Not wanting to escalate the situation, Tim got down on his knees just in front of the two and pleaded once again, "Put down the knife."

The seconds felt like hours, but finally the wild-eyed dirt bag complied with Tim and placed the knife on the floor directly in front of them. Tim immediately took the opportunity to scoot the knife away.

Now the tables had turned, and Tim was face to face with the unarmed man. It took about a nanosecond before Tim had him prone on the floor and completely subdued.

Where's a cop when you need one? While lying on the floor, the now somewhat compliant ex-knife-wielding assailant decided he would make a break for it, so Tim subdued him again.

The Azusa police arrived, took him into custody, and as they say, the rest was history.

I spoke to Tim days after the incident, and asked him what the hell he was thinking, kneeling down in front of a knife-wielding madman?"

His response was what I had come to expect from this mild-mannered friend. *"Aah, I wasn't going to let him hurt her."*

That afternoon Tim displayed courage that others don't possess. He could have stayed in the safety of the kitchen with the rest of the crew after he dialed for help, but instead he chose to put his own life in danger and return to the apparatus floor. He assisted a young woman whom he did not know, and in all likelihood would never see again.

John Wayne had an expression that summed up Tim's actions: *"Courage is being scared to death, but saddling up anyway."*

The California State Firefighters Association awarded Tim the Medal of Valor for his actions.

It had been a number of years since I last spoke with Tim, so to make sure all my facts were correct, I telephoned him. The minute he answered, it was as if I were transported back over the years by a flux capacitor with 1.21 gigawatts of power. Logic tells me many things have changed, but for the next hour, Tim and I spoke as if we were sitting across the table from each other, in a brand-new county fire station. It was great catching up on old times.

Both of us are retired now, and he assured me life has indeed been good to him and his family. He said he pretty much looks the same, with one exception; gray hair, and his forehead is three inches larger.

It only took a second to realize his humor was still completely intact.

I listened silently, awestruck, as he related the story about the man with a knife. He was still entirely reserved and humble as the day it occurred, and then he caught me by surprise when he related the rest of the story.

Some ten years after the incident, Tim received a telephone call from the Riverside County District Attorney regarding new charges filed against this poor devil. As with many of the wayward, prone to drug use, this seditious perpetrator failed to take responsibility for his actions and never changed his ways.

He came from a middle-class home in Hacienda Heights, and had all the opportunities any child could desire. He was now on trial for shooting his girlfriend in the head, once again proving there is no cure for stupid.

Unfortunately, life experiences were teaching me there is no shortage of evil people.

The good Lord works in strange and magnificent ways. Significant life-changing events come from countless experiences in ways you would least expect.

⁂

Hardcore firefighters and police officers have an expression they use frequently to separate themselves from the public. They refer to some as *"those people"*. I learned this expression early in my career, and uttered it many times myself.

Those people are like that! What do you expect from *those people*?

I eventually came to detest the phrase, and would often ask others, "Who are you talking about," a question that was often met with a blank stare.

The expression is meant to divorce you from those with whom you feel you have absolutely nothing in common. When others are unlike you, they become less significant and entirely un-relatable. How can you empathize with someone to whom you cannot relate?

It is easy to look at people from different backgrounds and assume they are not at all like you, when in reality most of the time they are. It is a rare person with whom we do not share at least some type of commonality. Misfortune is not just reserved for the underprivileged. This was not something I inherently knew; I was starting to understand we have more in common than those things that divide us.

People are drawn to those most like themselves, groups with which we share some similarities. Those with whom we never interact will draw our suspicion.

The fire service eventually brings you in contact with every race, ethnicity, and economic background you can imagine. It was becoming almost impossible to divorce myself from the suffering of others. Tragedies know no boundaries. Consequently, some of my long-held beliefs were starting to fade. I was starting to look at life and people differently; viewing life through a shifting prism shapes you in unexpected ways.

Engine and Squad 32 responded to the scene of a drug overdose in a poor section of town, one of those rundown houses with a dirt lawn and about half a paint job. The kind of place where the front door is generally left standing open day or night, and you get the feeling livestock would be right at home in the living room.

The victim was enough to make Mother Teresa vote Republican. The thirty-something dirt bag was a total down and outer, with a scraggly, puke-filled beard, filthy clothes, and a monkey on his back the size of King Kong.

He was unconscious when we arrived, so an opiate inhibitor was administered in hopes of blocking the effects of whatever drug he'd taken. Whenever that's done, the transformation is amazing to watch. The person will go from an absolute stupor into an immediate state of awareness. It usually happens rapidly, and our victim was no exception.

He quickly sat up, suddenly bright-eyed and bushy-tailed, and then tears appeared in his eyes, so I turned my head to see where he was looking.

His daughter, who looked to be around fifteen, had been fearfully wringing her hands and watching us work on her father. When his eyes found hers, she rushed into his arms as if she hadn't seen him for years. She ran to this filthy, smelly, drug addict and melted into his embrace like a child on Christmas morning. I heard him whisper into her ear, "I love you, baby. Thank you for being here."

There was absolutely nothing about him I could relate to only a moment before; he was truly one of *those people.*

Witnessing his love for his daughter struck me like a ton of bricks. In that one moment, I could see his humanity and understand him as a father who loved his child. That single, tiny instant probably softened the hard edges of my conservatism more than a thousand speeches by a thousand bleeding-heart politicians ever could.

We forget we all share common feelings, such as the love a parent has for a child, even if that love is coming from a down and outer. It becomes easy to dismiss people, even those within your own family, when they become completely unrelatable. Perhaps it is just a defense mechanism to keep them at arm's length, not wanting them to touch your heart.

As I was becoming older, with more and more incidents and family turmoil under my belt, my views toward life were shifting in ways I had never expected. My rigid stance regarding the fine line between right and wrong was starting to blur. Life was not as simple as youth dictated. I still held firm to my beliefs of personal responsibility, but I was starting to realize not everyone in life had the same advantages.

The fire service has a way of exposing you to groups from every lifestyle and ethnicity. The one inescapable fact is everyone has problems. After all, we are human beings.

Once I started to shed my blinders from my childhood, the lessons for life did not end with the drug addict or family members. Within a few short months, we responded to the home of a woman who was having difficulty breathing.

The woman must have been close to six hundred pounds. She was in her mid-thirties and was confined to her bed due to her weight.

She was another person who was just hard to relate to because of her condition.

Her caretaker was her niece, who was always at her bedside. She was about the same age as the daughter of the earlier drug overdose.

You cannot imagine how a person could get to be that size. It took six of us to get her on the gurney. I am sure it was an embarrassing thing for her to endure. Once we had evaluated her, and determined nothing could be done in the field, the ambulance transported her to the hospital.

The rescue squad went along, not because of any medical need, but we knew the hospital staff would need help getting her off the gurney.

Late the same night, we received another call to the same address, but this time it was for a person not breathing. Apparently, the hospital did not feel the need to keep the morbidly obese woman overnight, and had released her the same afternoon.

On the way to the call, I have to admit I thought this was just another *"frequent flyer,"* a term used for people who call us frequently as their own personal medical provider.

I fight it, but sometimes you can develop a cynical view of human nature. She was definitely another one who had joined the ranks of *those people.*

When we arrived, the woman was dead. The little fifteen-year-old niece was sobbing over her aunt's body, holding on to her for dear life. Her tears ran unabated. There was a human being under those mounds of flesh, and someone who loved her dearly was kneeling next to her, not wanting to let her go.

Like the drug addict, it was another reminder there is always more to someone than meets the eye. The most unrelatable or irredeemable person you can imagine probably has someone somewhere who loves them, and I suppose that has to count for something in this irrational world.

CHAPTER TWENTY-FOUR

THEY'RE FAMILY,
YOU GOTTA LOVE 'EM

Many of the areas I have worked in are much like the idyllic Eagle Rock of my youth. I found shootings and other acts of violence happen in all communities. There is always a "more than meets the eye" principle, and it applied to cities as well as people.

There will always be diversity in people; some you can relate to, but others, for a variety of reasons, will always remain at a distance.

My innate sense of fairness would no longer allow me to pass judgment regarding someone just because of how he initially appeared. You see things one day that make you cynical about human nature, and then the very next you experience something that restores your faith in humanity. Each incident leaves an indelible mark that is then conveniently filed away, and if you are lucky helps you grow.

The more heartbreak I witnessed, the more I tried to distance myself from them. I always found a way to disguise misfortune as something that happened to others, because after all, there was no common ground between us. The harder I tried, the more I found that tragedies don't just happen to others. Life's inequities were surfacing in my own family. The lives of Debbie's brothers were rapidly collapsing.

It was easy to look at others and put them into the *those people* category until I took a hard look at my own family. Call it an epiphany or just a blinding glimpse of the obvious, but my long-held attitudes were changing.

It went unnoticed by the rest of the family for a long while, but Royce, Debbie's older brother, was starting to have issues (that's a popular, in-vogue way of saying his life was turning to shit). The problems were becoming catastrophic until finally Royce and his wife, Nancy, separated and divorced. It was a first for the family.

After graduating from high school, both Royce and Nancy became Mormon missionaries. They met in England while on their missions and married shortly after returning home.

The divorce was particularly painful for devout Mom and Dad. They tried not to let on, but in one way or another, their feelings bubbled to the surface.

Royce and Nancy's sons, Jackson and Samuel, were young when their folks separated. Divorce was no longer all that unique, so they both appeared to be adjusting.

Nancy found a small place in town so Sam and Jackson split their time between parents. It wasn't long before Nancy remarried a local dentist.

Royce, the ever-handsome cowboy, who never had trouble finding female companionship, was dating again. He stayed on their twenty-acre ranch, sixteen-plus miles southeast of Sacramento.

Kevin, Royce's younger brother, lived just down the street, and was always there to lend a hand on Royce's ranch. His life wasn't faring much better.

The outskirts of Sacramento is wide-open cattle-grazing land, tailor-made for cowboys. It only took a short while before both had adopted that lifestyle. Everyone loves a cowboy, which made the transformation all that easier.

The styles worn earlier in the big city morphed into wearing nothing but blue jeans, cowboy boots, and a large-brimmed hat. For formal occasions, they wore clean blue jeans, cowboy boots, and a newer hat, minus the sweat ring.

Kevin was never without his silver trophy belt buckle he and his brother had won for wild cow milking. Yes, there is such a rodeo contest!

When I heard about it, I had to look it up. The event consists of a mugger, a cowboy, and a cow. The cowboy ropes the cow around the neck and the mugger attempts to steady the cow. The cowboy tries to milk the cow into an empty beer bottle (what else). The cowboy then runs to the side of the arena with the milk to stop the clock. The bottle is checked for milk, and then receives a time. The best time wins the event.

Come on, this is great stuff. It's great to be a cowboy. With political correctness, do you think they should now be called cow-persons?

As if to make up for lost time in their youth, both Royce and Kevin doubled down on drinking. What a change in lifestyle for a couple of kids brought up in Burbank.

Both were changing, and not for the better. The cowboy's life had a stronger pull on the two than their childhood upbringing.

Kevin's life, like Royce's, was also in turmoil. His life had all the ingredients of a good country and western song. His truck was always in the need of repair, it had bald tires, and rarely did he have a spare dime in his pocket. He had a faithful dog, and was always between loves.

Kevin's wife Belinda, after giving birth to Janice, had health problems. First complications related to appendicitis, and then dental work that went wrong. She was in constant pain. She quickly became hooked on painkillers she obtained from various doctors. She was a bright star in the family for way too short of a time. If any signs of her drug dependency were visible, no one in the family recognized them.

Kevin had left for work when Belinda accidentally took a few too many painkillers and died.

Poor little Janice was left unattended with her dead mom until Kevin's return home that evening. Janice was only three years old. Up until then, there had been no untimely deaths in the family, but that was going to change, and way too soon.

Belinda's death hit everyone in the family hard, first because we missed her, and second because it was so unnecessary. She was only twenty-four when she passed away. The entire family assembled in Sacramento for Belinda's services, and soon after everything in our lives was back to normal, whatever normal is.

Kevin was not as sophisticated as his brother, but he did have all the charm Royce possessed, and within a few years, he was married again.

The brothers' lives were becoming just another episode of *COPS*. Both were perched on the precipice and just inches away from finding themselves stars of the law enforcement melodrama.

Poor decisions were starting to catch up with both them; each day they would painfully write another line in the continuing saga of their hard-luck country and western song.

The stability in their lives came from visiting the same old watering hole! They spent many hours there at the bar, socializing and hashing over old stories.

Kevin's life could only be described as tumultuous. The highs never reached high, and the lows always reached new levels. When he branched out, venturing from under the watchful eye of his father, he landed right back in the shadow of his brother, perhaps by necessity; however, someone was still always there to dictate his life.

The walls of the perfect family were beginning to crumble. No one knows for sure why things happen, but once the downward spiral started, it continued out of control for years, taking a horrible toll on the entire family.

The family hoped for the best, but perhaps the die had already been cast. Royce's life was out of control, and his tragedies made Kevin's life look normal.

I was learning my extended family was the same as *those people* I helped every day at work.

CHAPTER TWENTY-FIVE

WE ESCAPE DEATH
NOT ONCE, BUT TWICE

Station 61 is in the city of Walnut, a beautiful residential community close to just about everything. It is surrounded by a cluster of other smaller cities.

When I first arrived at 61's however, I got a sinking feeling in my stomach. I should have done a little more research before putting in my transfer request to this depressing little station.

It was on Old Valley Boulevard, within feet of the main railroad yard that serviced the San Gabriel Valley industrial areas. It also had a mainline track that headed in all directions out of town. As you would expect, it operated on an around-the-clock basis. To say it was noisy would be a colossal understatement.

The station itself was old and small; the staffing was three on the fire engine, and two on the paramedic rescue squad, so everyone was cramped.

I felt lucky. It had indoor toilet facilities!

The only salvation was that a new station was being built, and we were going to move in within the next ninety days. It couldn't happen quickly enough. Those ninety days were the worst days I ever spent in a fire station.

Once we were in the new station, everything fell into place.

The station was surrounded by other fire stations, so we were designated as a move-up company. We were the first to respond anywhere in the county where there was a major emergency.

Every shift in the summer brought something new. When we would head out on a response, and we could see a giant smoke plume in the distance, I'd think, *we're gonna see some action now!* By my second year I'd see the same thing and think, *we're gonna get our butts kicked again today!*

Extended wildland fire assignments earlier in my career were exciting; now being wet, dirty, hungry, and tired to the bone was not fun anymore. It was just hard work.

As the years passed, and I was getting more and more assignments under my belt, the allure of the fire station was losing its luster. Age has a way of catching up with you. I was wearing down.

Gradually, but ever so surly, a thought was creeping into my mind: *maybe I should start studying for the next battalion chief's exam.* I had watched for years while captains were promoted to the rank of battalion chief, their only qualification being they had a chief officer as a golf partner.

When I arrived at Station 61, I was in those middle years of life. Some call it the middle-age crazies. I was forty years old, and had been in the fire service for nineteen years, seven of those years as a captain. I had a beautiful wife and two great kids at home, and life in general was first-rate. The crew I was working with was excellent.

Everything was coming together, including my confidence. Being part of the best fire department in the world only adds to your self-assurance; unfortunately, it also adds to your arrogance.

When working with other firefighters from smaller cities, especially from departments with only a few employees, you can't help but feel a little bit superior. You try not to, but it is hard when all of the smaller departments look up to you. It's easy to get the mindset that you're better. As a rule, smaller departments have excellent and highly qualified firefighters, so arrogance is unjustified.

∴

Fire Station 61 had several automatic aid agreements with surrounding communities.

The automatic aid is exactly what it sounds like. Agreements between departments allow fire personnel to respond into adjacent jurisdictions on an initial response basis, without regard to political boundaries. Communities can now work together seamlessly on a day-to-day basis. Over the past thirty years, the fire service has made great strides in the standardization of equipment, communications, and procedures, so working together is much easier. Automatic aid is an excellent example of how adjoining cities can share resources and work together.

On a hot day in the middle of summer, we received an automatic aid response to a structure fire in the neighboring community of West Covina. There were three of us on Engine 61. Tom was the engineer, Mike the firefighter, and myself. We had worked together for some time and we were a close-knit group.

It took less than five minutes to arrive at the scene.

The area was an attractive two-story condominium project. Units were attached in groups of three. This home was at the end of a cul-de-sac, surrounded by other buildings.

West Covina's first arriving fire engine stopped directly in front of the building and had a hose line going in the front entry. Heavy black smoke was pouring from the top of the entry door. The windows on the second floor were closed, and as a result no smoke was escaping from the upper floors.

West Covina's captain was standing at the front of his rig directing operations when Mike and I approached him. Tom was busy parking our fire engine.

Emergency scenes always look disorganized, but nothing could be further from the truth. There is some confusion, but it is always being managed, if that makes sense. Incidents unfold quickly, so tactics change rapidly.

Your first action as an assisting unit is to check in with the incident commander. In this case, it was the first arriving West Covina captain.

"How can we help?" I asked.

"Nobody's searched the condo yet. Take your men in and see if the building is clear."

This was where my arrogance came in. My first thought was this captain wasn't all that bright.

It was a nice working-class neighborhood with all the condo's windows closed. The whole place was locked up as tight as a drum. No way was anyone in that structure; everybody would be at work. At one thirty in the afternoon, if anyone were at home, he would be up and around and would have easily left the house.

This idiot captain wanted us to go in there and look for possible victims when it was obvious to me that the building was clear.

I could not help but roll my eyes as we all donned our protective gear.

What was this guy thinking?

However, we did as we were asked.

Mike was the first to get all his equipment on, so he entered first, followed almost immediately by Tom and then me.

It was a nice condominium; the entry led into the living room. The kitchen and family room were to the rear of the first floor. A staircase led to the second floor right off the entry. Mike took the stairs, and Tom and I quickly made our way to the back area of the first floor to search for victims, each going a different way.

By the time we went in, the conditions had rapidly deteriorated; it was hot, very hot, with thick black smoke down to waist level on the first floor. You could hardly see your hand in front of your face downstairs; there was probably more light in the bowels of the Timpanogos Caves than there was on the second floor. The smoke was pitch black, we had a tough time negotiating our way.

Even with the light beam from my flashlight, I could barely see a foot in front of me.

Heat rises, and as it hits the ceiling, it starts to move downward. The closer you are to the floor, the cooler it is, so we began to crawl along, hugging the floor. It's also easier to see, although not by much, I grant you. The smoke was so dense, I bumped my breathing mask on the base of a toilet before I realized I was in the bathroom.

We continued to crawl along the floor and started to make our way upstairs. Still in the back of my mind I was thinking how stupid this whole operation was, jeopardizing my men for some long-gone mythical victim.

After Tom and I cleared the first floor, we were halfway up the stairs to check on Mike when we heard a muffled sound coming from the direction where we thought he was.

Listening more closely, it was evident the sound we heard was Mike; he was saying something, but we couldn't make it out over the dull roar of all the firefighting operations. Whatever he was yelling, I could hear panic in his voice, and that sent a chill up my spine.

The air in our self-contained breathing apparatus was down to about half, and I did not have a clue where Mike was, or if he was all right.

We all decorate and furnish our homes to suit our own taste, and after a while I'm sure we can make our way around in the dark if we have to. Everyone's different. Imagine walking into the house of a stranger in complete darkness, making your way around small rooms with furniture you can't see. It was almost impossible to find our way around in the dark, deplorable conditions, and now we could not hear Mike at all.

I grabbed Tom by the arm and we both stopped for a moment, listening for his voice. We heard him again. It was definitely a muffled cry for help.

Tom and I finally found the room Mike was in, but it was still difficult to find him.

The heat from the smoke had intensified and made it impossible to stand upright even if we wanted to, so we still had to crawl into the room. I could tell by the sound of his voice he was within feet of us, but I still did not know exactly where he was.

Tom and I felt a bed, and crawled around the edge and found him.

Mike was pinned to the floor between the wall and the bed, underneath a 350-pound woman who was either dead or unconscious.

While Mike was searching the upstairs bedrooms, he had found this rather *rotund* woman, lying lifeless on the bed. Trying to place her in a position where he could put his arms around her and drag her outside, they both slipped down between the wall and the bed, trapping Mike beneath 350-plus pounds of essentially dead weight. Dead human weight!

Mike did exactly as his training commanded. All he knew was he had a victim. In that environment, he didn't know if it was a male or female or a hundred pounds or five hundred pounds. According to his training, he lay next to the victim and rolled over, pulling the person onto his back so he could crawl or carry the person to safety. Mike's problem was that his victim was almost twice his weight and the space was too small for one, let alone two.

He could tell the woman was breathing, but unconscious. Once we got Mike free of his burden, the task at hand was getting the victim out of the bedroom, downstairs and into the fresh air.

Tom and I pulled on the woman while Mike pushed, but she was still wedged tight against the wall. It was like trying to move a 350-pound plastic bag of Jello. It was as if she had no bones in her body, and whatever we did seemed to be useless.

The alarm bells for low air supply in our breathing apparatus were starting to sound, so we knew we only had a few minutes to move the mountain of flesh.

Finally, after pushing and pulling our victim with all our strength, we managed to get her past the bed and across the floor and through the bedroom door onto the landing at the top of the stairs.

We were all exhausted; we scarcely had enough energy left to finish our rescue. We had managed to get her to the top of the stairs, but that was it.

The only thing left for us to do was to just roll her down the stairs.

Well, more like pull her down. Even with two of us below her pulling and the other at the top pushing, we could barely move her. After each step, there was an awful thump when she hit the next step. Finally, we reached a landing where the stairs turned, and we all started yelling for help as we descended below the hot, black smoke.

A group of West Covina firefighters heard us and came to the rescue of our rescue. With their help, we got the poor woman outside into the fresh air and onto a gurney. It took six of us.

At this point, any arrogance I may have felt was a distant memory. So was the iconic image of a beautiful damsel clutching the neck of a firefighter as they ran from a building with smoke and flames licking at their heels, the waiting crowd cheering as they emerged from the building. I like the image much more than reality.

Paramedics took it from there and quickly got an oxygen mask on her and rushed her to the hospital. Her breathing was labored, but she was breathing, and for that, I was grateful.

The three of us collapsed on the front lawn, glad to be out in the cool fresh air and now with new respect for the West Covina Fire Department. Had I followed my initial instinct, that woman might have died.

The three of us probably lost quite a few pounds between us during that enterprise. I later heard after a lengthy hospital stay, she finally recovered, probably having lost a few pounds herself.

At the fire station, we sat around the kitchen table with a cup of coffee (wishing it were a beer), and analyzed our rescue. We all told our side, and we all made more than a few jokes at the expense of both the victim and one another.

It was Mike who summed up the day.

"The only thing I could think of," he said, "was after all that I've been through as a firefighter, all anyone would ever remember about me was a headline that would read 'Firefighter Dies After Being Flattened by Three-Hundred-and-Fifty-Pound Woman.'"

"Yeah," I laughed, "probably in the *West Covina Times!*"

Gallows humor, indeed.

⁎⁎⁎

Unfortunately, that wouldn't be the last time Tom, Mike, and I would have our lives flash in front of us.

If I would ever have let my thoughts stray to dying on the job, it would have been from injuries suffered in a massive fire or explosion, or from rescuing a small child from an overflowing river, not from crashing in a fire engine.

One rainy evening we responded to a vehicle accident on the westbound side of the 60 Freeway. As with many incidents, the victim refused aid, and we quickly returned to service.

With the first rains of the season, the streets become slippery with a buildup of oil and grease from months of use. Freeways are especially dangerous, mainly because drivers do not see the dangers in a wet roadway, and instead of reducing their speed, it appears they speed up.

It was a little later in the evening, so most of the rush-hour traffic had subsided. Traffic was beginning to return to its normal flow.

Engine 61 was a four-year-old rig at the time, but its design was ancient by today's standards. The firefighters would ride looking toward the rear of the rig, and the roof covered only half of the area where they sat. They were subjected to the elements; in other words, they got wet when it rained.

The front cab had enough room for three, so returning from calls, they sat in the front between the captain and engineer. It was a little cramped, but well worth it, especially for the firefighter.

The rig had two electric fans mounted on the dashboard, the same as you see with some long-haul trucks, one pointed to the driver's side and one to the passengers. They did a good job of keeping the windshield clear. The fan on the driver's side wasn't working, so earlier in the day the mechanic removed it, with a promise to replace it the following morning.

When we returned to the rig, we placed our helmets on the dashboard between the two fans; they were locked in place, or so we thought, a fact that will become important in a moment.

It was still raining quite heavily as we made our way back to the fire station. We took the off-ramp that circled around and led to a bridge that crossed over the freeway. As we rounded the long sweeping curve, Tom's helmet slid across the dashboard and became firmly lodged underneath the steering wheel. As he turned the wheel, the helmet only wedged tighter. The harder he turned, the more the helmet wedged between the wheel and dashboard.

When we got to the top of the off-ramp, we were doing about forty-five miles per hour, with Tom frantically trying to straighten the rig out. The steering wheel was literally locked in a hard right position, doing what felt like a bazillion miles per hour.

Tom hit the brakes hard. The back end tried to catch up with the front, and we slid around 180 degrees into oncoming traffic. The rig still had plenty of momentum, so we weren't quite done yet. We continued to slide in a right turn, somewhat slower but still with enough speed to hit the curb and jump on to the sidewalk.

The only noise you could hear in the cab was three grown men yelling, "Oh shit!" in unison.

We slid across the sidewalk and came to a stop in a muddy area just inches before we would have tumbled back down onto the freeway below.

I imagine it was quite a sight for the people driving by to see a fire engine pull a donut in the middle of the bridge, but their reaction was the last thing we were worried about at that instant.

When the rig finally stopped moving, we just looked at each other for a moment, realizing how close we had come to disaster. Tom yanked his helmet out and we drove back to the station in dead silence.

We laughed about it later—nervous laughter at first, and then it became humorous when each of us told the others back at the station what we had just been through.

Mike thought we all were going to die, as we all did for a split-second, or at least we would have to spend weeks in the hospital. Tom said he was too busy trying to stop the rig to think of anything, and I was pondering how many accident reports I was going to have to file.

I guess that says something about our varying degrees of optimism. Like so many calls, little things could have either caused or averted a tragedy if we had only paid closer attention to the details. Sometimes there's neither rhyme nor reason at all. We were lucky that night. The only damage was to our egos.

I was fortunate to have the crew I did. It remains one of the best groups of guys I worked with my entire career.

The time I spent there had a big impact me. I hit my stride as a captain, and grew tremendously into the job.

Mistakes have a way of teaching you more than your victories ever could. Most of my accomplishments were directly related to the caliber of the crews I worked with; they are the ones that deserve the credit.

I am proud of the time I spent in the fire department, but I learned just enough modesty to give credit where credit is due. Firefighting at its core is always a team effort.

I have worked with many great people, whom I've already mentioned, and many others whom I have not, but each has pointed me in the right direction and supported me over the years.

It is a foolish man who thinks he does it all on his own!

CHAPTER TWENTY-SIX

FROM THE MOUTHS
OF BABES

Growing up in Eagle Rock in the fifties and sixties appears old-fashioned by today's standards. Single-parent households were almost unheard of, and single-income families were the norm. The men worked nine to five while the stay-at-home moms took care of the house and met their husband at the door with a kiss and a drink, which was the first of several on the way to dinner with the entire family. Smoking and drinking was the rule rather than the exception. My wife, Debbie, would always take exception to this; her Mormon upbringing was completely the opposite of mine.

During my time in the fire service, so far, I was keeping alive that old Ashby tradition of imbibing. I was drinking quite regularly during my time off. This was nothing out of the ordinary, especially considering my upbringing. It is only hindsight that makes me see the error of my way's.

Like the drug addict and the obese woman, there is always more than meets the eye. I am sure the idyllic families in my neighborhood growing up had their share of problems they kept from the world, just as any family does. There is a reason some skeletons are kept in the closet, and it was certainly easier to do back then.

Today, with Facebook, YouTube, and the ubiquity of social media, I am amazed there are any secrets left at all. I have great sympathy for kids growing up in a society where people know about your mistakes before you even get a chance to make them, but that is one tidal wave I'm afraid it's impossible to stem.

The fact remains, I grew up around some heavy drinkers, and it was perfectly acceptable as part of the social discourse of the day.

Fortunately, I was brought up with strong family values based on sound moral principles, as was Debbie, which is one of the reasons we have been together for over four decades. In spite of the differences over smoking and drinking, we were both for the most part on parallel tracks.

My father was a man of his generation, a hard worker with a stressful job and a propensity for the two-martini lunch and two-fisted dinners. My mom, as I've mentioned, was right behind him in the alcohol department, eventually, sadly, surpassing him.

The fire service has its share of macho men to whom heavy drinking comes naturally, and coming right out of fraternity life in college, only solidified alcohol as a natural part of my everyday life. What had been normal in my younger years was starting to become a problem in midlife.

During the early eighties, my sons Chris and Colton, and I were on a Sunday drive through rural Orange County. It was my day off, a beautiful day. The sun was out, the windows were down, and my two boys were looking up at their dad as if he could do no wrong. What could be better?

Naturally, I had a beer as we drove along, holding it between my legs as we wound through the narrow, winding roads. My sons had their sodas, and Dad had his beer. What could be wrong with that?

When I lifted my beer straight up, took a quick drink, and replaced it between my legs, Chris piped up brightly and said, "We know why you drink like that, Dad!"

Startled, I turned to my son and asked, "What do you mean?"

"Like this," he said, and turned to face the front of the car like a rigid little soldier. Then Chris lifted his soda straight up to his mouth and took a swig before replacing the can back down between his legs.

I looked at him, a little puzzled. When he'd first spoke up, it had seemed oddly ominous, but now it just appeared as if he was doing a cartoon-like impression of his father.

"So why do I drink like that?" I asked, slightly amused. I still wasn't quite getting the message.

"So if there's a cop behind you, he won't know you're drinking!" Chris was seven.

The message hit me like a ton of bricks. What a thing for a father to teach his child!

The seed had been planted. It took several more years to germinate. In the meantime, I continued drinking as I always had, but that afternoons drive stayed in the back of my mind.

,

In July 1985, I took my family on a vacation up to my sister's house in South Lake Tahoe. We did this as often as we could. The trip always included several nights at the casinos. It was always a special time when we got away as a family (to my sister's house, not the casinos). A firefighter's work schedule keeps you away from your family both days and nights, so uninterrupted time with Debbie and the boys was always prized.

Our vacation began as they always did, time with my sister and her family at their home. We would go on bike rides, hike, and take trips out on the lake in my brother-in-law's boat, and of course, we fished. Nights were spent at the casinos. As was my habit, I was in a drinking mood, and that is exactly what I did. I had a good time in the casino, and as always, I enjoyed more than my share of free drinks as I gambled.

More and more as I got older, the aftermath of a fun evening was a dreadful thing. My drinking was becoming a problem as the years passed, and the days after were appalling.

I was setting a horrible example for my boys, who were no longer so young they couldn't understand what was happening. The ghosts of my past were starting to weigh heavily on my mind, and this trip was about to bring them into focus.

It isn't just about being a drunk driver. Alcohol can damage your family in other ways.

On Sunday morning after a fun-filled night at the casino, we piled everyone into the car to go to breakfast. I was feeling miserable, terribly hung-over, and I did something I had somehow managed not to do during previous events. I threw up in front of my kids.

I literally slowed the car to a stop in traffic, opened my door, and tossed my cookies all over the street on a beautiful Sunday morning. I can't imagine what any passersby must have thought—possibly nothing at all, given the fact there were bars everywhere, but more important to me were my sons. What kind of an impression was I making on my boys?

Debbie tried to cover for me, telling them I had the flu, but the damage had been done in my mind, even if my sons believed her story.

I was feeling more comfortable in my position at work; more was expected of me, and I was asking more from myself. I have learned as a fire captain, you need to lead by example, hopefully good ones. Yet at home, I was failing to supply them to my sons. The truth is, I was providing examples, some very poor ones.

I found it hard to look my family in the eye over breakfast. The boys were their usual, rambunctious selves, oblivious to what they had witnessed. I felt truly terrible. The shame of my inexcusable behavior was a thousand times worse than the pain of any hangover.

I was failing my sons. Colton would be driving soon, and Chris would be right behind him. I thought back to that day when Chris told me how I was fooling any cop who happened to be following me.

I wasn't fooling any cop, I was fooling myself. What kind of example would I set for my sons? How would I lead them?

Debbie had protected me without a word as she always did, but I knew I had let her down as well. She had always been there for me, and it was time to return the support.

Moments like this show the true measure of your character. When you look into the abyss and realize there is only one choice, you decide to surrender or to fight for change. I knew I was a better person than what my actions were dictating.

That day proved to be a benchmark in my life. I quit drinking and have not had a drop since. The decision was simple; I owed it to myself and to my family.

The choice to quit drinking was mine, and mine alone. It was a personal issue. It is said that in life you only have two choices: you accept things the way they are, or you take responsibility and change them. I could either keep going down the path I was on, or accept a new lifestyle my wife and her family had adopted many years ago.

I just recently read the parable of the two wolves." It has been around for some time; however, it was new to me. It best describes my dilemma:

A Cherokee elder was teaching his grandchildren about life.

He said to them, "A fight is going on inside me…it is a terrible fight between two wolves. One wolf represents fear, anger, envy, sorrow, regret, greed, arrogance, hatefulness, and lies. The other stands for joy, peace, love, hope, humbleness, kindness, friendship, generosity, faith, and truth. This same fight is going on inside of you, and inside every other person too."

The children thought about it for a minute. Then one child asked his grandfather, "Which wolf will win?"

The Cherokee elder replied…

"The one you feed."

I could say I am proud that I no longer drink, and I suppose I am, but I want to convey it with the humility of someone who knows how close he came to being a full-fledged drunk. How can you take credit for something when the good example has always been in front of you all along? I just chose to ignore it.

They do not give out awards for being the husband and father you are supposed to be. It is nothing more than personal choice. The reward is your wife and kids.

A seven-year-old boy planted the tiny seed, and it finally flowered after a drunken night in a gaudy casino. It took some time, but I finally got the message.

CHAPTER TWENTY-SEVEN

IF I COULD HAVE ONLY TOUCHED THEM

I didn't truly recognize how large the County was until I moved around into a variety of assignments. I hope history is a good teacher. I was starting to feel more self-assured than I ever had in my entire life, which is a good thing—that is, if you leave the arrogance behind. I had conquered most of the ghosts of my past, and everything was continuing to gel.

Other than the two years I spent in fire prevention, all of my assignments were in the fire station. Life was becoming routine, something I have fought my entire life. I wanted to be surprised every day, and the surprises I was getting were starting to have a sameness to them.

I never thought it could happen, but I was growing tired of fire station life.

Leaving a crew to go to a new assignment is always disconcerting, especially when the personnel you are leaving behind rank as some of the best with which you have ever worked.

Fire Station 61 was a first-class assignment, unsurpassed in the entire county fire department; being a captain there had to rank in the top ten of the most sought-after positions. Not just because of the station, but because of the caliber of those who worked there.

Time flew by. Some days nothing had an effect on us; we just laughed our way through the entire shift. It must have been my early Christian upbringing, because I was starting to feel guilty about having so much fun. I wasn't encouraging the firefighters to better themselves. I had been promoted up the ranks with the help of some good people. I knew part of my job was to inspire others to advance.

I should have been more like a Jewish mother. *"You're having too much fun! Life is not always enjoyable! You need to study! Make something more of yourselves!"*

Oy vey.

As a fire captain, I was becoming complacent. A leader should encourage and motivate, but somewhere along the line, I had lost my ability to persuade others to prepare themselves for advancement.

In one of my weaker moments, I drove to LA headquarters and put in a transfer request for the Valley Communications Center.

My first clue regarding the wisdom of this move should have been I was the only one requesting the position.

At month's end, the transfers were processed, and mine was accepted. I left one of the most satisfying and comfortable positions I ever had to work at the ugly stepchild of the department. One of the least desirable assignments imaginable. Communications.

In 1986 the fire department had three communications centers.

The Los Angeles Communications Center, known simply as LA, was the largest. It served most of the metropolitan area in the Los Angeles basin within county jurisdiction. It was located in the downstairs area of the headquarters building. It was also referred to as the dungeon. That alone should have been a clue regarding my new assignment.

"Antelope" adjoined old Fire Station 129 in the Antelope Valley. All of the area north of the Angeles National Forest to the county line was served by Antelope Valley Communications.

Valley Communications Center, or Valley, served four battalions that stretched from the northern tip of Los Angeles City, along the foothills of the Angeles National Forest, to the

San Bernardino county line, and most of the area in the San Gabriel Valley not served by local fire departments.

The three centers covered over two thousand square miles of Los Angeles County, which was a formidable task.

Each center would be considered extremely active in its own right when compared to communications centers across the country.

Walking in the door my first day, I can remember feeling sick as I looked around the room.

Boy, did I make a mistake.

Another clue as to the attractiveness of my new position was that I would have to be there for two years. When transferring from fire station to fire station, you were only required to stay for one year. Since no one was beating down the door to get communications, they figured once they had you, they'd better keep you for as long as possible.

My thoughts of misery quickly evaporated when I saw my old friend Greg Bates. He was the captain whose shift was just ending. I had met him when I was a newly promoted captain at Station 19. Greg's reasoning for being at Valley probably made more sense than mine. He received his captain's promotion to a fire station on the Kern County border, some 150 miles from his home in Anaheim Hills. To get closer to home, he filed two hundred transfer requests, the last one being Valley Communications.

Now we would be working together for the next two years.

Greg was a deep thinker, one of those thoughtful people who naturally promote great discussions. He was more liberal than conservative. We had many spirited debates while we were in the fire station. He probably served to moderate some of my positions, and maybe I had an effect on him as well; at least, I hope so.

He was one of those considerate people who listened to you when you were speaking, and considered every word before he spoke. Not like me. I usually had both feet in my mouth before I engaged my brain. We didn't always agree, but he had a profound influence on my thinking. We remain good friends to this day.

＊＊＊

The center itself was located at the end of a long drive at the rear of an old abandoned fire station. It was a one-story building probably built in the early fifties. The dispatch floor was about five hundred square feet, with phones and radio equipment on a long desk-type console.

On the left side of the building was a small kitchen, maybe twenty square feet, just big enough for a small stove, sink, and refrigerator. A little farther down the hall was an equipment room. The last room was what they called the captain's dorm, because squeezed in among the electronic equipment was a single lumpy bed. The room even had a locker to go with it.

On the opposite side of the building were two locker rooms with beds, showers, and toilets.

Each room had windows, but they had long before been painted shut, or were just plain encrusted by dirt, and would not open. The only fresh air that came into the center was in the spring when we'd prop open the front door.

Electronic and radio equipment generate a lot of heat, so to cool the center, window air-conditioners were added one by one as needed. A total of eight were finally installed, not because we reached the maximum cooling temperature, but because we ran out of windows to put them in. Needless to say, the sound of all those air-conditioners added to the general clamor.

A gaudy old Las Vegas casino had nothing on the center. The noise was akin to the clamor of a casino floor, never ending night or day. The smell was the same, minus the stench of spilled beer. The air was always filled with secondhand smoke, and the walls, ceiling, and floors were covered with a thin brown crust from years of exhaled smoke. It was hard to tell the original color of the walls.

The smoking ban in county buildings was still years away.

∴

"The phone is ringing, pitch in and answer it!" That was the extent of the training I received.

Valley Communications was located in the city of El Monte. The county fire department didn't serve the city until years later, so if the center caught fire, or we needed help of any kind, we would have had to call the El Monte Fire Department. I always thought that was amusing; what are the chances of a fire department facility burning down?

I found out about a year later while I was answering 911 calls.

It was in the latter months of 1987. The day's 911 activity had been fairly light and I answered the call quickly; the phone scarcely rang.

"Fire Department—"

"The fire station is on fire." It was the voice of a youthful caller.

I could tell from the information on the 911 screen the kid was calling from a pay phone.

"Yea," I said in my most sarcastic voice.

"No, really, I started pounding on the fire station's front door, and as soon as I did, the lights went out. There's black smoke coming from the back of the fire station.

"Uh-oh." I had lulled myself into thinking this was just a prank call from a pay phone; boy, did I reverse course instantly.

Several minutes before, we had dispatched Station 145 to a traffic collision a couple of blocks away from their station, so I knew the station was empty.

I took the rest of the information and sent the ticket to the radio position. A full structure fire assignment was dispatched. Not wanting to leave the station captain out of the loop, we radioed him the information. As we expected, he cleared the call he was on and started responding.

Station 145's crew must have been beamed to the scene. They made it there quicker than any of us could have imagined.

The captain's first report was, "Light smoke showing from the front of the building."

Building…right! He was still having trouble digesting the fact his fire station was on fire, and wanted to downplay this incident as much as possible.

Of course, firefighters being what they are, the unit responding to the rear said, "I don't know where you are, but we have fire and heavy smoke coming from the rear of your fire station."

Right about now, the captain was thinking, *This is not going to look good on my next resume!*

The protocol for the outlying centers was to notify LA Communications regarding any noteworthy incidents. This fit pretty well into that category. I also asked for the news media to be notified.

They said they would get back to me regarding the news notification.

Within seconds the phone rang again, and it was an angry assistant chief. He told me in no uncertain terms, "The news media *was not* to be notified." I guess he thought you could keep the local fire station burning down under your hat, or helmet, in his case.

The nightly news broadcast from the three network television's stations carried the full story regarding the $250,000 dollars of damage to the fire station. The fire was caused by an electric stove mistakenly being turned to high instead of off. That night's dinner was going to be taquitos.

The next morning's local newspaper read, "Three-Alarm Taquito Fire Destroys Roland Heights Fire Station."

To this day, I still don't have a clue how that story slipped out to the media!

In the early eighties, personal computers and cell phones were in their infancy; the 911 system was almost nonexistent, and all the emergency calls were received over the seven-digit telephone lines.

One need look no further than your own personal computer and cell phone to understand how communications has progressed over the past twenty-five years. By comparison, we were one step ahead of two tin cans and a taut string between them.

Whenever a radio technician would come to work on our system, he would have to take the tubes out and go to the local drugstore where they still had a tube tester. I am guessing that today a teenager doesn't have a clue what a tube is, let alone a tube tester.

The only computer we had was for street searches.

The center was staffed with three firefighters and a captain, not nearly enough for the workload. Communications is a twenty-four-hour, seven-day-a-week, 365-day-a-year operation. The bulk of the call load is from sunrise to midnight, depending of the day of the week. Weekends are always busy. Weather also played a huge role in call load.

I have always been lucky to have excellent firefighters working with me. Two of the dispatchers I worked with in the field, Mike Botenhagen and Gary, both had an excellent work ethic. Every day they gave more than was asked. They were also paramedics, so they were especially good in giving instructions over the phone. They made my job a lot easier.

Mike was shorter than most, something I would never let him forget, and he was built as solid as his character. He loved his coffee and cigarettes and had a great sense of humor. He was the type of good-natured, hardworking firefighter any captain would love to have on his crew. Mike was a dispatcher the entire time I spent at Valley Communications.

All of the communications centers were shorthanded, so on each shift you knew you were going to be on the dispatch floor for extended periods, usually fourteen to sixteen hours per day.

The top staff didn't have a clue what went on in communications. They were convinced all we did in the centers was answer phones and dispatch equipment. As long as there weren't any problems, they were comfortable with not knowing. The hours were long and hard and the work was often unappreciated. Since most of the firefighters didn't want to be there, there was a constant turnover, and due to the stress there were always problems with personnel.

A dispatcher could easily be overwhelmed by the volume of emergency calls. Listening to people scream and cry from seven in the morning until ten at night could be pretty taxing, and that was just from their fellow firefighters! After hearing all the troubles in the centers, you might wonder why on earth I transferred. To be honest, I've often wondered the same thing myself. Sometimes you just have to marvel at things you survive.

Aside from being misunderstood and undesirable, communications also served as an easy scapegoat. When errors occurred, or an emergency-response call was dropped, the first stop on the headhunting expedition was the communications center. It was easy to blame the faulty communications center because there was no one single person who would suffer the slings and arrows. The "system" was to blame.

This was all before the 911 system was in full effect. We had twenty or thirty landlines (a foreign term in an age before cell phones). The calls came in from everywhere, and a person had to dial a telephone number to get us. We received telephone calls from citizens, hospitals, and from many other agencies. You name it and we got it.

When a call was received, the first thing the dispatcher would do is was ask what the problem was. Once the dispatcher knew it was indeed an emergency, he would get the number from where the person was calling, and then quickly get the address. By having the callback number, you would at least be able to reconnect with them in case you were disconnected for any reason, or if you needed additional information.

During a true emergency, people are excited and sometimes confused. When you ask questions, the dispatcher also has to be specific.

"What's the address of your emergency?" If you ask, "What's your address?" you might get just that, their home address, and not the location of the emergency. The same was true with phone numbers.

When the 9-1-1 system was first introduced, some areas of the country referred to the system as nine-eleven. The feedback was quick and comical; an errant few were complaining their telephone did not have an eleven button on it.

Dispatching, field operations, and unit-to-unit radio communications were all done on a single radio frequency. It could be quite hectic at times.

Imagine a brush fire with a battalion chief, five engine companies, four camp crews, a tractor crew, two helicopters, and two fixed-wing airplanes all arriving at the scene of a wildland fire, and everyone wanting to talk on the radio at the same time. All of this while on the other side of town, units were working on a structure fire. Both incident commanders believing their incident was the most important. With all the emergency activity, normal fire business does not come to a halt; dispatching other emergencies needs to be squeezed in between the field chatter. Calling it chaotic does not do it justice. Fortunately, most of the dispatchers were quick to adapt; they were excellent at multitasking.

We eventually received more radio frequencies, which was one major improvement.

After many years of planning, false starts, and millions of dollars being invested, one of the most unique buildings and communications centers in the world was finally up and running. The Fire Command and Control Facility, FCCF, better known as LA Dispatch, was completed. In 1991 the most state-of-the-art communications facility began operations.

The command and control center was constructed on enormous shock absorbers so the ground could move and shake, but the building would remain stationary, and hopefully the center would remain fully functional, ensuring emergency communications would be uninterrupted no matter what circumstances occurred. So far it has withstood the many earthquakes we have in California without a hiccup.

I was on duty at Valley when the Whittier Narrows earthquake hit in 1987.

At 7:42 a.m. the 5.9 temblor hit beneath the city of Rosemead, and by 7:43 our system was overwhelmed. It amazed me how instantly, even while the ground was still shaking, people would be on the telephone requesting help.

While I was at Valley, we had earthquakes, wildland fires, floods, river rescues, high winds with extremely hot weather, and an upswing in normal day-to-day activity, all using the rudimentary equipment that was completely out of date and prone to breaking down.

I settled in for my two-year journey in dispatch and just went along for the ride.

As much as you tried not to let it happen, emergency calls could get personal. The worst fear of any emergency dispatcher is to receive a call from someone you know.

During one warm afternoon, when emergency activity was busier than normal, I received a call from a frantic, screaming woman. I had a terrible time getting coherent information from her, at least initially. She finally told me her husband had just walked in the house and collapsed, and wasn't breathing.

I managed to get her address and assured her help was on the way. Suddenly she blurted out, "You know who this is, don't you?"

Many people believe they are calling the local fire station instead of a communications center, so in my most arrogant voice I said, "Lady, I don't have a clue *who* this is!" Sometimes my arrogance would surface at the most inappropriate times.

She said that her husband was one of our captains.

I felt terrible. We dispatched the equipment, and they arrived in record time, but none of our efforts could save him.

One of our beloved captains passed away that afternoon, and now his name is inscribed on the memorial wall.

That was an unforgettable day.

It took a constant effort to divorce yourself from the caller; but when the person in need was someone familiar to you, the situation took on an entirely new dimension. Names and faces became real, and you came to realize that every day there was someone out there, a lot of someones, and they all needed help. In some small way, your job was to lend a hand.

You realized every call was personal whether you recognized the name or not. Like the addict with his daughter or the heavy woman and her niece, someone always knows their name and loves the person who answers to it.

It is difficult to describe a job where you come in to work every day knowing the call you take will be someone who is anxious and in need of help, and it could well be someone you know. You are fully aware that one transposed number or one misspelled street name could easily prevent someone from receiving help in a timely manner.

From the moment you walk in the door in the morning until your shift is completed the next day, you are in a situation where the pressure and anxiety levels are extreme. Your day consists of receiving requests for every conceivable type of emergency.

There is a sense of helplessness speaking to people on the telephone when all you can do is envision their emergency. In the field you can see them and have an effect on the outcome; you see the fruits of your labor. In communications, you are left guessing. We were dealing with small fragments of the call, pieces of a story in which we never knew the ending. Sometimes you would follow up, but most of the time, they were just one call in a never-ending series of calls.

Not knowing the outcome is a completely different kind of stress.

I learned quickly communications was not at all what I had expected when I arrived that first day. It was a lot more complicated than even most people within the department realized.

Not all calls were nerve-racking; some brought a smile to your face. The voices on the radio became familiar. You learned quickly who the good field captains were. Just like all professions, you had the winners and the losers.

We dispatched a call to a fire at the top of a five-story building. The caller didn't know the exact address, but the building was on the southwest corner of a prominent intersection. The informant could see smoke coming from the top of the building. High-rise fire incidents require a lot of equipment, so many units responded to the location.

Within minutes the captain from the first arriving unit reported at the scene and said, "Valley, do you have any additional information regarding this call?"

You always felt like saying, "Yup! But we thought we would hold it back, just to keep you guessing."

"There's no five-story building on the southwest corner."

As the dispatcher double-checked the information and tried to reach the reporting party, he heard the voice of the captain continue.

"There's a five-story building across the street, though. Could that be it?"

Never overlook the obvious! Sometimes all you could do was laugh.

I am sure that captain probably complained about communications sending him to the wrong address. When I was in the field, I complained about communications, and when I was in communications, I complained about the guys in the field. Loyalty sometimes is where you hang your hat.

You never knew what call would stay in your mind; there were certainly enough calls to fill a library. All of these years later, an incident in Bassett still is stuck in my memory banks; as hard as I try, it pops up every now and then. Maybe it is because I had worked in that area, or maybe just because it was haunting.

One evening I received a call from a composed woman. In a calm voice, she said she was in the back bedroom of her mobile home and could see small flames in the living room area. I took all of the information as fast as I could, and as with all fire calls, I said, "The fire department is on the way. *Get out of the house.*"

She said, "Okay," and then hung up.

The first responding units reported they were still several miles away, but could see smoke and fire. Hearing that gave me a very uncomfortable feeling.

The fire was controlled in less than five minutes, and then the captain stated this incident was a *Code F*. That radio communication made my uncomfortable feeling quickly turn to chills going up my spine.

The woman I had just spoken with minutes before was now dead. I had never met her, didn't even know what she looked like or even her name. Our conversation lasted less than a minute, yet she left an unforgettable impression on me.

Perhaps if I hadn't kept her on the telephone so long, she could have gotten out safely. Maybe if I were just a little more forceful in telling her to leave, she would have survived. The good Lord is the only one who knows the answers to those questions, but in the meantime, years later, I can still hear her voice.

As in all aspects of the fire service, but particularly in communications, tragedy could mix with comedy at almost any turn. How could an incident be tragic, painful, and humorous all at the same time? I guess if you take enough calls, some are going to fit in this category.

"Fire Department," Gary barked into the telephone.

"My boyfriend shot himself." The voice belonged to a youthful-sounding female. She was calm.

You could hear faint groans in the background. It didn't sound like a mortal moan, if that makes sense.

"He shot himself in the end of his…you know!"

"Where did he shoot himself?" Gary was completely puzzled, and at this point was at a loss for words. I half expected her to answer, "In the kitchen."

"Well…," she hesitated. "He's bleeding."

The groans changed and became commands. "Just tell them to get here."

After taking all the information, Gary didn't have a clue what to say next, and was completely buffaloed regarding how to give emergency instructions. Being a former paramedic, he started searching his memory banks for the proper protocol; unfortunately, his mind was completely devoid of treatment on how to stop the bleeding from, as the caller put it, "a bullet hole in the end of his…you know."

If nothing else would work, he thought back to direct pressure, and told the caller to use a clean cloth to press as hard as she could on the wound; that should stop the bleeding, although, of course, it might cause a little pain.

He then stated, "Help is on the way," and hung up. As he gazed around the room, everyone—or should I say, every man—sat there with a grimace on his face and repeated his last words. "Just a little pain?"

It's hard to imagine what might occur to cause someone to shoot himself in the penis. We never called the fire station to find out the particulars regarding the call; some things are best left unknown!

∴

If you can live your entire life without hearing the screams of a person in need, you are truly fortunate. The nature of the job puts first responders in a position where they will hear those unforgettable screams many times during their career.

Dispatchers are the first link to an emergency and are every bit a part of the emergency response team.

It was busy when I arrived at the center, so immediately I sat down and starting taking calls. I scarcely got out the words "Fire Department—" when a terrified voice on the other end of the line screamed, "My baby's not breathing, please help me!"

Scarier words were never spoken nor heard.

The only tool the dispatcher has is his voice—unlike in the field, where you are fully hands-on with a crew. There is only you and the sound of your voice to do as much as you can for the person in distress. At that moment, endorphins run through your body just as if you were an integral component of that team in the field.

The first order of business is to calm yourself and then try to calm the caller so you can get the essential information.

The young woman stopped crying long enough to tell me she had found her baby face down in the bathtub, and the child was not breathing.

The entire center came to a dead hush while I tried to walk the mother through instructions to save her baby.

I visualized sitting beside her as I told her what to do. I closed my eyes and began to recall the classes I had attended in child CPR. I could see her in my mind, frantic, and I placed my mental hand on her shoulder as I instructed her as calmly as I could to place the baby on her lap.

"That's good," I said. "Now tilt his head back just a little and gently place your mouth over the baby's nose and mouth."

"Over the nose and mouth," she repeated like a prayer, which I suppose it was.

"Give the baby two or three short quick puffs of air."

"Okay," she said when it was done.

"Take two fingers and push gently on the baby's chest between his nipples."

The time between my commands felt like an eternity. I used the pauses to take a deep breath myself.

The others in the call center were huddled around me like at a campfire, although I didn't realize it at the time.

Just as I would catch my breath, the mother would come back on the phone for more instructions and reassurance. We fell into an uneasy rhythm. Instruction. Pause. Breathe. Instruction. Pause. Breathe. I thought there had to be something more that I could do, but if there was, it had completely escaped me.

Between instructions I could hear the mother crying, "Breathe, baby, breathe, breathe, oh God, please breathe." She was mimicking my own thoughts.

I was utterly frustrated about what to do next. It was as if I could see everything so clearly, but I was prevented from touching the mom and baby by a glass partition. Have you ever had one of those dreams where you wanted to scream or run but you couldn't? I was living that dream. I could not give the woman or her child the help they so desperately needed. It was like a slow-motion nightmare unfolding right before me. A nightmare that would stay with me for a long time.

The minutes passed slowly until finally I could hear the faint sound of sirens in the background.

What took you so long? I shouted in my head, but what the mother heard was, "Help is coming, hang on, help is coming."

Just before the phone went dead, I heard the muffled cries of a little baby.

I sat there for several minutes before I took another call, wondering if that child lived or died and whether I had made a difference. The others went back to their jobs. I had the callback telephone number of the mom, and I knew the firefighters who had responded to the incident; all I had to do was call and I could find out if that baby survived.

I stared at the phone for a long time before I went back to work.

I never made the call.

Sometimes it's better to imagine the outcome. This was one I just couldn't bear to know. I didn't want another addition to my mind's filing cabinet that day, although I guess it went in there after all.

The phone rang again and I quickly took another call; it diverted me from thinking about the mom and little baby. That's pretty much the way a day went in communications—one call pushed the last into your memory banks. We do all we can, and I guess that has to be enough.

One of the worst emergency calls I ever took involved senseless bloodshed and loss of life so tragic, it shocked me to my very core.

The caller was my wife.

CHAPTER TWENTY-EIGHT

JUST PLAIN EVIL

It was a typically hectic day at Valley Communications. It was a warm July day in 1986, so we knew it was going to be busy.

I answered the phone expecting to take just another call in a long list of emergency calls for the day. The frantic woman choking back tears on the line was Debbie. She had just received word that her older brother, Royce, and his two teenage sons had been brutally attacked at their ranch outside Sacramento in what would become one of the most grisly and fascinating murder cases the area had ever seen.

I immediately tried to wrap things up as best I could so I could leave. It took a little while, but I eventually made it home. Debbie had managed to find a friend to stay with the boys for a couple of days. Information was a little sketchy about the situation up at Royce's, as you might imagine, so we didn't want to take Chris and Colt along with us under those circumstances. We literally did not know what to expect. This was before cell phones, and since we were on the road, all we could do was listen to the news.

The reports on the radio only increased our anguish, as we heard the terrible news repeated with each broadcast: "Three people had been killed near Sacramento." We were totally in the dark as to who was dead. When Debbie first received the call, she was told Sam was dead and Royce had been shot. For all we knew, Royce and Jackson were the other two.

Normal life for Debbie's older brother Royce only lasted for brief periods.

Since Royce's divorce, he had pretty much been between loves, until he met an attractive barmaid named Laurie. She was eighteen years Royce's junior. It did not take long for that relationship to grow, and soon they had moved in together. Things were starting to settle down, and they were beginning to have a normal life. (I have used the expression *normal* several times referring to families, and now as I get older, I am coming to the realization I don't have a clue what normal really is.)

Royce's life was once again growing into a routine, so he naturally thought things were finally getting better, until he came home one evening and found a note taped to the refrigerator door. Laurie had packed up and left him for a new guy, one with a nicer car and thicker wallet.

Laurie and her new beau, Frankie S*****, had left town.

We could not imagined the heartache Royce must have been going through. He was tough as nails on the outside, but the internal conflict and pain must have been unbearable.

Royce's tenacity again rose to the surface, and he outwardly took things in stride and got on with his life. He promptly hit it off with another pretty woman, whom he quickly invited to bunk at his ranch. Things were getting right back on track, almost back to where they were; only the names had changed.

Laurie's new boyfriend was a mysterious man, having shown up in cowboy country driving a fancy car and sporting a big-city attitude. The rumor was he operated on the shady side of the law; no one knew for sure the depth of his illegal activities. Reality was much worse than rumor, and time would prove Frankie to be a stone-cold psychopathic killer.

Royce should have had an internal warning device that would activate when things started running smoothly. Periods of tranquility only lasted for brief periods, and this time was no different.

The nine-month stay in flyover country for Laurie and her newfound love must have been tempestuous. She was miles away from home, and torn between two lovers.

It did not take long before her heart turned toward Royce, and she returned to the Sacramento area. Things have a habit of never staying the same, and she quickly found the bed she had once occupied was now taken by another.

Nothing is fair in love and war, so the new girlfriend's things ended up on the barn floor.

Royce's now ex-girlfriend made what might have been the most intelligent decision of her life; she gathered her things and moved back into town.

Royce's broken heart was on the mend again. Laurie was back.

Several months went by, with Royce and Laurie's relationship again growing stronger, and a wedding date was set for the near future.

Mom and Dad were reduced to bystanders. It was like watching a train wreck in slow motion. Dad was more vocal than Mom; she tended to internalize most of her feelings. The plans they had for their firstborn were much less than ideal, and certainly more tumultuous than they ever could have anticipated.

Kevin was living nearby with his family and continued to live in the shadow of his big brother.

As you can imagine, this was not the beginning of a love story where they all lived happily ever after. It was the beginning of a tragic ending, one that up until then was reserved for nighttime television dramas.

Determined to get his lost girlfriend back, Frankie showed up in town again. He began making threats against Royce, both veiled and overt, which Royce pretty much ignored. That turned out to be a bad decision.

Perhaps the straw that broke the proverbial camel's back was that Royce and Laurie announced they were expecting a baby.

Royce lived out in the country, and like most folks, they never locked their doors at night.

Jackson and Samuel split time between Royce's place and their mother's. She lived closer to town, and unfortunately on this night, both boys were with their father.

Frankie, dressed in black and wearing a bulletproof vest, parked his car in a field about a mile away from the ranch. Under a three-quarter summer moon, he hiked toward the house through cow pastures and vacant fields, with two pistols in his belt and a semi-automatic rifle slung over his shoulder.

Sometime a little after midnight, he calmly cut the telephone lines, and entered through the service porch at the back of the house, just off the kitchen.

No one knows why the dogs did not bark.

The only noise in the house was the hum of the refrigerator. Idle kitchen appliances produced a tiny amount of light. Frankie cautiously, and ever so quietly, walked down the hallway, past Sam's room.

At the end of the hallway was the master bedroom where Royce and Laurie were lying next to each other in bed.

Standing in the darkened hallway, still not making a sound, he burst into the room and switched on the lights, as if he wanted to say, "I want you to see the face of the person who is going to kill you!"

No one knows if Laurie ever woke up as Frankie pointed the gun at her and sprayed the bed with bullets. Two found their mark, killing Laurie and her unborn baby instantly. He re-aimed his weapon and pulled the trigger once again, hitting Royce in the leg, just above the knee. One of the ejecting shells from the salvo jammed in the firing mechanism, and now Royce was looking into the eyes of a cold-blooded murderer.

It only took Frankie a second to abandon his misfiring weapon and grab a pistol from his waistband. That tiny pause gave Royce the chance to save his own life. He quickly threw the bed covers up as a distraction, and jumped out of bed and grabbed Frankie in a bear hug, yelling for Sam as he did. I am sure that will haunt him until the day he dies, because Sam heard his name being called and ran to support his father.

Frankie and Royce fiercely struggled to gain control over the weapon. Royce had just awaking from a deep sleep and was no match for the killer. He quickly lost control and was pummeled on the top of his head with the butt of the Frankie's gun. Temporarily stunned, he fell back onto the bedroom floor. Frankie took aim and shot Royce in the face as Sam ran into the room.

Samuel also courageously fought with the attacker, but was quickly overpowered by the more experienced and bigger man. Frankie manhandled him down the hallway, back into the family room. He pushed Sam to the floor and made him kneel. He shot the nineteen-year-old once in the face, killing him instantly.

All of the commotion awakened Jackson from a dead sleep. He heard the dreadful sounds of his brother being shot, and waited in his room for the ideal time to investigate.

While Frankie was unfocused, Jackson ran into his father's bedroom, only to see what he thought were the dead bodies of his father and Laurie.

Royce kept an unloaded .22 caliber, nine-shot revolver in his nightstand, unloaded for safety reasons. The ammunition was in the nightstand on the opposite side of the bed.

Jackson quickly rushed around to his father's side, grabbed a handful of bullets from the nightstand, and tried to load the gun as he ran back to his room.

He could hear the pounding footsteps coming down the hall, and knew he was going to be the next victim.

Crouched down in the closet, still fumbling with the bullets as he tried to load the pistol, he reached out and hurriedly closed the bedroom door. Holding the pistol with two hands and carefully aiming at his bedroom door, he suddenly realizing he left the bedroom lights on. Possibly a fatal mistake. With only a few seconds to spare, he jumped out and hit the switch.

Frankie stopped momentarily to listen outside Jackson's bedroom door. With the full force of his body, he leaned back and kicked in the door, but saw no one. Now, standing in the darkened room, backlit by the hallway light, Jackson took aim at the figure dressed in black and fired, hitting Frankie with a glancing shot to the head knocking him down.

The shot was not fatal, but the force was enough to knock him to the floor. Knowing he was still in grave danger, Jackson carefully took aim and fired again; this time the bullet hit the side of Frankie's head.

Jackson heard his father moaning from the other room, and for the first time realized, his father was still alive.

"Dad, Dad," he yelled, leaping over Frankie's body and running to his father's side. "I got him, I got him, but I think he's still alive!"

Royce, lying on his bedroom floor and barely able to crawl, told his son, "Get me a gun."

Royce was unsteady and fighting to stay conscious. It was all Jackson could do to help his father into the other bedroom, where Frankie lay moaning, still a deadly threat to his family.

Royce placed the muzzle against Frankie's temple and pulled the trigger, just before he blacked out again.

The sparsely populated area had few neighbors close by. Jackson, now by himself, ran to the telephone to call for help, but the line was dead.

The mind of this seventh grader was now in overdrive, trying to make sense out what had transpired over the past few minutes. Not knowing what his next few steps should be, he ran to his brother's side hoping desperately for the comfort that his brother had always provided. He hugged him briefly while he formulated his next move. The respite only took seconds before he ran to his father's truck and sped toward his Uncle Kevin's house.

The banging on the front door and Jackson's frantic cries jarred Kevin from a sound sleep. Jackson could hardly speak, but eventually got the words out that his dad, Sam, and Laurie had been shot.

Kevin yelled to his wife to call the police as they both jumped into the truck and sped back to Royce's ranch.

Royce's emotions were running wild as he sat there in the now-quiet house. Drifting in and out of consciousness, he also was having a difficult time comprehending what had just taken place. The throbbing from his bullet wounds were minuscule compared to the ache in his heart. He cradled Sam in his lap while waiting for help to arrive.

I cannot envision the horror Kevin saw as he entered the house.

The sheriff finally arrived, but the carnage was complete; there was nothing that could be done for Laurie or Samuel.

Royce was rushed to the hospital, and the remaining family was left to sort out the details for the sheriff's department.

The next morning a helicopter search found Frankie's car. In the trunk was a cooler packed with the equivalent of twenty-five pounds of dynamite and more guns. Later the sheriff's bomb expert would say there were enough explosives in the vehicle to "remove the home from the immediate vicinity."

What wasn't found was any type of triggering device or blasting caps. They knew that somewhere in town was a motel room filled with more explosives.

Terrible news like this is tailor-made for the news media, and they wasted no time filling the airwaves with the tragic story. They also televised the pictures of Frankie in an effort to find his ill-fated motel room.

After several hours, his room was located, and it did indeed contain more explosives.

Reality is different from the fantasies we see at the movies and on television. When our nightly heroes get into shootouts, and a fistful of bad guys bites the dust, there are no consequences. In life, real people, from real families suffer tremendously. Time will soften the memory, but it never entirely goes away.

⁘

The news spread quickly within the family, so it didn't take long before they all assembled in Sacramento.

Debbie's mom and dad arrived not long before us, having flown immediately from St. George, Utah. They were devastated at the loss of their oldest grandson, as were we all, but were relieved Royce and Jackson were still alive.

When Debbie and I arrived, we went directly to the hospital and met with everyone. It was quite a crowd; all the visitors plus the hospital staff made the environment chaotic.

Among the group was Royce's ex-wife, Nancy, Sam's mom. The tension in the room was so thick; you could almost cut it with a knife.

With two almost-fatal bullet wounds, Royce was lying in the hospital bed not looking well at all, as you might expect. It was hard to tell what injury he suffered from the most, the loss of his loved ones or his physical injuries.

The first shot fired at Royce hit him just above his knee. The second tore into his cheek, taking out several teeth on the way to its final resting place in his neck, near the spinal cord. Had the bullet continued its path, he could have been easily killed or paralyzed. The doctors decided it would be too dangerous to try to remove the bullet, so it remains in his neck. His bullet wounds would heal, but the loss of his loved ones would last forever.

For the next several days, family and friends gathered around Royce's bedside to provide whatever comfort they could to try to help Royce minimize his grief.

After days of sitting in the hospital, I volunteered to help take care of the funeral arrangements. Nancy's new husband went along.

:':

It was difficult planning Sam's funeral, but we did the best we could.

Anything to do with the funeral of a loved one is painful, especially with such a tragic and untimely death.

Timing was critical; Royce had two families, and having services at the same cemetery, at the same time, would have been adding untold grief to the family members. Even though several days had gone by, tension was still palpable.

The weather was perfect for a mid-July day in Sacramento. There were hundreds of people at the services so they were conducted outside at the gravesite. Loudspeakers were used to amplify the eulogy.

As a father, and having sons close to Sam's age, I couldn't bear to sit with the family during the services; it was just too painful. I sat in my car several blocks away, but I was still on the cemetery grounds.

Every word spoken brought tears to my eyes. I had to be by myself and left alone to deal with my thoughts in my own way.

The funeral goers unhurriedly left the cemetery and returned to their lives, and within days they were back to a normal routine. Our family was unable to do that; life does not have a reverse, and past events can never be completely erased from your mind. They are indelibly written.

:':

The day following the funeral Kevin, Craig, a close friend of the family, and I went back to the house to clean up and repair things. It was a job everyone dreaded doing, but it still needed to be done.

It was a ghostly feeling being in the house. The last time I was there was when Debbie and I were first married, and we spent the weekend with Nancy, Royce, and the boys. It was a happy house then, filled with good memories. Now the carnage was pushing those memories aside, and I am afraid they won the battle for space in mine.

Brutally evident were the events which had occurred. They were almost as clear as if we had been there.

Tragedy was everywhere. You could see the bullet-ridden bedroom where Laurie and Royce had been shot. As you walked down the hallway, Royce's bloody handprints were still visible along the wall where he steadied himself as he made his way to be with Sam. There was a large stain of blood on the carpet where Royce cradled his son for the last time.

I was having trouble coping with being there, and I was hoping the others didn't see how upset I was. I think they were going through the same roller coaster of feeling, but none of us wanted to speak about it.

It took a while to clean the house. Painting, patching holes, and removing blood-soaked carpet was the easy part. When we were done, the house looked as if nothing had ever happened; if only the terrible memories could be erased so easily.

The sheriff's department later disclosed that Frankie S***** was a suspect in unsolved murders in other states. He was truly an evil man.

The fate of Frankie is now in God's hands, and for our family, I guess that will have to be enough.

The newspaper gave graphic details regarding the tragedy. Within days, it fell from the front page; fortunately, the reporters moved on to other stories. There had been only a few small passing references to Jackson's heroic actions.

Thirteen-year-old Jackson was abruptly awakened from what should have been just another night at his father's house. Instead, he heard shots he thought had killed his entire family, and still had the courage and presence of mind to confront the intruder. Not knowing where the attacker might be, he ran to his father's bedside to retrieve a gun and armed himself. He never thought about his own safety, he just reacted. That is the mark of a *true hero*.

Royce's incident is scarcely mentioned within the family in the hopes the silence will help heal the wounds. I think about Jackson all the time, and how he saved his father's life. He is truly a remarkable young man.

Royce moved from the Sacramento area and is living a somewhat uneventful life in the northwest. Jackson and his family live nearby.

Significant emotional events occur in everyone's lives. No two people process them the same. They can help you grow, or they can destroy you. Debbie chose to receive professional counseling; it helped her immensely. I bury the events in the far reaches of my mind, and try to never visit them.

Kevin was an affable chap, didn't easily share his emotions with anyone. He maintained his macho cowboy persona. Suppressing his feelings just drove him further into the bottle. He and his small family moved from state to state, and job to job, never staying in any one area for long. His needs from life were minimal; as long as he had a cold beer in the refrigerator, and fresh packs of smokes in his shirt pocket, he was content.

His second marriage only lasted ten years. He was again raising his daughter by himself. He married a third time and moved to Nevada with his new wife and her young son in tow.

Time goes by in the blink of an eye, and soon his daughter was starting a family of her own. Janice married and quickly divorced, but not before having two children of her own. It didn't take long before she was living with Kevin and his family.

Most times the family would squeeze into a small rental home or trailer, in some out-of-the-way town in Nevada. His new wife gave some stability to the family, but the environment was still something less than desirable.

Kevin's love for his granddaughters was the driving force in his life, but his health began to dramatically decline. The consequences of the cowboy lifestyle, heavy smoking, and drinking finally took its toll. He was fifty-four when he died, thus writing the final verse in his country and western song.

His death went completely unnoticed by the world around him; however, he left a wide gaping space in the hearts of those who loved him.

ADDITIONAL AUTHORS NOTE

The above narrative, as well as the other descriptions in this book are true and as accurate as humanly possible. Royce's story unfolded several years ago, but the hurting and heartache has not grown any less over time. Sensitivity and pain still exists amongst family members, so it was difficult to tell their story. Out of respect for the family, and for their security, I have changed the names of each family member. The names used are the product of the author's imagination and are used fictitiously. Any resemblance to other organizations or persons, living or dead, past or present, is purely coincidental.

The individual in this story is so evil; I have limited him to only a first fictitious name.

Debbie's nightly prayer is that the terrible memories of this family episode will fade into obscurity and the good family recollections will replace them, and once again the family will become whole.

CHAPTER TWENTY-NINE

FOR BETTER OR WORSE

After Royce and Sam's horrible tragedy, life was not the same. Debbie's mom and dad were starting to show the effects of years of family stress, slowly at first, but then quickly picking up speed.

May internalized most of her emotions. She gradually started showing symptoms of dementia. Nobody knows what causes Alzheimer's, but she was rapidly showing more and more signs of the disease. I am sure the tragic death of her grandson helped push her into the deep recesses of her own mind and away from reality.

You could see Mom's mental acuteness decline almost on a daily basis; nevertheless, Ron took care of her at home the best he could, for as long as he could. Eventually it was too much for him and he was forced to put her in a nursing home.

Ron showed love and compassion for his wife the likes of which I have never seen before. Without fail each day, he would go to the nursing home and dress his beloved wife, fix her hair, put on her makeup, and feed her breakfast. He would say, "Just because she is sick, there is no reason she shouldn't look beautiful. That's the woman I married."

He would sit and visit with her until lunch. The conversations were always one-way. He couldn't tell if she understood, but it made him feel happy they were sitting there together.

He would return at the end of the day before dinner, and get her ready for bed, removing her clothes and putting on her nightgown, kissing her cheek as he tucked her in for the night. He never missed a day. She was his sweetheart.

The last several years of her life, she did not recognize him or her family. Who's to say that behind those loving and ever-so-dimming eyes, that deep within she wasn't beaming with pride, and saying, "That's the man I married, he's still taking care of me, for better or worse." The devastation of Alzheimer's disease could never break the bond that was created over sixty-two years of marriage. The love they shared had absolutely no limits.

Mom passed away in 2002.

Debbie visited her father as much as time would allow. Being with him was enjoyable and painful at the same time. Every visit brought the same remark from Ron: "Why am I still here? I am ready to go."

Debbie has always been strong, but she would remark it was difficult to describe the pain of watching her father giving up on life. He too was hiding from past memories.

In the latter part of 2010, Ron's prayers were answered, and he joined the love of his life, his sweetheart, in death. Both were finally at peace.

The funeral was modest and simple, perhaps the most fitting ceremony for a man that through his life was humble and giving.

I try to convince myself that we as firefighters are different, but in reality, we are the same as the people we serve every day—rich, poor, or just in the middle. Once again I am reminded there is no such thing as *those people*. After all, we are still just people, and beneath the surface, we are not all that different.

CHAPTER THIRTY

THE BURN WARD IS A HEARTBREAKING PLACE

The new Command and Control building was in the latter days of construction when I left Valley Communications. I kicked around in the field for another year before the lack of activity started to get to me. Being in communications with its long hours and constant activity left an indelible impression, so when I returned to station life, I again had to adjust, this time to the slower pace of the fire station. At first it was a welcome change, but after a short while, I was starting to climb the walls.

I switched to another station in the field, hoping for more activity. Station 17 proved to be just that, very active. I had some of my more unforgettable incidents in the year I spent there.

The transition from firefighter to civilian dispatchers was well underway. My old friend Richard Land was a battalion chief now, and headed the transition team. We had not worked together since our time in Azusa at Station 32.

I had discussed with him how fire station life was taking a toll on me, so he asked if I would be interested in coming back to help training the new dispatchers.

I never thought it would happen, but the activity in communications is infectious, so I jumped at the opportunity.

∗∗∗

The department has not only been on the cutting edge of firefighting, but it has also led the industry in every aspect of emergency operations. They bring cost-effective services to the public, and have taken community fire protection to new heights.

Change comes slowly—in the fire service, even slower. Professional civilian dispatchers replaced firefighters in communications over twenty years ago now. The new dispatchers have proven themselves a valuable asset and part of the team. The financial savings and improved quality of service has added immeasurably to the system.

Today dispatchers are fully trained for their role as communications specialists, including pre-arrival instructions. They have detailed directions for every imaginable emergency scenario. If you call 911 to report a rabid duck has bitten your ear off, once equipment is dispatched, the dispatcher keeps the caller on the line and walks them through step-by-step instructions on any conceivable emergency, from childbirth to CPR to crazed waterfowl.

It takes only seconds, instead of minutes, to process a call with the computers used in today's centers.

The organization is much more specialized and sophisticated than the rudimentary system I endured. The lengthy training and comprehensive training now is tailored to the job. The days of "the phone's ringing, you'd better answer it" are finally over.

In early 1991, Valley and Antelope Communications centers were phased out, and the new state-of-the-art facility was finally up and running.

At first the field units were somewhat reluctant about the new changes. Change intimidates people, and this was a whole lot of change.

In today's communications center, the staff totals eighty dispatchers, with thirteen supervising fire dispatchers.

Each day the center is staffed with nineteen dispatchers and three supervisors to handle all the activity. A fire captain and battalion chief are on duty at the center on a twenty-four-hour-a-day basis to ensure harmony between the field and the communications center.

Fire Command and Control dispatchers receive calls from throughout Los Angeles County's borders, including the fifty-nine contract cities, all unincorporated areas, and the Angeles and Los Padres National Forests. Calls are received through the 911 telephone system, seven-digit emergency numbers, and local ring-down lines.

Last year nearly a half-million business telephone calls were received, in addition to the daily total of over 650 emergency incidents. It is considered one of the busiest centers in the nation.

The firefighter-dispatchers were gradually displaced and returned to the field. Some looked forward to returning, and others went back reluctantly.

Mike Botenhagen, stayed at Valley until the transition was completed and the center was closed. He then transferred to Station 85, my old stomping grounds. He also had mixed emotions, but nothing in life stays the same, so he was looking forward to returning to station life. He had spent so much of his career as a paramedic in that battalion, it was akin to returning home. After several months, Mike suffered as I did; the lack of constant activity wears on you.

Two fire stations serve the majority of Glendora. The 210 Freeway almost equally divided the districts. It had a little bit of everything, from high-rise buildings and light industry, to wildland areas. The 57 Freeway served as its eastern boundary. The two freeways were a source of many calls. If it wasn't a vehicle crash, it was a vehicle fire.

Late one afternoon, Engine 85 was dispatched to a vehicle fire on the westbound 210 Freeway. Motorists in distress used a large area on the side of the freeway just past the Sunflower off-ramp frequently. Mike knew it well; he had dispatched units to this area for years.

As they approached, they could see from the amount of smoke and flame this wasn't just an ordinary vehicle fire, it was a limousine. There is no such thing as a normal incident, but after responding to many vehicle fires, they do become repetitive. The commuters even thought so that day, because the freeway traffic was running almost at normal speed; traffic had barely slowed down for rubberneckers.

Times were changing, and the auto industry in an effort to make cars lighter and more efficient was using plastics at an amazing rate. The fire fighting tactics had been slow to change, and a lackadaisical attitude persisted toward this type of fire. Full turnout clothing was rarely worn, and self-contained breathing was almost never used.

Mike's approach to everything was at full speed, and that day was no exception. He donned his gear and went right to work.

Vehicle fires are usually extinguished within minutes with a single small hose line and the water carried on the rig. This one was particularly stubborn, perhaps because of the size of the vehicle. Mike started working his hose line from the front of the vehicle and moved in a sweeping motion toward the rear.

To make cars safer, the auto safety engineers have designed and installed shock absorbers on front and back bumpers, safer for the driving public in low-speed accidents, but terribly dangerous for firefighters. When shock absorbers are heated, they have a propensity to explode. Mike knew this, so he was being extra cautious and was keeping away from the front bumper.

No one knows for sure how long the fire had been burning, but it was long enough to super heat the gas in the tank.

Timing is everything, and today it was not on Mike's side. While he was bending over to extinguish the fire under the rear of the limo, his face squarely in front of the gas tank inlet, it exploded, sending a fireball into the air and completely engulfing Mike with fire.

As Mike relayed the story to me, he said the first thing that went through his mind was to run. He had been trained differently, but nonetheless, all he wanted to do is run. In a nanosecond his training took over. He knew if he ran, it would be into the fast-moving traffic of the freeway. He dropped to the ground and began rolling. His captain rushed over and smothered him with his body, trying to extinguish the remaining flames.

Mike was badly burned on his face, neck, and hands.

Firefighters are used to the routine of an emergency response, but when it is one of your own, time slows and everything takes forever.

He was transported to the burn center at Sherman Oaks Hospital.

As soon as I heard the news, my son Colton and I went to the hospital to visit with him. Colton was a Fire Explorer and vividly remembers his visit.

Nothing could have prepared us for what we were about to see.

When we walked into the hospital room, poor Mike looked like a mummy, with bandages covering all the areas of his body that could be seen. His head was bandaged, with slits for his eyes, nose, and mouth. His hands were covered. His lips were huge and swollen, and he looked like he must be miserable and in great pain, which I'm sure he was.

The first words out of his mouth when he saw us were, "I feel fine, but don't make me laugh, that hurts like hell!"

We sat there together for some time as he relayed what had happened. He also spoke of the treatment he had just gone through that morning.

To clean the wounds and promote healing, all the burnt and dead skin must be removed. They gave him the maximum amount of painkilling drugs and began cleaning the burns, literally scrubbing them with a brush. He said it was like having your face placed over an open burner on a stove and then just held there. It was the most painful experience he had ever gone through.

Mike's narrative was captivating; I had completely forgotten Colton was there in the room with us. He sat there engrossed with the sights and sounds in front of him. He did not speak. He didn't speak at all while we were driving home either.

Everyone did his share of second-guessing regarding Mike and his burns. As you can imagine, it had a devastating effect on his captain, as well as on me. It is every captain's nightmare to have someone injured or even killed on an incident. Mike blames no one for his accident. The policy for the use of safety equipment on a vehicle fire has changed. Firefighters are now completely encapsulated with turnouts, flash hood, and breathing apparatus.

He didn't return to work for months, and if you saw him today, you'd never know he was burned. Time heals all wounds, almost. The psychological scars remain. Certain sounds, like dragging a chair across the floor, can cause him to flash back to that day. That sound is like the low rumble he heard just before he felt the fireball blow across his face. He still has nightmares.

Finally, he returned to duty. He appeared to be unchanged; he was still the optimistic and aggressive firefighter he always was. I can't imagine the butterflies he must have felt every time they responded to another vehicle fire.

CHAPTER THIRTY-ONE

YOU LEARN FROM EVERYONE, EVEN IF YOU DON'T ALWAYS AGREE

The irony regarding busy areas is invariably they come with more memories you want to suppress. It meant dealing with more human tragedy. With great responsibility comes great opportunity, and with more incidences come more chances to do something beneficial, and the memories that go along with them as well.

The old proverb, *"May you live in interesting times,"* can be either a blessing or a curse, depending on your point of view.

My last station assignment as a captain before I was promoted to battalion chief was at Station 17 in Whittier. I have many strong memories, both good and bad.

Every station has unforgettable calls and the busier the station, the more of those you get; but invariably it's the people who make the difference. Sometimes I have to pinch myself regarding my career. I was truly fortunate to have worked with many outstanding people. As a captain and a battalion chief, it sure made each assignment all the more pleasurable.

Everyone in life has something to offer. Unfortunately, some serve as nothing more than a poor example; I have learned immensely from them also. It didn't take me long to learn that everyone who passed through my office door pleased me—some by entering, and others by leaving.

You hope each person you work with adds to the team, and at the end of the day, you can say you made a difference. If you are truly lucky, as I have been, you can say one of the firefighters not only made a difference in your life, but also added tremendously to the fire service.

I was fortunate to work with a fellow firefighter named Dallas Jones. His given name was William, and I have no idea why everyone called him Dallas. I never thought to ask. He was a guy who always had a friendly smile beneath the mustache that stopped just short of handlebar territory.

Dallas was someone who met his calling early in life; he was a union guy. As I have mentioned many times before in this book, firefighters love to help people, and Dallas took it one-step further and strived to help those he worked with by improving their work environment. He was instrumental in having the Whittier Fire Department join the consolidated fire protection district, a decision beneficial to both the city of Whittier and the Los Angeles County Fire Department.

It didn't take Dallas long before he learned all the county ways, and again he was up and running and assisting others. As they say, "You can't keep a good man down."

Dallas was soon elected president of the Los Angeles County Firefighters Local 1014.

Lifetime experiences have taught me power and authority vested solely in one side could lead to abuse. Local 1014 and the administrators of the fire department appeared to have a balance that was advantageous for all. One group would keep the other in check; it appeared to be a perfect balance. That did not mean there was always harmony between the two groups. It just meant those on both sides worked diligently to support the fire department and in the end firefighters belonged to a better organization. His hard work paying off.

My attitude toward Dallas changed quite a bit, as well as my view towards unions.

The good Lord gave us one mouth, and two ears, and intended for us to use them in that proportion. After I tried to adopt this formula, some of Dallas's long held beliefs became clearer to me. It was a pleasure working with him at Station 17.

During the days, Dallas would work at the union office, then at night return to the fire station. He would usually return to the fire station dog-tired. He never complained; he just kept doing his job. I could usually tell by looking at him what a tough day he had. Union business could sometimes be even more wearisome than fighting fires.

It made the days long for him; however, it worked well for both the department and the union alike. He never lost touch of the feelings and attitudes that came from those in the field.

When he would arrive at night, the greeting was always the same, "The union THUG is back in quarters."

Dallas would smile, and tell us how proud he was to be a union *THUG.* He said it stood for "*Those Helpful Union Guys.*"

I would only bump into Dallas occasionally after I was promoted to battalion chief. Several times a year the Battalion 8 captains would meet at the headquarters station for a captains' meeting. As luck would have it, during the meeting I received a call from Dallas while he was cleaning out his locker at Station 17. After thirty-two years of service and many years as the president of Local 1014, he was retiring. I invited him to the meeting so we all could wish him well and say good-bye. We all had a good visit.

I didn't know it then, but it would be the last time I would ever speak with him.

Dallas was a maverick when it came to union business, and he became well-known in California politics. Gray Davis, probably best known as the politician who was kicked out of the governor's office by the Terminator (with a little assist from the voters of the state of California), appointed Dallas to head the state's Office of Emergency Services. Dallas became a nationally recognized emergency services manager.

After a few years there, Dallas went back to work for the California Professional Firefighters, serving even after he was diagnosed with lung cancer, a disease from which he died in 2008, at the age of sixty-four. Governor Arnold Schwarzenegger ordered the Capitol flags to be flown at half-mast in Dallas's honor.

Over a thousand mourners attended his funeral, with full firefighter honors.

Two years later, with the signature of Arnold Schwarzenegger, the California legislature enacted the William Dallas Jones Cancer Presumption Act of 2010, which doubled the statute of limitations that governed job-related cancer claims for firefighters and other public employees exposed to carcinogens in the line of duty. Some of the dangers to which firefighters and others are exposed can take years to show their nasty results, so it was an important improvement to existing laws.

I didn't always agree with Dallas, and I don't always agree with public employee unions today, but I did admire a guy who did so much good for his fellow firefighters, even after his death.

Dallas was a union man to the day he died and beyond, and no matter what your political leanings, it is impressive when the impact you have lives on long after you've left this earth. He definitely made his mark.

While I was writing these memoirs, my friend Tim Murphy's wife, Patty, sent me a quote by Albert Pike; it couldn't have been more timely:

> *"What we do for ourselves dies with us. What we do for others and the world remains and is immortal."*

CHAPTER THIRTY-TWO

A TERRIBLE WAY TO START THE NEW YEAR

F ire stations can be separated by miles and be in different cities, yet have many comparable type of incidents. Perhaps because people are pretty much the same no matter what part of town they live in. It does not matter how nice the city might be; there is always the "other side of the tracks." Fire Station17 served some of the most beautiful neighborhoods in Whittier, but it also had a dangerous part, one where most of the crime took place.

There is a fine line between serving the public quickly and keeping your crew safe. Pictures of a firefighter rushing to the scene and saving the day are great images, but there are times when a little bit of caution is necessary. We are there to serve the public, not be part of the problem.

Police and firefighters are similar, but a big divide exists in the jobs we perform. Police arrest the bad guys. Nothing good can happen if firefighters arrive at the scene before it is secured, and the bad guys are not in custody.

During the summer, when the nights are still warm, drinking beer goes on into the wee hours of the morning. If it is a weekend, it never stops. Now throw in the part of town where there is notorious Mexican gang activity and you have the stage set for trouble.

We were dispatched to a shooting at the liquor store on Whittier Boulevard, just east of the 605 Freeway. As we left the station, I reminded the engineer, when we get close, to slow down a block away and to shut off the red lights and siren so I could get a better look at what might be awaiting us. I wanted to make sure the police had the area secured. If the shooter was still around, I didn't want to get in the way of any of those pesky bullets, and drive into an ambush.

While responding, the location was changed to just south of the boulevard, in a residential area. When things change, they change rapidly. We made a few turns and went down a couple of side streets, and before we knew it, we had run right up on the scene with red lights ablaze and sirens blaring, arriving like gangbusters while all the sheriff's deputies, our security blanket, were back at the liquor store.

We were immediately surrounded by enough angry gang members to constitute a good-sized Cinco de Mayo parade. We didn't want or expect to see two hundred angry Mexican-Americans on a hot, sticky Saturday night after they'd run out of beer, which was exactly what precipitated the crisis.

In the middle of the party when the keg had run dry, a couple of somewhat sober souls (yeah, right) were elected to go to the liquor store, *on the north side of Whittier Boulevard*—a territory claimed by members of a rival gang, who, and I am guessing here, were not invited to the party. Gangs are protective of their area of the 'hood, and in this case, were not willing to share their preferred supplier of spirits with a rival gang.

Things like this happen in Los Angeles County all the time. The situation has gotten a little better since its height of gang activity in the nineties, but there are close to 100,000 gang members roaming around, and sometimes it seems like they all live in your district. They claim territory literally right across the street from each other. The only people who know the boundaries are the gangs and sometimes the cops.

The beer run was cut short when the rival gang members saw the two partygoers on their way into the liquor store and pulled out guns and shot one of them dead-center sternum before hightailing into the shadows. The wounded buddy was quickly heaved into the back of a pickup and driven back to the party and the safety of being on the south side of Whittier Boulevard.

As I mentioned, nothing good can come from being alone in a situation like this. The rescue squad and ambulance arrived shortly after we did, and increased our numbers, but we were still greatly outnumbered, and without law enforcement.

As we arrived, the first thing I noticed as I got out of the fire engine was a skinny little Mexican fellow, dressed up as a typical gang member, thrown in the back of a pickup. He was just as dead as Elvis Presley and half the size.

At first, the crowd pulled back a little, allowing us enough time to put their wounded friend on the gurney. There were still no cops on the scene, and the crowd, now feeling a little braver, started to close back in to see what was happening. I radioed communications and informed them I needed the sheriff immediately. The pilot of the sheriff's helicopter heard my plea for help and was over the scene in an eye blink.

As a general rule, drunk and angry gang members tend to have a dislike for police. When it comes right down to it, they hate anyone in a uniform, especially those in helicopters shining a spotlight down on them from on high. It tends to interfere with the ambiance of their party.

The pilot sensed our dilemma and flew as close as he could. He used his siren and dispersed some of the crowd, which was getting more agitated by the second. The helicopter got so low, it appeared to be pulling leaves off the treetops. With the engine noise of the helicopter, its siren, and with the bright lights shining in their eyes, some of the partygoers parted like Moses and the Red Sea. However, most of them did not.

The spectators who were left were the brave ones. Several notorious-looking banditos, with their colorful bandanas drawn tight around their foreheads, who looked like they might have taken a few bullets in their day, were particularly resolute in their insistence we save their friend's life.

I don't know if you've seen the movie *Weekend at Bernie's*, but if I ever meet the man who produced the film, I'm definitely going to buy him a drink.[7]

We got old Bernie, AKA dead gang member, into the back of the ambulance, and I asked one of the apprehensive-looking paramedics if he'd ever seen the movie. He knew what I meant immediately, and as that ambulance made its way through the crowd, I could see him sitting next to our victim in the back of the ambulance, waving the arm of our newly departed gang member, in a gesture of the living. All the while, he was using his best gang member accent saying, "I'm okay! I'm fine!"

That was just enough to calm the crowd.

Normally we do not transport dead bodies to the hospital, but this evening it was the better part of valor.

Not all the images in your mind are traumatic ones. This one surfaces quite frequently for me, and puts a smile on my face every time.

Just as the ambulance was leaving, the sheriff started to arrive, and arrive they did. I don't know how they do it, but they always manage to screech to a stop. I think among the two-hundred-plus people at the scene, the fire guys were the only ones not armed.

A sheriff's deputy came up and asked about the victim, and I played the movie trivia game with him too, which put a large grin on his face.

The only thing left at the scene was police business, so we left just as quickly as we arrived.

The scene we left behind was a traumatic one for the families involved, but it is a lifestyle they have chosen. The gang population in the county stands at one less as the gene pool continues to purge itself.

The year was ending, and Christmas was behind us for another year. The closing months of 1989 had been exciting, and little did I know how tragically 1990 would begin. It should have been a time for celebrating the coming New Year; however, it marked the most heartbreaking day I ever spent in the fire service.

Working on New Year's Day should have been a time for relaxing and reflecting on what great things the new year would bring.

We had already had our day planned: watch the Rose Parade in Pasadena and view a couple of bowl games. A tranquil day before the start of a busy year.

Our plans never materialized.

We were jolted back into the reality of the fire service by the day's first response, a structure fire in Station 96's district. It was just a few miles south of our station.

The entire crew was hoping the alarm was for a minor incident like morning eggs burning on a forgotten stove. With a little luck, we would be back in quarters within a few minutes, as soon as the first unit arrived and gave their report.

Protocol dictates the first arriving units give an account of conditions as soon as possible, so responding units will be more informed and prepared as they arrive, or if the fire is small, the assisting units can return to quarters.

A small fire was not to be. Responding units could see smoke on the horizon and knew there must be some type of substantial structure fire. The first arriving unit was so inundated, they failed to give a first report.

Engine 96 arrived within minutes, and saw what every firefighter fears—family members and neighbors standing on the front lawn, not knowing what to do and overcome with horror, screaming their loved ones were trapped in the burning building.

Fire and black smoke was billowing from the windows and doors of the two-story home.

Arriving firefighters had all of their protective gear on and made entry, only to discover the horror that was thrust upon this multi-generational family.

The initial fire did not take long to extinguish.

Inside the front door and below the stairway stood the family Christmas tree. It had long since been cut from the forest and was completely dried from weeks of display in a warm home. It had all the ingredients for tragedy.

As the family was busy preparing for the day, Grandma noticed a spark from the tree's lights—small at first, but due to its condition, the tree was rapidly engulfed with fire. All of her efforts to extinguish the fire were in vain, and overcome by smoke and fire, she literally collapsed into the burning tree.

The flames and hot smoke rose directly up the stairway into the bedrooms and killed two more family members, as well as another person who died downstairs trying to save the grandma.

Four family members were dead, with four more injured and transported to the hospital.

A terrible way to start the new year.

Even the most hardened, macho firefighters among us were moved by the tragedy. The fact that one family had been so devastated this soon after Christmas was disturbing. The events we had just witnessed were a lot to comprehend.

Critical incident stress debriefing was new to the fire department, and the battalion chief decided this was a perfect time to use this resource. He scheduled a debriefing session for that afternoon.

I was dog-tired, both from the day's activities and from sitting in our newfound therapy session. I couldn't help but wonder how much good it did; after all, I was one of those macho fire guys! The universal sentiment from my fire buds after the session was that a good New Year's Day bowl game would have done us just as much good. As I have said before, firefighters are slow to change.

⁎

It was a few hours later, just after one in the morning, when we received another structure fire alarm. This time it was the other side of our district, just inside Station 40's area, in Pico Rivera.

As we arrived, there were no screaming neighbors or victims, just somber-looking faces. The mood was grave.

The house was small and typical for the neighborhood, so it did not take the first arriving unit long to extinguish yet another Christmas tree fire. The burning tree quickly filled the house with smoke and fire, and killed three people. This time a mother, father, and an uncle.

The dead we left where they lay. There were other injured family members to worry about. They were rushed outside to the cool night air.

The first to be transported to the hospital was a little five-year-old girl, the daughter of the couple who had just perished. She clung desperately to the neck of the firefighter who was holding her as she was placed onto the gurney. She didn't want to let go. It was the only security she knew. A yellow rescue blanket was gently tucked around her, which made her look even smaller and more helpless.

She was dressed in pink pajamas, the kind with feet in them. They were charred on one side. Her hair was matted from the heat. Her little PJs smelled like flannel that someone had left a hot iron on for too long. She looked at me with the most innocent, beautiful brown eyes and never uttered a word. You could see the bewilderment etched on the face of that little girl, asking where her parents where and why am I here. I squeezed her little hand, held it for just a second, and said nothing. I couldn't summon any words. It's probably a good thing I didn't speak, because my own cracking voice would have given away my emotions.

As we placed her in the back of the ambulance, she still never spoke a word.

Her whole life was ahead of her and that night would change everything in it; she didn't have any understanding of what she and her family had just gone through.

I thought again of my own children and how lucky I was to have them. My heart broke for that sweet little girl, and for all the heartache I knew she had just suffered.

I can still see her face, with a strange, puzzled look, and I knew it would turn to the worst possible grief anyone could imagine. No one that young should ever have to feel the way she was feeling, and there was absolutely nothing I could do to change it.

Now many years later when my wife takes our granddaughter's pajamas out of the dryer and the air is filled with the smell of warm flannel, I can't help but see the face of that little girl and wonder how her life has turned out.

In a matter of hours, we had lost seven human beings, seven people whose lives were snuffed out. Those events would send ripples across generations and change many lives for generations to come.

Thank goodness, I never had another day like that one. This had to rank right up there as the most heartbreaking day I have ever experienced—one of those days that makes me both proud and sad because of my chosen profession; proud of the job we do every day and so terribly, terribly sad we can only do so much. That day left a mark.

The personnel at Station 17 would change, but the gang activity would not. The dispute over territory and the senseless violence continued at an alarming rate.

Responding to shooting victims was becoming a staple for us, this time on the north side of Whittier Boulevard.

When Engine 17 arrived, they found they had two victims, not just one. This incident was just as senseless as when "old Bernie" passed on a few years earlier, but the stakes were getting higher. Two young men dressed in gang attire in the wrong part of town were shot in the back of the head by a rival gang member.

Many medical emergencies are labor intensive. With multiple victims, the responding EMS units can become quickly overwhelmed, so additional resources are needed. When the first arriving captain requests more equipment, the local battalion chief is notified.

Knowing the captain very well, and being a graduate of Station 17, I decided to respond to the incident.

As I drove up, through the closed windows on my SUV, I could hear the bloodcurdling screams of a young woman. Before I could get out of my car, the captain came up and met me.

"Hi, Gary, what's going on?"

"Another gang shooting, this time two guys, both shot in the back of the head. We are working on both of them, but it doesn't look like either will make it."

"What's wrong with that woman who's screaming? How badly is she hurt?'

"Not at all, Chief. She just witnessed the whole thing and can identify the shooter. She knows what her life is worth now."

So goes the battle in the 'hood.' The victims that night indeed didn't make it, and we never heard another thing regarding our young witness. We can only hope she has a long and healthy life.

As firefighters, we see endless human suffering. The days of retrieving a cat from a tree, or lifting a young child up onto the fire engine while the mother stands by watching with a smile from ear to ear, are now all too rare.

CHAPTER THIRTY-THREE

A PROMOTION WILL MAKE YOUR DAY

Los Angeles County has always been at the forefront of affirmative action. The county has enacted many changes to assure discrimination did not, nor would not, exist. The most visible change within the fire department was the promotional process.

After the first exam was given under the new rules, everyone adapted, and as they say, that's all history now. There was some grumbling, but no single system will satisfy everyone.

I was fortunate and passed yet another battalion chief exam and was on Fire Chief P. Michael Freeman's first chief officer's promotional list.

He had only been with the county for a short time, so he would have to rely on the opinions of his top staff regarding the candidates. I thought I was doomed! Being outspoken was going to catch up with me once again.

The fire chief did not know a soul on the list, so he decided to have an interview with each candidate in the promotable band. The names were arranged alphabetically, so I was one of the first to be interviewed, again.

I was sitting in the fire chief's outer office when the chief deputy walked by. I had known him for many years. He looked at me and said, "Doug, what are you doing here?"

"I have an interview with the fire chief."

"You sure it's today?"

Oh man, that's all I need to do is show up on the wrong day. I am sure that would make a great first impression. I thought I was

281

anxious before. This put me into the high digits on the old stress scale.

It felt like forever, but I am sure it was only couple of minutes, when the chief's secretary came over and said, "Follow me, the chief is ready to see you."

I was down to just sweaty palms and a dry mouth, but at least I was there on the right day.

As I walked into his office, he stood up, walked around his enormous desk, and greeted me with a warm handshake and a smile. I let him sit down before I did.

Unfortunately, this wouldn't be the last time I was in front of him with sweaty palms.

We started the interview with some small talk, and he did a great job of bringing me back down to earth.

He looked at me and said, "This isn't another oral interview. It's just my way of getting to know the candidates."

Yea, right! In later interviews, he dropped that remark.

He asked questions and then gave you as much time as you needed to answer. Most good interviewers will allow time after you have answered a question. Silent pauses are uncomfortable, so most start rambling, including me, and you usually utter things you wish you wouldn't have said.

All in all, our one-to-one interview went well, or at least I thought it did.

Promotional lists are active for two years. The fire chief had been promoting from my list for twenty-two months now. Plenty of well-qualified candidates were still left in my band.

There is no guarantee as to how many promotions will be made. It is left to the discretion of the fire chief.

In a typical year, five or six battalion chiefs are promoted. This year, there had already been ten promotions. Chances were becoming slimmer and time was running out.

It looked like I was going to die on another list!

In a large organization, there are many retirements in a year, and this tends to make promotions plentiful. In some departments, if you are *not* the number one candidate, you *will not* be promoted.

During my career, there have been several captain promotional lists, where the entire list was exhausted, and all two hundred candidates received promotions.

It was the end of the month, transfers had been processed, and rumors were flying the fire chief was about to promote two new battalion chiefs.

For the next two days, there were no promotions. Waiting was the pits.

The promotions would fill all the vacant positions, and then the list would die. If I didn't get the nod this round, I would be left on the list and have to go through the whole process again. Maybe the fourth time would be my lucky charm.

I arrived in communications around six thirty in the morning. The assistant chief was on the dispatch floor, something which didn't happen often this early in the morning. They must have had a big fire during the night.

As I approached the supervisor's area, the assistant chief approached me, put his arm around my shoulder, and got the attention of the twenty or so people milling around the dispatch floor.

I couldn't help but think, *this can't be good.* Promotions were the last thing on my mind. I guess that early in the morning, my mind hadn't fully awakened.

He looked at everyone, and then announced I was the newest battalion chief in the department.

Boy, that'll sure make your day!

Within the next few days, I learned where my new assignment would be—Battalion 10, the same battalion where I started my career twenty-two years before. What a great assignment.

Promotion day is truly unforgettable. You are filled with mixed emotions, including both excitement and apprehension.

The exhilaration and optimism outweighs any anxious thoughts you might have. Your enthusiasm is electrifying.

There was one more promotion off the list before it died, removing me from the unenviable position of being the last promoted. I have always maintained it was better to be last promoted from the existing list, than the first from any future list!

I was a battalion chief for twelve years, and the euphoria I felt the day I was promoted still stays with me to this day.

CHAPTER THIRTY-FOUR

THERE IS NO SUCH THING AS AN ORDINARY DAY

It was hard for me to admit, but at forty-five years old, I was in the middle of my life. Both the boys were somewhat established, and were no longer dependent upon Debbie or me. We were empty nesters.

The kids were out of sight, but certainly not out of mind. One day around the kitchen table at the fire station, a group of older firefighters tossed around the question, "When do you stop worrying about your kids?" The answer was striking: "When they close the lid to your casket!"

I had a difficult time admitting it, but I was middle age. It was a real shock when I looked around the fire station and saw nothing but young kids. Most were the age of my sons.

My career was in full swing, and I had just received my last promotion. Knowing you are no longer upwardly mobile brings a sense of tranquility. One I had not experienced. Debbie and I started doing things that we had put off while the kids were younger. We started taking a few vacations, and were doing things around the yard that up until now time hadn't allowed. I couldn't believe it, but I actually got excited about the mulching function on my new lawnmower.

Life was good.

My new assignment was Battalion 10.

The first day you walk in the door, everyone knows everything about you, both the good and bad. That has always amazed me; firefighters believed that was a one-way street. The day I arrived, I knew everything about every captain in my new battalion.

The crews I have worked with over the years have always been top drawer. Well, almost—maybe one or two exceptions. After all, no one bats a thousand.

The headquarters station was in Temple City, at Fire Station 47.

The battalion was large in both fire stations and geographical area. Nine fire stations served several contract cities in the San Gabriel Valley, and all of the unincorporated areas in between.

The battalion chief's quarters were at the rear of the fire station in a small thousand-square-foot house. It was perfect. It gave privacy to the firefighters and to me.

One of the benefits of being a chief officer is your quarters are cleaned from one end to the other each morning. Not that chiefs are any dirtier than the rest, but it is nice to have it done by others. It's like your own private motel room each shift. One night I even had my bed turned down and a mint placed on my pillow.

The first few months were uneventful. I got through the warm weather and winds without any major incidents.

The activity level was picking up, with small structure fires from one end of the battalion to the other—nothing extremely large, just enough for me to get my feet wet as a battalion chief and become familiar with to my new role as an incident commander.

The weather was starting to turn cold, and the rains were coming. It was a cold January morning, and a good day to stay close to my office.

The alarm we received was for a structure fire in an area that was quite some distance from my headquarters. It was on the outskirts of all three stations that were responding.

As we got closer, the dispatcher said they were receiving many calls regarding the incident. On a clear day, smoke rising can be seen from miles away. This day was different; the low clouds and the persistent light rain were keeping an inversion layer over the area, so there was no large plume of smoke pointing out the fire.

The first arriving engine company gave a report about heavy smoke in a residential area.

I thought the report was a little vague; we knew it was a residential area. The captain said nothing regarding the fire or the type of structure. Those are crucial to a first report.

The basic tool of a firefighter is water, the kind that comes from a hose line, not the heavy rain inundating us at the moment. The captain ordered his firefighter to take the hydrant at the corner, and they laid a supply line for water as they drove into the smoke that was hugging the ground. By sheer instinct they made their way down the street into the thick dark smoke.

The firefighter and the captain took a smaller hose line and prepared to attack the fire as the engineer set up at his pump panel. All was going well so far, just as they had been trained.

They reached the front door, the dark smoke still cutting down the visibility to mere feet. Again reaching back into the bag of tricks taught during training, they checked the front door to make sure it wasn't locked before they literally kicked it in.

Just as the firefighter balanced himself for the kick, it opened. The firefighting crew was looking directly into the eyes of a completely shocked and baffled neighbor. He was almost unable to speak the words, "It's the house next door!"

As quickly as the smoke covered the area, it lifted, revealing a fully involved house just south of the stunned neighbor.

I often wondered what the captain might have said as he left: "Excuse me, boy, all of these houses look alike."

As I said, no one bats a thousand.

⁘

Every firefighter dreams of his son seeing him in action. My son Colton had the opportunity to ride along with me and see firsthand exactly how firefighters save lives.

It was April 1, 1992, and I had just picked up my oldest son Colt and his friend for a ride-along. Colton was in his early twenties and was at the beginning of his firefighting career, so I enjoyed taking him with me whenever I could. He no sooner got into the car when we started getting calls. It was going to be a busy day.

The Los Angeles area is a desert, and as such, the annual rainfall is meager compared to other parts of the country. But as it says on the Morton's Salt package, *"when it rains, it pours."* A thunderstorm was passing to the north of us at the base of the Angeles National Forest Mountains, and the rain hadn't reached any farther down into the valley yet, so where we were, it was still dry.

Los Angeles County is crisscrossed by countless creeks, streams, and flood canals, all eventually making their way to the Pacific Ocean.

Not long after I picked Colton up, we received a call regarding three kids who'd fallen into the swelling waters of the Rubio Wash near Valley Boulevard, which wasn't too far from where we were. A reliable source, an employee of the Southern California Gas Company, called it in.

The protocol for swift-water rescue was almost nonexistent; most of your actions were flying by the seat of your pants. Now the department has an established procedure for swift-water rescue.

However, back then rudimentary techniques were employed, which was to send engine companies to cover the bridges downstream to observe and try to rescue anyone in the water.

I could see the water was running fast and furious.

As luck would have it, the battalion just south of us was preparing for the upcoming wildland season and had two of our helicopters present at their exercise. That's what is so great about Southern California; the rain was pouring, and we were preparing for wildland fires!

The first company arrived where the kids were spotted entering the channel, and the informant said the two got out on their own. The captain was comfortable there was no one left in the channel and cancelled all the responding equipment.

I guess it was just the mind of a worrisome dad, or because I was in a new position as a battalion chief and incident commander, I did not want anything to go wrong.

Something just didn't feel right.

The original report was that *three* kids had fallen into the wash. Informants are not always correct, but this came from a reliable source. I couldn't shake that uneasy feeling. I did some quick mathematical calculations: three in the water, and two out. Hmm.

Two helicopters were still in the air, so I asked one to fly north along the wash and the other to fly south. That way, if anyone was still in the water, hopefully we would find them.

It has been said the good Lord looks after children, drunks, and fools, and I have been all three. Today he was again watching over me, and of course the victim. Within minutes, one of the pilots radioed and said he could see the third kid, traveling downstream in the swift water of the flood control canal.

Immediately many things needed to happen. You feel like the old one-armed paperhanger.

First, we needed an accurate location regarding the victim. Our pilots were good but, as they would remind us from time to time, it's hard to read street signs at 1,500 feet.

Once we knew for sure our victim's location, I placed equipment at bridges downstream. They needed to be far enough away so the crew could set up for a rescue. If we didn't allow enough time, they would become bystanders and merely watch as the victim continued his trip to the Pacific Ocean. If we took too much time, our victim could drown.

I asked communications to notify the Long Beach Fire Department and to place units downstream, just in case our efforts failed, and we missed him.

The battalion chief's vehicle is set up with every electronic gadget known to man.

Responding with red lights and siren through traffic and looking at the map would have been easier if I were not busy with radio traffic. One radio frequency is for communicating with ground units, the other with the helicopter, and all along, I was on my cell phone with the communications center. If the California Highway Patrol could only see me now.

I had my hands full, to say the least.

Colton thought this was all incredibly exciting. I wish I had time to see the look his face.

Colt, being the good kid that he is, and always wanting to help, said, "Dad, can I do anything for you?"

"Nope, I got it."

We had entered several intersections where the traffic had backed up for blocks due to the rain, and Colt asked, "Why don't you use the PA system to clear the traffic?" Using your red lights and siren sometimes just jams people up in an intersection; they forget they should pull to the right.

That was a good idea. "Go ahead, Colt."

He looked at the dashboard with all its switches, buttons, and small flashing lights and said, "How do you turn it on?"

"Just handle it for me."

He again looked at all the knobs and dials, turned to me with a puzzled look on his face, and said, "How does it work?"

"Hey, I'm a little busy here. Just handle it."

"You don't know how to turn it on, do you, Dad?"

I was reduced to saying, "Nope, not a clue."

He was crushed. How could I have all of this cool equipment and not know how everything worked?

It took a while before we arrived at the bridge downstream where the crews were setting up. We did arrive safely. I now had time to give my full attention to the rescue.

Long Beach Fire Department reported they didn't know what flood control channel I was requesting them to monitor; all of their channels were as dry as the Mohave Desert in July!

Whoa, that was strange. With all the thunderstorm activity, their channels were dry? I had placed equipment on several of our bridges where the water was running rapidly, so I felt comfortable they wouldn't be needed. As fast as the water was running, I was sure it had time to reach Long Beach and the Pacific Ocean.

Southern California is one of the nation's largest hot beds for news. It has many televisions and radio stations vigilantly watching for sensational news worthy items. Not only do they have a horde of reporters with well-equipped news vans, there is also a fleet of helicopters constantly in the air to cover any breaking tragedies.

Once a dispatch goes out over the airwaves, it is picked up by the news agencies and monitored. If it becomes news worthy it only takes seconds before the air and ground is converged upon by reporters. Rainy days, and swift running flood control channels are tailored made for the news media.

One of Los Angeles's major network television helicopters was in the air and over our developing swift-water rescue within seconds. On board the helicopter was a world-famous helicopter pilot and videographer with many awards under his belt. Instantly he was broadcasting to the entire Los Angeles County audience and had them riveted to their radios and televisions as he narrated the drama as it was unfolding. The footage he captured that day has been used all over the country hundreds, if not thousands of times regarding swift-water rescues. The footage is that dramatic.

The reporter flew just feet above our helicopter and started his dramatic account.

Several people saw the television broadcast, and were coming out of their houses to assist the fire department. They were throwing ropes into the channel in hopes of rescuing this young man as he washed by.

The skies were dark with turbulent rain clouds. Thundershowers continued to produce more rain and lightning kept striking nearby…

Our helicopter was setting up for a river rescue for what is known in our organization as "dope on a rope." A paramedic is lowered down in a harness, dangling from a line attached to the boom just outside the door of the flying helicopter. The plan is to catch the victim floating downstream. Our pilots are some of the most skilled in the world, but under the best of circumstances, this operation is downright dangerous.

Talk about stress. The pilot would have to fly his helicopter with his firefighter dangling two hundred feet below, hovering the craft just high enough above the water to allow for the rescue. All the while maneuvering between power lines and avoiding bridges that cross the river at regular intervals. It wouldn't look good on a résumé if the pilot smacked his firefighter against a bridge, or swung him into some high-voltage power lines.

I sat in my suburban and continued to watch and listen to this incident unfold. I could see more lighting strike, one about a quarter a mile away.

The firefighter was just above the raging water, dangling from a hoist, as the pilot was trying to position for the rescue. They are going to try to intercept him…Slowly they were getting closer. The pilot was trying to match his speed with the flow of water. Finally they were within a hundred yards, now within feet, they were close enough for the firefighter to grasp him.

The firefighter quickly grabbed him. But with wet gloved hands, the movement of the helicopter and turbulent water, the lifesaving bond was broken. The victim fell back into the water.

The helicopter tried to reposition for another try. They had to move higher and clear the power lines, and the next bridge. They were doing everything they could to save him. The man is going twenty-five to thirty miles-an-hour and headed for the spillway, which leads to a larger channel.

The distance between the air rescue and the units on the ground was getting shorter. The ground crews positioned a line across the river as a last effort to catch the victim.

The fire department, sheriff's department, and many citizens packed the bank; tightly holding a lifeline that was stretched across the river. Hopefully the victim had enough strength left to garb the rope as he washed by.

As the incident commander, I was watching a multitude of resources converging to save a life. Everyone pitched in to help a man they never knew and would probably never meet again.

Finally, he reached out and caught the line. Several rescuers' knee deep in water grabbed him and pulled him to safety. After what must have seemed like an eternity, he was on the bank of the river. Wet, scared, and completely exhausted, but safe, and alive.

Everyone involved in the river rescue won that day. The victim eventually dried out and was okay; my son saw firsthand what his dad does at work; and I got a nice mention in my personnel file regarding the positive outcome of the incident.

Well, almost everyone won; there is still that image in the back of Colton's mind that his good old dad didn't know how to work all the knobs and buttons on the dashboard.

You can only bask in the sun for so long before reality hits and you are back into a normal routine.

❉

Summer was just starting, and it was a beautiful day. I was tired of being in my office, so I thought I would finish out the afternoon with a quick drive around the battalion.

I was at the far end of my district, sitting at a traffic light, when I heard a dispatch go out for a drowning child. The address and engine company number quickly followed.

Stored memories are not hidden too far from the surface. It doesn't take much to have them come roaring back to life. When they appear, they are just as vivid as the day they happened. Certain situations activate memories which are best left in the recesses of your mind. Hearing that dispatch I quickly flashed back to the unforgettable days in communications.

The incident was close to where I was. I quickly glanced into my rearview mirror and saw two Azusa police cars race into a driveway. I turned on my red lights and responded right behind them.

No sooner had I gotten out of my car when a police officer passed a sixteen-month-old baby into my arms. The baby was soaking wet and not breathing.

The officer's expression said everything that needed to be said.

I could scarcely believe what was happening; just seconds ago I was driving along admiring how great the weather was and how good fortune had smiled upon me, and within an eye blink, I was standing there with a dying child in my arms.

I clutched the little baby close to my chest for just enough time to let my brain kick into gear. Your mind races and millions of bytes on information flash before you in a nanosecond.

I cradled the little guy in my arms and tilted his head back, just as I had told that frightened mother to do all those years ago. I placed my mouth over the baby's nose and mouth, just as she had done. I breathed into that child's tiny month and nose, just as I had instructed that terrified woman to do. At that moment we were connected across the years, mother to me, me to my younger self. It was as if time had somehow evaporated, and all of us were together at the precise instant.

As I was about to start pushing on the child's chest, I heard the faint sound of the tiny baby in my arms gasping for air.

Suddenly I noticed everything about that child, as if looking at him through a magnifying glass. He was one of God's perfect little creatures, as all babies are. I could see tiny water droplets on his eyelashes like little sparkling stars. When he opened his eyes and looked at me, I just stared back at his pale blue eyes and almost forgot all my surroundings. It was just for a small moment, and then he began breathing on his own and started to cry.

I was aware of sound again, as if the mute button was pushed. The sirens, voices, and crying all came flooding back into my ears.

The mom and dad were good parents. They had only let the baby out of their sight for a minute, and he toddled down the steps of their apartment and into the pool.

It only takes a second.

As I was writing this account, and reflecting upon those memories, the phone rang.

It was my son Colton. Whether it was the timing of his call or the memory of that drowning child, I don't know which, but I was especially glad to hear his voice.

"What's going on?" I asked. It's a nice generic opening—covers just about everything.

"I just got back from an interesting call, Dad," he said without much prelude.

As soon as he spoke, I could tell something was weighing on his mind. He often calls to share unique incidents with me. He knows I like hearing about interesting calls. It takes me back to the days when I was working.

"We were just on a call for a drowning baby."

My jaw dropped.

"A little two-year-old baby, Dad. Her parents found her in the pool."

He was quiet for a moment, so I waited for him to continue.

The silence was uncomfortable, and then he again began to speak. The pace of the conversation accelerated. It was as if he got the words out quickly, it would somehow change the outcome.

"Early this afternoon we received a call for a child not breathing. I was hoping this was going to be just another false alarm from an over protective parent. As we arrived, every detail told us it was going to be just that. The front door wasn't open, and there was no one outside waiting. No panicking neighbor waving their arms in the air and telling us to hurry. I had lulled myself into a sense of false security."

"As we got closer to the house the front door suddenly flew open and a young woman ran out with a baby draped in her arms instantly snapping me back into reality."

"I jumped out of the cab, took the baby from the mothers grasp and laid her lifeless body on the front lawn. I was just reacting to the circumstances; my brain hadn't fully kicked into gear yet. I placed an oxygen mask over the babies tiny little mouth and nose, and started CPR."

"The ambulance and our rescue unit arrived minutes after we did."

"I cradled the baby in my arms and rushed to the back of the ambulance. I almost threw the child into the arms of the paramedic waiting there. He continued CPR all the way to the hospital."

"Dad, I can still see the little baby. She was wet, and her hair was all matted down around her face. I can feel her skin on my fingertips."

I was speechless.

"She was barely alive when we got her to the hospital. I don't think she's gonna make it."

The calls that hit you the hardest are always the ones closest to home. Colton has a little blue-eyed blonde-haired girl at home the same age. My granddaughter.

I felt a lump in my throat.

I asked Colton if I could share with him what I'd just written. "Sure, Dad."

As I read to him, my voice broke, and I could hardly get the words out. It was as if it had just happened, as if there had been no intervening time.

I finished reading and there was dead silence on the phone. "Colt?"

"I'm here, Dad."

We talked for a while longer, and as I hung up the telephone I had the awful feeling I hadn't made him feel any better. As a father, you want to guide your children through troubled times. In life, you cannot alleviate some issues, no matter how hard you try.

The same thoughts go through the mind of every first responder—did I do everything? Could I have done more? Those thoughts continue and go unabated.

Time heals most heartbreaking experiences. Eventually the helplessness does subside.

I know the sight of that poor little baby is imprinted within the mind of my son, and will live there forever. If he is lucky, he'll be able to file it away in the deep recess of his minds filing cabinet. The one he has created out of necessity, and hopefully he will never visit it again.

It was a reminder for Colton just how precious life is.

He went home the next morning and held both of his kids just a little closer, and hugged them just a little longer, just as I had done many times before.

My mornings have evolved into a time where I can relax by myself for a few minutes before the hectic day starts. The only sound in the house is the crackling coming from the fireplace. My overstuffed leather chair is just close enough to the hearth so I can feel the radiated heat from the fire.

Emily, my two-year-old granddaughter, had just awoken, and came downstairs and snuggled up next to me. We both sat there in silence for a few minutes and then unexpectedly she said, *"Granddad, stop hugging me so tight, it hurts."*

Memories flood back in the unexpected ways; I wish I could protect her from life's hardships by just hugging her tightly.

CHAPTER THIRTY-FIVE

A LIFE TIME OF SERVING

The fire service attracts a certain type of individual. The hands on type, that wants to make a difference with their lives. I do not know if it is something that is inherently in their character, or if it grows each day. The one thing I do know, is that it becomes a dynamic part of their makeup.

Day after day, you train and hone your skills. Many hours are spent on the drill field and in the classroom preparing.

You never want a tragedy to befall anyone. Your most fervent prayer is that none of these misfortunes will ever touch you or your family. However, if they do, firefighters want to be there, and be first to arrive.

No one is immune. As your family grows and your experiences broaden, this single issue is what keeps you awake at night.

Everyone hopes retirement will be filled with many years of healthy and happy times. Unfortunately, that is not always one of life's realities.

Tragedies do strike close to home, way to close.

Walter Meagher was a deputy chief in charge of the operations bureau for the Los Angeles County Fire Department. He was third in command of the fire department.

He and his family were reminiscent of everything good about America. He was one of this countries success stories.

He joined the department in late1940's and rose through the ranks quickly. He was a loving and caring father who's son also became a firefighter.

He served the department for twenty-seven years, and then retired. When you retire you don't quit working, you just start a new vocation. For the last twenty-five years, he was the neighborhoods surrogate grandfather. The unofficial position he held for at least two generations. Everyone loved him, especially the kids. He was the role model.

Chief Meagher and his wife Anna, had been married for fifty-one years. Her health was beginning to decline due to her emphysema. She also had difficulty walking, even with the help of a walker. After many years of helping others, he was now caring for the one he loved most, his wife. He was her sole caretaker.

The New Year's Eve fire went unnoticed by the neighbors, so it was able to gain a foothold.

It wasn't discovered until a couple driving on a nearby street saw the flames and called 911. Eventually the bright flames emanating from the house, and the sounds of small explosions awakened several neighbors.

They tried desperately to douse the fire with garden hoses, and made several attempts to enter the burning house, but were turned back by the heat.

Chief Meagher was abruptly awakened shortly before midnight by smoke coming down the hallway. It didn't take long before heavy smoke and fire were quickly spreading through his entire home. Spry for his eighty-one years, he could have easily left the house through the entrance to the garage near his bedroom.

He had just seconds to make a decision, which for a firefighter, is no decision at all. He instinctively made his way down the smoke filled hall, to Anna's bedroom. His first thought was to save the life of his loved one.

It was difficult for him to rescue her because she was on oxygen and had a difficult time walking.

They tried to make their way through the front of the house, but the hallway was now fully engulfed in flames.

Her small bedroom was quickly filling with supper-heated smoke. The power had failed and dense smoke made visibility difficult or nonexistent.

Both weak from the fire, Chief Meagher knew he could escape alone from the small window, but his love for his wife made him stay.

Firefighters found the couple on the floor under the window. He had spread his body out the best he could to protect her from the impinging heat.

The couple died of smoke and heat inhalation. His last efforts were trying to save her. He died the way he lived his life, helping others. He made the ultimate sacrifice—his life—in an attempt to save a loved one.

Chief Meagher had been retired for many years, but still belonged to the fire department family. Many of the firefighters who responded that evening had worked with him during the course of their careers. He touched many, both in life and in his sudden death.

The fire department had just lost a loved one.

CHAPTER THIRTY-SIX

SOME NEED TO CHANGE MORE THAN OTHERS

Each year chief officers are reviewed, evaluated, and subjected to transfer. During a typical year, about a dozen battalion chiefs are transferred, and one or two assistant chiefs. The transfer process starts with your deputy chief, and ultimately the fire chief has the last say.

Transfers are met with mixed reviews. Just like the old saying, "Where you stand on a subject, depends on where you sit." I enjoyed my assignment and didn't want to be transferred; it was a good assignment, with good people.

I was just getting comfortable and starting to enjoy my position, when my assistant chief came in my office and said, "We need to talk."

Ahh, man, that's never good, and it wasn't.

My boss just looked at me for a minute, and blurted out, "I just spoke with the fire chief and because of your background, he thought you would be perfect for the job he has in mind. Starting Monday, you will be transferred to the LA office for the next year."

The die was cast, and there was nothing I could do. I was leaving an assignment I loved, and a schedule I had worked for years, to become a downtown headquarters office worker.

To say I was unhappy about my transfer would be an understatement. I loved the field, my crew, and my new responsibilities. If I wanted to be an office guy, I'd throw my hat in the ring for another promotion, the assistant chief position.

The fire chief was still new to the department and wanted to evaluate every aspect.

He did not accept the attitude, *"That's the way we have always done things."* He believed if it is the right way, prove it.

My new project was an extension of that philosophy. It took a year to complete.

The department had dispatched the same amount of equipment to medical aid calls for years. The time had come to evaluate the way we dispatched equipment. Regrettably, my new assignment would bring a sense of uneasiness to me for the remainder of my career and beyond.

The one-size-fits-all attitude was starting to be scrutinized across the country, and since we wanted to remain a leader in all aspects of the fire service, new ways of dispatching equipment needed to be evaluated.

"Response to Alarms" was an all-encompassing assignment, and included everything from pre-arrival instructions given by dispatchers, to the evaluation of response times. No stone was left unturned.

When an emergency call is received in communications, it is classified as to the type of incident it is, and then the appropriate level of equipment is dispatched from a predetermined response matrix. The amount of equipment sent to an incident can differ greatly.

Firefighting is labor-intensive, so more staffing is needed for a fire in a high-rise than for an emergency on the freeway. By classifying an incident correctly, resources can be more efficiently utilized.

Rescue responses are different; they receive the same level of equipment whether it is a child injured in the park or an elderly person not breathing. All responses are dispatched red light and siren, Code 3.

This area needed further study, hence my project.

The basic philosophy regarding tiered dispatching is to correctly evaluate the initial call and establish the true nature of the emergency. Emergency medical calls had become 80-plus percent of the department's total workload. By matching the correct response level, red light, and siren responses, and the amount of equipment could be reduced.

Our system was the Cadillac of dispatching procedures, and also the simplest. We sent the closest resources and a paramedic rescue squad to all medical emergencies. Our department did not transport patients, so a private ambulance was also dispatched. It was as uncomplicated as you can get. It assured the closest help would arrive as quickly as possible.

Responding red light and siren is dangerous, especially in highly populated areas. Fire departments across the country have had their share of accidents while responding, but they have maintained a reasonable safety record. It is common for a county rescue squad to have twenty or more Code 3 responses in a single shift. The higher the response load, the more exposure there is to having a vehicle accident.

Police departments across the country have an atrocious record regarding vehicle accidents. They are killing the public and themselves at an alarming rate. It is directly related to their attitude they are above the law, including the law of gravity. There is literally no one to keep them in check.

Firefighters deal with true emergencies on a daily basis, and adjust to changing circumstances quickly. Experience has taught me police do not. Most of their day is routine, and when presented with a true emergency with rapidly changing circumstances, they go into overload and brain fade. (That is a clinical diagnosis, which was created in the fire station.) As we have discussed, their bag of tricks contains few tools. The one they rely upon the most is force and intimidation, and with many incidents, this only escalates the situation, and does not alleviate it. It pains me to say this, but the remainder of my career would bear it out.

According to the 2010 preliminary data from the National Law Enforcement Officers Memorial Fund, for thirteen years in a row, traffic fatalities were the leading cause of police officer fatalities. They are dying by their own hands and in most cases, it is completely preventable.

They are in desperate need of overhauling police driving practices. They make changes slower than we do in the fire service.

Some of the most heartfelt incidents are those in which a fellow emergency responder is involved in an accident. My apparatus driver, when I was a captain at the "Three-Alarm Taquito" fire station, hit and killed a driver in an intersection while responding. He learned a lesson the hard way. Needless to say, I never needed to tell him to slow down.

Fire departments fare somewhat better than policing agencies, but their driving record is still in need of improvement.

Most large municipal fire departments have professional drivers responsible for fire equipment.

Apparatus drivers are firefighter specialists, most commonly called engineers. It's a promotable position. This position is above the firefighter rank, and reports directly to the captain. Their duties include knowing every aspect of their first in district, including temporary street closures. They know the location of every fire hydrant and what type of water main to which it is connected. They are responsible for pumping safe water pressure to hose lines at the scene of a fire. They know every detail about that rig, from the front bumper to the back, including every aspect of the rig's maintenance.

The engineer's primary responsibility is to get the crew to the scene of an emergency safely.

Police organizations are only fooling themselves by driving at excessive speeds. High rates of speed versus driving safely shaves little time off responses. The risk-to-reward ratio needs to be balanced against public safety.

Many departments use a new response matrix and send fire department emergency units to the scene without their red lights activated. A call about an injured person may sound ominous, but if it is not a life-threatening injury, adding a few minutes to the call is justified in order to keep the public safe.

A victim not breathing is a true medical emergency; red lights and sirens are justified when the response time is critical.

In order to keep the public and responding firefighters safe, no matter what type of emergency call, responding units must come to a *complete stop* before entering an intersection against the red traffic light.

The new communications center ushered in many innovative policies, including a pre-arrival instruction. These detailed directions help close the time gap while units are responding.

The project also established a better understanding of communications and the "why" behind what we do. New procedures helped ensure a balance between public safety and response times.

When I finished the project, I was ready to return to the field.

The day I walked into Valley Communications, I had a sinking feeling in my stomach, thinking I had made a terrible mistake. Never did I realize the coming years would prove to be some of the most exciting and fulfilling times in my career. At the end of my project, I was considered the department's expert on emergency responses.

CHAPTER THIRTY-SEVEN

THE PEOPLE OF THE STATE OF CALIFORNIA VS. DOUGLAS BOYD ASHBY

Perhaps it's just pride, but when I left my "Response to Alarms" office assignment, I was awarded one of the best battalions in the county, Battalion 8. Again I was in the swing of things. I hit yet another of life's trifectas—a good battalion close to home, in an excellent division, surrounded by good people. All headed by a great boss. What could be better?

Station 28, the Battalion 8 headquarters, was a large station, with a lot of equipment and guys. It was the Whittier Fire Department's Station 1, before they transitioned into the county. It had four apparatus bays. My bay was the first and closest to the offices. In the middle two bays were the engine and truck. Truck 28 was a tillered hundred-foot aerial. In the last stall was the paramedic rescue squad.

The battalion chief's vehicles were Chevy Suburbans. They were beautiful SUVs, and all the emergency warning devices made the vehicles look even more impressive and intimidating while driving down the street with red lights and sirens blazing. It was the little boy in all of us that made responding so much fun.

Being a first-line piece of equipment, every two years we received a new vehicle. That's another blessing of a big organization.

With many calls per day, weariness can creep in, and attitudes can change.

I detested the attitude that some emergencies were just another routine call. When the alarm bell sounded, I wanted everyone out the door and on the road immediately.

No matter how minor the incident might sound, the requests for service, was always an emergency to someone.

⁂

When a response for a structure fire was received, all of the station's equipment would respond. I would typically hang back and be the last one out the station.

We had been running calls all day, so when I went to bed, I fell asleep right away. When the alarm sounded at two in the morning, I wasn't happy.

I was the first to be dressed, completely in my protective clothing, and sat in my Suburban waiting for the rest of the crew to leave the station. The seconds turned into minutes, and the longer I waited, the angrier I became. Finally, I decided to show my displeasure by driving out onto the front ramp and waiting outside the station.

So much for well-laid plans. I had forgotten the front door was on a timer. When the apparatus door came down, it only took a millisecond for it to act as a guillotine and sheer off my light bar and siren. It also destroyed the apparatus door as I drove onto the front ramp.

My anger quickly transformed into embarrassment and then back to anger. How could I be so stupid!

When I started with the Pasadena Fire Department, the apparatus doors were left wide open when the rigs left on a response. However, over the last twenty-five years, attitudes and the culture have changed, and fire stations have become easy targets for burglars and thefts. Today firefighters take the time to lock the stations up, tighter than a drum before the units leave.

Shift change was at eight o'clock in the morning, and Ken, my relief that day, was a little early. We enjoyed the mornings discussing the activity, which had taken place the day before, and swapping a few fire department stories.

It was a beautiful November morning in 1998, and I left my office in a good mood. I jumped into my truck and headed for home. That was where my normal routine ended. Five miles into my commute, I had a chance encounter with a young California Highway Patrol officer that would change my career and life immeasurably for the next year and beyond.

I was driving on a quiet residential street when I passed a CHP vehicle on the side of the road with his red lights flashing. Like most people, as I passed I looked over briefly, out of curiosity. I wished I hadn't. It was just some poor devil getting a ticket, and so it barely registered with me, except the officer looked directly at me and gave me a "you scum ball" look.

He had my attention. It was one of those moments that made me feel odd, as if I had just been caught doing something wrong. I hadn't had a cop look at me like that since I was a car guy back in high school. It was only a split second before I focused my attention back on the road. The uneasy feeling remained, and I couldn't help but wonder if there was more on his mind.

Yep, there was. The next time our eyes met was when I glanced into my rearview mirror; this time his flashing red lights were requesting me to pull over.

What the hell...?

I pulled over to the side of the road, more annoyed than worried. After all, I hadn't done anything wrong.

I was on Imperial Highway, and the morning traffic was heavy, so I rolled down the window on the passenger side so he could approach without being in traffic. I also placed both my hands on the steering wheel so he could see them. I watched as he approached.

Police officers are trained to get out of their vehicle and go toward the rear of their car and approach from the opposite side. This way they have time to view the driver and approach safely.

He didn't advance toward my truck that way; he just got out of his vehicle and walked between our cars and came up to the open window. I took this as a good sign. Whatever he thought I had done, at least he didn't feel threatened.

I remained silent until he spoke; I did not want to appear annoyed. Maybe one of my brake lights was out.

He peered through the open window, giving me a once-over. I was in a sweatshirt and shorts, appearing exactly like what I was—a regular guy, minding my own business, and just going home.

"Can I see some identification?"

"It's in the briefcase," I said, nodding toward it on the seat next to me. Before I opened it, I looked at him for approval. I gently lifted back the top on the briefcase, reached in, and retrieved my wallet. I handed him my driver's license and my gold fire department badge identifying me as a Los Angeles County Fire Department Battalion Chief.

"Do you have any weapons in the car? Someone driving a white pickup like yours was seen brandishing a gun at another driver not far from here."

It might be a good time for a brief review of my family history.

I was raised in a hunting family where firearms were second nature, and my wife's brother and his family would have *all* been murdered if they had not had the foresight to be prepared with a gun in the house. I received my captain's promotion while I was working at Fire Station 14. The station is located just blocks from Florence and Normandy Avenues, where Reginald Denny was almost beaten to death at the start of the Los Angeles riots.

As a firefighter we are always prepared.

"Do I have a gun in the car?" I repeated his question. "Nope," I answered, completely surprised. *Did this idiot think I had been flashing a gun at other drivers?*

"I want to search your car."

Again I answered, "Nope. I haven't done anything wrong; you may *not* search my car."

"I have to call my supervisor then," he said.

As I was relaying this part of the story to a friend of mine, his only response was, "Can you imagine what would have happened if you were Black?" Boy that was sobering.

Another four or five additional CHP cars slid to a stop, and several sheriff's deputies arrived on the scene, all with the "You are a guilty dirt bag look" on their faces.

Man, this was getting serious. I called back to my office and asked Kenny, whom I'd just left, to respond to where I was, I'd been pulled over and things were getting out of hand.

Within the next five minutes, I heard the original CHP officer on his radio requesting his supervisor and then running my license. I also heard, "Code four."

"Code four" is police jargon for "situation stable, emergency no longer exists." Perhaps they had figured out I wasn't the guy they were looking for, or at least that is what I was hoping.

During the buildup of police, I got out of my car and walked to the curb and watched the circus in which I was the main attraction.

When the CHP sergeant arrived, I remember thinking, "Perhaps now cooler and maybe smarter heads will prevail." Nope, they are all cut from the same cloth.

Kenny arrived and told the officers I had just left the office five minutes ago.

"How could he have flashed a gun at a motorist an hour ago and ten miles away?" Damn, those confusing facts; you can't let them get in the way.

The sergeant approached me and said, "Do you mind if we search the vehicle, sir?"

"Yes, I do."

He just looked at me and I noticed a couple of other officers ears prick up.

"Excuse me?"

"Yes, I do mind," I repeated evenly.

"Are you refusing to allow me to search your vehicle? Sir?"

This guy was sharp.

I had inadvertently done the unthinkable; I doubted their authority, and told them again they could not search my car. Things were going downhill again.

I felt like General Custer at Little Bighorn; more cops kept arriving, probably because it had gone out over the radio that they had snagged a battalion chief. Just as I'd feared, things were blowing up way out of proportion.

The sergeant left, had a little powwow with some of his cronies, and returned to where I was standing. He informed me they were going to search anyway. So much for the Fourth Amendment. Double damn this time; another annoying rule.

Facts at this point did not matter; I had to be hiding something. After a few minutes of the police searching my vehicle, they found on the backseat floorboard a black canvas satchel that contained my loaded 9mm Beretta 92FS blue steel semi-automatic handgun.

Oh boy, you should have seen the glee in their eyes. They looked like kids who had just opened their first gift on Christmas morning.

I stood there watching as they put the items from my gun case on the hood of my truck. Meticulously they placed the gun, the magazine, and all of the ammunition out to be displayed for the entire commuting public to see. With each item, their smiles got bigger.

I instantly became one of *those people*. One of the those on the wrong side of the law.

A CHP lieutenant showed up, spoke to me briefly, and said that within a few days someone would get in touch with me. I was then released and was free to go.

I've mentioned I had a slight problem with authority in general and police in particular. I have been a little naive about law enforcement; naive is a polite word for saying I was *stupid*. I believed police officers would respect their oath and tell the truth.

My values were about to be tested to the fullest. I hate it when that happens; I am comfortable with simplistic views toward life. Many of my long-held beliefs were about to be tested via the court system. I was about to find out just how suspected criminals were treated. It is almost funny to me, and I stress the word *almost*, because even now it gets my shorts in a bunch. It was an ordeal at the time, and it consumed thousands of dollars and a year of my life before it was over.

It took me about an hour to get home. Debbie and I sat down and discussed what had just happened. She shares my distrust of authority, and as a loving wife, supported me and was just as appalled.

Later that evening I received a call from Ken asking how I was doing, and he wondered if I had informed our assistant chief.

I told him I hadn't, this was an off-duty incident, and I was embarrassed by the whole thing, and just wanted to keep it as low-key as possible.

Ken took a deep breath and said, "It's all over the department."

Astonished, I said, "How could that be?"

He was a little subdued and said, "Some of our battalion units were on a traffic incident today, and the CHP officers wanted to know if they had heard about the battalion chief they arrested."

Oh man, I didn't think things could get worse, but they did.

As a courtesy, the commissioner of the California Highway Patrol telephoned the fire chief and informed him they had arrested one of his battalion chiefs that morning.

I was caught square in the middle—the firefighters in the ranks, and the fire chief on the top, and everyone in the middle. How embarrassing.

⁎

I had not been at work long the next shift when the phone stared to ring, and ring it did, nonstop. I was getting calls from all over the county. I could not believe the stories I was hearing, everything from me being locked up in jail for a couple of days, to having a shoot-out with several CHP officers.

One of the calls I received was from my old nemesis Deputy Chief "Hang 'Em High." It was a very unpleasant conversation.

He and I were about the same age, and came on the job about the same time. He moved up the ranks quickly. For some unknown reason, he is the one that unsuccessfully tried each year to have me transferred. He was almost joyful in delineating all the rules and regulations I had violated. He shared with me how I was looking at some serious disciplinary actions. During his rant, he never asked how I was handling all of this.

I desperately tried not to think about it, but as the days past, my thoughts became a fertile field of possible scenarios.

I had envisioned a CHP officer coming to my office with an arrest warrant in hand, and handcuffing me before the station crew. Then make me preform the ceremonious "perp" walk to a waiting patrol car.

My thoughts were endless. I even imagined having to surrender myself to the local police station, and have the famous booking mug shots taken. Then being incarcerated until I could find an attorney and post bail.

After a torturous week of playing mind games, I received a certified envelope containing a litany of charges which had been filed in the Whittier municipal court. They included brandishing a weapon, pointing a loaded gun at an occupied vehicle (a felony), carrying a concealed and loaded handgun in my vehicle, driving on a suspended driver's license, and not playing nice with others. As bullies are inclined to do, they tacked on a multitude of other charges in the hopes that at least one would stick. (Just kidding about playing nice, but I am sure if it were in California's legal code, they would have tacked it on.)

The arrest report was like reading a story from Aesop's Fables; any resemblance between what had happened and the truth was completely coincidental. They were acting as if they had just caught the Unabomber. They filed so many criminal charges, I wondered if I was at the same incident.

Facts didn't matter, they had their man. It wasn't about justice anymore, it was about winning...at any cost.

In my wildest imagination, I never thought there would come a time when I would need the help of the man upstairs. I am speaking of the fire chief, not the good Lord, although I am sure he did help me quite a bit.

I requested a meeting with the fire chief, which he granted.

The executive bureau offices are located at the far end on the headquarters building. Two glass doors were installed at the entrance so it is impossible to accidently stumble into the forbidden territory. Few firefighters ever make it past the glass doors.

The fire chief's office is at the far end of all the other bureau offices.

In an effort to familiarize himself with future chief officers, the fire chief conducted a series of interviews with candidates that successfully passed the battalion chiefs exam. My first visit to never-never land was for one of those interviews. My career path was predicated upon that exchange, needless to say it was stressful. Nothing compared to this, my second visit. Not much had changed; he still held my future in his hands.

It had been several days since I had been arrested, and rumors were running wild in the field. I didn't know how far up the department's chain of command the stories went, so I couldn't wait to share my side with the fire chief.

Sitting in the outer office was nerve-racking, it was like being in the preverbal fish bowl; there is no place to hide. I could feel the eyes of everyone in the office staring at me. In reality, they were all going about their own business, and I was just being paranoid.

The constant commotion and hubbub of the bureau presented the opportunity for several chief officers to walk by, none of which would look directly at me or make eye contact. Boy was I glad, because my mouth was dry, hands were sweaty, knees wobbly and I was as nervous as hell. If someone had stopped to say hello, I would have stumbled for a coherent response. I am sure any word I would have uttered, would have come out in a high-pitched squeak.

Finally, his office door slowly opened, and I could swear I heard the door hinges creaking in protest.

Chief Freeman was gracious as we discussed the specifics of what had happened. The meeting was completely the opposite of the one with my deputy chief.

He was concerned regarding the conversation he had with the commissioner of the California Highway Patrol. He had relayed that I had copped an attitude, and "had whipped out my badge and tried to pull rank" on his poor officer. He said I was "visibly disturbed" when they asked to search my vehicle.

I was learning when you assert your rights as a citizen in the *Law enforcement world*, that's copping an attitude.

Just as I was about to leave, the fire chief asked me if there was anything he could do to help. That statement went to the caliber of the man.

My assistant chief, Skip Bennett, was as supportive as the fire chief.

After my conversations with Skip and the fire chief, I was starting to feel a little more comfortable. I thought I had evolved to a point in my life where sweaty palms and a dry mouth were a thing of the past, but as nerve-racking as it was, the real test still lay ahead. I needed to address my entire battalion regarding the rumors that were running rampant.

Early in the morning of my next on duty shift, I assembled half of the battalion in one fire station, and in the afternoon the remaining half in another.

It was uncomfortable standing in front of a group of firefighters and fielding questions. By nature firefighters have active minds, and for an hour, I responded to questions that were beyond my wildest imagination. I couldn't believe the stories that were being spread. At least by the end of the day the entire battalion was armed (perhaps that's a bad word to use) with the facts.

Later that month I would learn facts never got in the way of a good story. I was still the topic of conversation. I received an arsenal, perhaps another inappropriate word, of plastic toy guns in our battalion mail. Firefighters are so sensitive.

Tim my trusted friend and attorney discussed the specifics of my case at length, and he suggested a good criminal defense attorney; trust me, they do not come cheap. Richard A. Leonard and his brother Mike had an extensive background in criminal law. They were perfect for the case.

It took almost a full year before my case came in front of a judge. It wasn't my actual trial. It was a motion to suppress evidence. To keep illegal or irrelevant information from being admitted during trial, my attorney submitted the motion—specifically, an illegal search and seizure, that annoying Fourth Amendment.

As you enter the courthouse, there is a directory that lists the proceedings for the day and in which courtroom they will appear. There it was, prominently displayed for all to read:

"The People of the State of California v. Douglas Boyd Ashby."

Seeing that still gives me chills.

I had my entire family with me, plus Tim and my boss, Chief Bennett. Boy, was I glad Skip was there. He literally saved the day.

I sat up front at the defendant's table with my attorney, Mike Leonard.

You sit inside the little fenced area, placed so you are separated from the common folks. To my left was the prosecuting attorney. Right in front of us was *the judge,* elevated and peering down on the court. The whole environment is designed to make you anxious. They certainly achieved their goal.

To say I was nervous is an understatement!

The deputy district attorney didn't waste any time calling her first witness, the man who had the gun pointed at him. She did a good job of preparing him; she had obviously told him this case involved a Los Angeles County Fire Department battalion chief.

After a few preliminary questions, she got right to the point.

"Do you see the person that pointed the gun at you here in the courtroom?"

Oh man, my heart sank; it doesn't take a brain surgeon to see the only one sitting in front of the witness was me, with a big sign that read *"Defendant."* I was here because of many mistakes; I just sat there and braced myself for yet another colossal screw-up.

The witness immediately responded, "I sure do."

I couldn't have felt any sicker.

"Please point him out to the court."

"That man right there." He pointed directly to my boss, the only man in the room with a fire department uniform.

Both my attorney and I jumped up. I felt like yelling, "Yes, there is a God!"

I surprised everyone, and Mike quietly whispered, "You should sit down."

"Sorry," I sat back down as quickly as I jumped up.

Being one of *those people* was starting to have more weight with me; so much for eyewitnesses. Another one of my long-held values was shattered!

Things were starting to pick up, and over the next hour testimony went fairly well, until the CHP officer started to testify.

The officer was, as they say, "on the horns of a dilemma."

He couldn't tell the truth—that he had just walked up to my window and started asking me questions.

He had already testified that he was nervous about stopping someone with a gun. Therefore, he had to start fabricating a story about how he conducted a felony traffic stop and got me out of my truck at gunpoint.

I was amazed at how effortlessly he spun his yarn.

Testimony went on for the full afternoon, and I couldn't wait to get on the stand and tell my story, especially regarding the CHP's statements and mistruths.

The objective of our court appearance was to get me off, not for me to make a statement. Both Tim and Mike felt we had already won. If I were to take the stand, I would be going against the advice of two outstanding attorneys.

I might be dumb, but I am not stupid. I bit my lip and just sat there.

By the end of the day, I was exhausted, and evidently so was the judge. Instead of giving her opinion, she took the case under advisement, which meant I would have to wait several days for her to render an opinion.

Great, my stomach would be tied in knots for another couple of days.

After the original witness could not identify my truck, my gun, or me, and the whole incident occurred ten miles away in a different direction, it became obvious to everyone I wasn't the perpetrator. Obvious to everyone except the deputy district attorney; she wasn't going to let facts get in her way either. This was about winning.

After a year and a lot of money and frustration, the judge ruled in my favor. The police did not have probable cause to search my truck, which meant the CHP conducted an illegal search. The evidence they discovered became what is known as *fruit from the poisons tree*, so it was all thrown out.

Don't think for one moment the system is about justice. They definitely receive their pound of flesh.

The judge did indeed throw the case out, however it is never over until it is over. The deputy district attorney, did not like the judge's decision, and certainly did not like losing. She informed the court, and my attorney, she had thirty days to file an appeal, and she would indeed file one.

That was just a little "screw you" from her.

The thirty days went by painfully slow. The appeal was never filed.

They still had my pistol, so I went to the lion's den, the CHP office that was holding my gun.

They still wanted to win.

I now needed a court order for the release of my gun, which meant another appearance by my attorney. As I said, good legal council is not cheap; The CHP kept my gun.

The stress of the last year wore me down. I was beginning to understand how many unfortunate people get trapped in the system.

I was blessed to have had the will and the resources to fight it all the way to the end; I cannot imagine what it would have been like for somebody without the finance's to pay for an excellent attorney.

After my case was dismissed, I continued to simmer. My sense of fair play wouldn't let me drop the issue, so I wrote a letter to the commissioner of the California Highway Patrol in Sacramento.

I should have heeded Mark Twain's advice; *"Confidence is the feeling you have before you understand the situation."*

Oh silly boy, I can't believe I thought you could fight city hall.

My inquiry was bounced down to the captain in the very office that handled my case when I was arrested.

The captain and his lieutenant came to my office to interview me and gather all the facts. Within a week, they had completed their disingenuous investigation and had absolved the CHP of any wrongdoing. I had thought I might actually get an honest reply from the commissioner of the California Highway Patrol.

The local captain failed to explain why the commissioner had informed the fire chief I was driving on a suspended driver's license. An issue, which had caused anguish with Deputy Chief Hang 'Em High.

So many questions went unanswered in his final report, I decided to call the CHP captain.

He was taken aback that I actually had the audacity to question him.

His response to my driving record was simple: "I guess our records were wrong." No explanation, no apology, just their database must have been wrong.

Our conversation took a turn for the worse when I said I thought his whole report tortured the truth, and was fraught with misstatements.

I thought nothing he could say would surprise me, however his parting statement was shocking.

"My officers handled themselves properly, and if the circumstances ever arose again, they would act in the same manner."

Their arrogance wouldn't let them learn from their mistakes. His egotistical defiance spoke volumes regarding his and the California Highway Patrol's core values.

This chapter in my life was finally coming to a close. It took a year, but finally it was over. Well, almost...

The judge saw the error of the CHP's ways. The deputy district attorney moved on to other issues, and the highway patrol kept my gun. There was only one loose end... Deputy Chief Hang

'Em High. He still wanted my hide nailed to his office wall. After all, there was the issue of driving on a suspended driver's license.

He could not gather support from anyone regarding punishing me, so he finally tired and dropped his quest for discipline. The issue was behind us, but he never forgot.

In a normal course of things, this should have been my last run-in with law enforcement, but unfortunately, it was not. After all, the life of a firefighter is not normal.

CHAPTER THIRTY-EIGHT

NO ONE LIKES A BULLY

No one likes a bully.

It has become such a problem in our schools, forty-seven states have passed anti-bullying legislation. Bullies run the risk of suspension or expulsion from school. The legislation also includes minor teasing. You might say these laws are bullying you into compliance.

It is an unfortunate part of life, but the strong will always pick on the weak; it is human nature.

You run into bullies in every occupation. The fire service has their share, in all ranks. Even our church-sponsored scouting program had bullies of all ages.

Both of my sons participated in the LDS scouting Program and became Eagle Scouts. I was proud to be their assistant scoutmaster for ten years while they were working toward those awards.

The scouting program exists to teach young men good values and responsibility.

There will always be a certain amount of bullying amongst the young; hopefully when it happens, it creates a teaching moment about relationships.

The scouts in our troop had a wide range of attitudes, from "I love it here, it's fun," to "The only reason I am here is because my parents make me." The latter mind-set was infectious to the rest of the group. Discipline and order was almost impossible if there were too many unruly kids.

One of the scouts was always pulling the rope in the wrong direction. He was detrimental to the entire program, and an unofficial leader of the weaker kids, and bully to boot. Unfortunately, I was going to be stuck with him for the next several years. Time only made his disruptive nature worse.

Twelve-year-olds have an innate sense of fairness. Their attitudes are quickly developing and changing. They know when their fellow scout is getting away with something they are not.

I knew the troublemaker's father and understood the origin of some of the attitude. The cocky kid's dad was a big man, some 350 pounds, with the height to carry it. Everyone has heard of the small man's complex; this father suffered from the big man's complex. He thought his size made his attitudes and opinions more important. He looked intimidating, and he was. He was also a community leader and a successful business executive.

I tried working with this disorderly scout, but he continued to try my patience. Finally, he had flouted the rules once too often. He was just too disruptive. I had exhausted every possible way I knew to keep him under control. The only avenue I had left was to throw him out of patrol meeting, and send him home.

His father took great umbrage to the fact his son had just been ejected from church-sanctioned program.

It didn't take long before his father's car came to a screeching stop in the parking lot. The thump of the car door slamming echoed off the walls of the church. After throwing open the main door to the church his heavy footsteps could be heard pounding down the hallway.

The scouts in our meeting room fell deadly silent, and their eyes were all fixed upon me.

I stepped out of the room to break the awestruck stares and to gain a little privacy. It wasn't that the walls were thin or that we were in a small area, but loud voices have a way of carrying. Even though our voices were loud, neither of us heard what the other was saying. The conversation became heated enough that the bishop came out of his office to investigate the ruckus.

I was about to learn a basic rule regarding church etiquette: it is never wise to have the bishop intervene between two scout fathers. With the bishop's help things were patched up, at least temporarily. The father started to pay more attention to his son's scouting activities, which I saw as a good sign.

After I graduated from college, I was faced with the decision of whether to start teaching in high school, or stay in the fire service; boy, did I choose well. In college, you are taught a lesson and then given a test. In life, you are given a test, which teaches you a lesson.

I'd just failed my tolerance and patience test.

Not more than two months later, the scoutmaster and I took the eight scouts on a weeklong camping outing at Cherry Valley on Catalina Island. Cherry Valley is one of the most popular Boy Scout camps in the western United States. It teaches many scouting values. The trip included a two-hour, twenty-two mile ferry ride across the channel from Long Beach. Once the scouts arrive on the island, there is a one-mile hike to the camp.

Cherry Valley is located on the leeward side of Catalina Island, on hundreds of acres of rolling hills, covered with oak and cherry trees.

Hundreds of scouts from all over the western states attended the camp.

The facility is well designed, with each troop having its own designated camping area. There is plenty of space between campsites.

The camping areas have six to eight two man tents arranged in a semicircle, with a small clearing in the center. They are constructed on a raised wood platform about a foot off the ground, with enough room for two old army cots. You can scarcely stand in each tent.

The outhouse was located far enough from camp to be readily available, or so we thought. When the warm wind blew during the evening, we wished they were located just a little bit further away.

In the center of the entire facility was a small store and canteen. Within walking distance of the campsites were shower facilities.

Each day the scouts had their fill of organized activities, so there was no time for cooking. All of the meals are prepared for the scouts in a large dining hall.

During the evening before dinner was the only time all the scouts at Cherry Valley congregated in one area. Each patrol would line up in front of the mess hall decked out in their proper uniforms and waited for inspection. The sharpest looking and best-behaved group would enter the mess hall first.

The protocol for our troop was to arrive in camp a few minutes before the evening meal to wash and don their scout uniform. It didn't take long before the kids were in a routine.

Randy, our scoutmaster, was a mild-mannered individual who probably never raised his voice in his entire life.

By Thursday, everyone was wearing down and the scouts were becoming a little cranky. The cocky little ringleader decided to test the will of the scoutmaster and refused to wear his uniform properly. When Randy mentioned it to him, he quickly went into a tirade and literally tore his shirt off in defiance, popping off all the buttons. It didn't go unnoticed by all the other scouts, who were amazed their unofficial leader could act so childish. The chaos between the two tainted the environment for the rest of the trip.

Just as common to the island as Boy Scouts were the wild boars. They were imported many years ago and had grown in number, and in legend. The two-hour ferry ride gave ample time to tell the story of how scouts had become the favorite meal of these ferocious wild animals.

One night a boar wandered through our section of the camp, as they did on occasion, snorting its way between the tents. All of the boys were peeking out, wide-eyed, as the massive, scary-looking pig went on his way.

I immediately saw my chance to resolve the problem with our cocky little troublemaker. His tent was close to mine, so it was easy for me to sneak around behind his. The kids were so engrossed in the meandering pig, they didn't hear me lift the rear tent flap. It only took a second to grab the little trouble makers ankles, and start shorting as loud as I could.

He catapulted himself outside the tent in two giant leaps, screaming and waving his arms—as the other kids would say, "just like a little girlie." It effectively ended his reign for the rest of the week.

You may ask if that wasn't a little cruel or if I felt bad afterward for embarrassing the little ringleader. I can honestly say, "Nope." That kid would have tried the patience of Mr. Rogers.

I am sure millions of scoutmasters out there would have done the same, if they had the chance.

By the time we disembarked from the ship in Long Beach, the weeklong trip had taken its toll on all of us. The ship had barely been moored at the dock, when the snot-nosed little ex-ringleader ran straight to his father and showed him the torn buttons on his scout shirt. He accused Scoutmaster Randy, Mister Non-confrontational, of manhandling him. I watched in disbelief as his father made a beeline for Randy, poked him in the chest, and started to berate him.

That was it for me. It was my general dislike of bullies or maybe the fact his kid was irritating me. I was sunburned, exhausted and had been living in a tent over a week, surrounded by hundreds of preteens. I was pushed to the edge, and something inside me snapped.

I stepped in between the two men and poked my finger right back in the big man's chest.

As we shouted at each other, the entire dock, filled with hundreds of scouts and their parents, over a thousand people in all, suddenly became quiet. We paid no attention; we kept right on arguing. There was no bishop this time to separate us.

Eventually the crowd tired of us, the ship pulled away from the dock, the crew went home, and most of the scouts and their families were gone by the time we stopped shouting. It was dead quiet. There was no one around except our wives, sons, and some guy pushing a broom by us as he swept up the trash on the dock. The sun was setting when we finally quit arguing, more out of exhaustion than resolution.

The next day, while I was at work, I received a call from a woman who announced herself as the big man's secretary. Would I please hold for his call?

I couldn't help but think, *how arrogant, why couldn't he just call me directly?*

"Sure," I said with a sigh. I didn't know what to expect. I figured he'd had time to hone his argument, and we were headed for round two.

I waited for what felt like a long while, but I am sure it was only a few minutes, imagining all the things he might have to say. Suddenly he came on the phone, cleared his throat, and apologized.

Whoa, I wasn't expecting that. If you can believe it, I became speechless.

We politely spoke for a few more minutes and then hung up.

I would see him and his family occasionally at different church events. Neither of us wished to speak of our confrontation ever again. I was out of scouting not long after Chris received his Eagle award, so I didn't see much of them after that.

I learned my lesson from this and other experiences; however as I've mentioned, I just can't overlook bullies.

Debbie can arch a single eyebrow that tells me to "just let it go," but somehow I still manage to find trouble for myself.

Both the boys were gone from home, and Debbie was visiting in St. George, which left me alone at home to fend for myself. This was a rare occurrence, since there is always some family member around.

I hate to cook, especially for myself, so I decided to go to the local sandwich shop for a bite to eat.

It was right at dinnertime, and the shop was packed with families. I stood in line waiting for my time to order, when the telephone behind the counter rang. The seventeen-year-old boy making sandwiches dropped everything to answer the phone. It always amazes me how everything stops when the phone rings.

The phone conversation was a brief one, lasting no more than a few seconds, and was terminated by the young man saying, "Oh yea, well, f— you," and then slamming the phone down.

It wasn't as if we were all eavesdropping; his voice was loud enough for everyone to hear.

I couldn't help but think, "Nice touch." I wondered if the owner knows what happens when he is away.

It wasn't more than a few minutes later when a car skidded to a stop in front of the shop and a huge guy kept getting out of the car. That is exactly what I meant; he was so big, it took him two tries to get out.

As he entered the shop, I was the only one between the somewhat-slight sandwich preparer and the big guy. He was red-faced, with veins in his neck protruding, and his fists were closed and white knuckled. He wanted to dot the little guy's eyes and between profanities, he said so.

I would have thought the better part of valor would have been for the little sandwich maker to button his lip, but nooo, he was spewing profanities back that would make a sailor blush.

I stepped between the two, as the shop became unnervingly quiet. I felt like I was going to get my butt kicked from both sides.

I asked the big guy to step outside with me. The environment wasn't the best for carrying on the way he was. Much to my surprise, he did, and I thought things were going to get better.

On our way out the front door, Goliath started to confide in me about the running battle he had with the sandwich shop employees. He lived in the houses just behind the store, and at night, there was constant racket filtering into his home that wasn't consistent with bringing up his family.

As I was nodding my head in agreement, one of the sandwich boy's cronies, who was standing outside the shop, came over and started to add his two cents. The kid was about sixteen, and obviously hadn't learned the proper etiquette regarding a little guy mouthing off to a pissed big guy. My newfound friend turned and without saying a word coldcocked the kid.

Now it was a real donnybrook. All the sandwich shop employees started for the door to help their fallen comrade. Had it not been for a 105-pound young woman, who was in the shop with her two kids, standing in front of the door and fighting to keep everyone inside, there would have been a real brawl just outside the front door with me in the middle.

I could hear the sirens in the background, and I didn't know if it was the sheriff responding or the fire department coming to help the now-awaking teenager, but it didn't matter; help was on the way. I was again standing between parties, trying not so much to keep peace as to keep from getting my own ass kicked. At least I had help from the young mom.

The sheriff and the fire department showed up at the same time, just as the mouthy boy regained consciousness and looked around. He thought flight would be in his best interest, so the last we saw of him was his backside as he ran for cover somewhere in the parking lot.

The big guy was quickly put into handcuffs and placed in the back of a police car. Sandwich Boy, who started the whole uproar, continued to spew profanities until the sheriff had a few words with him. I don't know what was said, but he immediately became humble and quiet.

I thanked the young woman for coming to my aid, and then left after having a few words with the sheriff's deputies.

I did not stick around to find out the final disposition of all the players. I was just glad I was in my truck headed home before anything more happened.

Later that evening when I related the story to Debbie. I could hear the sigh in her voice, and then she said, "You can't even have dinner without getting into trouble, can you?"

Shortly after I retired, Debbie and I took a short trip to Oregon. On our way home we drove through Susanville, California.

Susanville is a small city of eighteen thousand people in Lassen County. It is about one hundred miles north of Reno and surrounded by open desert and mountainous land.

We had just passed the city, and were in the middle of the desert.

Just ahead of us on the right shoulder was a sheriff's vehicle with its red lights on. I guess it is like the moth to the flame for a firefighter seeing an emergency vehicle; you just can't help wonder what is going on.

As we passed, I could see a little guy and a big guy standing just outside the patrol car. What a perfect mismatch.

It looked like the before and after pictures in a Charles Atlas AD, or maybe the poster for *Twins*, the film with Arnold Schwarzenegger and Danny DeVito.[8]

The problem was, the smaller of the two was the sheriff's deputy, and the big guy was, as police say, "the perp."

I was chuckling as we passed when suddenly Arnold made a break for it and hopped a barbwire fence, running out into the desert.

I couldn't help but comment to Debbie, "That poor deputy could get pummeled out here in the middle of nowhere."

Before we had completely passed the little doughnut-loving guy with a badge, he took off after him.

As I slowed and was about to pull over, Debbie asked me what I thought I was doing.

"You're not stopping, are you?" she asked, already knowing my answer.

I got out of the car, jumped over the fence, and took off after them. I came to another fence and kept moving, but I lost sight of them because of a slight incline. Suddenly I imagined getting to the top of the hill and seeing the portly one getting pistol-whipped with his own gun, which would then be turned on me. We were out in the middle of nowhere, and I didn't have a weapon with me at the moment. I left it in…well, never mind.

I took the lack of gunshots as a positive sign, and when I made it to the top of the hill, I saw the sheriff's deputy handcuffing the fleeing offender. He was huffing and puffing as he pulled him upright and back toward the road.

He looked relieved when he saw me, and said, "Hey, thanks for helping. I appreciate it. Not many people stop for us."

It was stupid of me to leave Debbie down on the roadway by herself. As we passed the car, I thought it was empty, but it wasn't. As we made our way back toward the road, I could see there had been someone else in the car, a woman.

When Debbie saw the three of us coming back out of the desert, she stepped outside the car with our camera.

I watched incredulously from sixty yards away as the pregnant woman got out of her car and chased towards my wife along the shoulder of the highway with undisguised fury in every step. Apparently, she took offense to being photographed.

After the three of us made it over the last barbwire fence, the woman was within three feet of Debbie, preparing to give Debbie a sucker punch.

Debbie, God bless her, raised the camera above her head and shouted, "Stop right there or I'll smack you with this!"

The woman, who was poised for a roundhouse, pulled her punch and missed my intrepid photojournalist by an inch or so. It is amazing, but sometimes if you bark an order with enough authority, people will obey it.

By that time we were close enough for the handcuffed suspect to start pleading with his girlfriend not to get him in any more trouble than he already was in.

I was proud of Debbie; all these years of being married to a firefighter must have worn off on her.

Other police started to arrive and the pair was quickly arrested. The deputy came over, shook my hand, and said, "You know, most people wouldn't pull over and offer to help. It's good to meet someone who supports us."

At some point, you have to ask the yourself, *why do we do the things we do?* Why do firefighters offer help to complete strangers?

The fight goes on between nature and nurture. Are we born with a propensity to help, and the days we spend as a firefighter stimulates those deep-seated feelings? One thing is for sure; firefighters are never afraid of getting involved. We want to make a difference.

We are proud of what we do, and usually have some type of decal or sign prominently placed on our vehicles showing the world we are firefighters.

CHAPTER THIRTY-NINE

SOME OF THE BIGGEST BULLIES ARE IN UNIFORM

Vivid lessons from your past never leave you, especially the ones learned the hard way. I am not speaking of the heartbreaks I have witnessed; those are filed in another special area. I am referring to different tactics and lessons learned to keep your fellow firefighters safe. After all, that's the number one job of a battalion chief.

Prior work experiences have a habit of floating around in your mind and do pop up every now and then.

I spent almost a full year in the Los Angeles office, laboring on a project to benefit the public, save money, help reduce wear and tear on equipment, and most of all help keep our firefighters safe. Never in my wildest imagination did I ever envision that after several years of retirement, those lessons would come back to haunt me.

Debbie and I moved to our home in Reno, Nevada, shortly after I retired. We love it here. Every day we realize how truly fortunate we have been.

Reno is different from California in many ways; people appear to be more open and friendly, the air is cleaner and the city much smaller. It has a small-town feel to it. I lived most of my life in Southern California, so the change is refreshing.

Another difference, much to my frustration, is the attitude of the Nevada policing agencies. I shouldn't have been surprised, after all, Nevada's history is rooted in the attitudes of the not so distant old west.

It didn't take long before I tired of having police cruisers fly by me at excessive speed, and realize they were out of control. No one is keeping them in check.

Our police officers were being injured and dying in vehicle accidents at an alarming rate. They were also killing the citizens they serve. What could be so important they would disregard public safety?

The seeds of their arrogance were planted when we arrived in this beautiful state, and would frustrate me for many months to come. Try as I might, I could not let their unsafe driving practices go.

I was approaching sixty and retired. The last thing I needed was to be frustrated about something over which I had absolutely no control. Perhaps my feelings could be traced to my own run-ins with the law, or my own deep-seated dislike for bullies. Whatever the origin, it didn't matter. Time made me all the more infuriated.

As always Debbie would say, "Just let it go."

This was the first time in our lives that Debbie and I lived in an area where you could actually see the changes in the four seasons. Winter was upon us, and Januarys here in Reno are cold. Snow had been falling for weeks. Coming from Southern California, Debbie and I had never experienced cabin fever.

The weather had cleared just enough for us to take advantage of the beautiful day so we drove into town for lunch.

We were worried about adjusting to the cold and snowy weather, but we adapted well, including driving on snowy roads.

The temperature was in the mid-twenties, with no more snow forecast for the next several days. The day was turning out perfect—we were out of the house for a while, had a great meal, and we were still enamored by the beautiful weather. We headed home without a care in the world.

We were on the southbound side of Highway 395, the main highway that runs through the middle of Reno. It is a three-lane, modern divided highway. The road was dry, but there were still pockets of ice here and there, which made driving hazardous.

It is amazing how quickly things change. When I glanced in my rearview mirror, I could see a Nevada Highway Patrol vehicle in the lane behind me, three quarters of a mile back. I was in the fast lane, driving at the posted speed limit of sixty-five miles an hour. It took only seconds for the cruiser to be ten feet behind me, so close I couldn't see his front bumper. His red lights flashing and siren wailing. Closing that distance that fast, he had to be traveling well in excess of hundred miles per hour.

A car was in the right lane next to me, so it was impossible to move over and let the officer pass.

I turned to Debbie and said, "What in the hell does this guy want me to do?"

I sped up and started to move over into the middle lane. We were now side by side, and I got another one of those *"you scum ball"* looks, as our eyes met. The last time I received that look from a cop, it landed me in court and cost me thousands of dollars.

Within milliseconds my past experiences and distaste for the highway patrol flashed before me. "Who does this a..hole think he is, driving so recklessly?"

Now it was personal, so I gave him the universal sign of disapproval. *I flipped him off.*

What happened next surprised me, and certainly Debbie; evidently, the emergency he was responding to became much less important, and quickly faded in his mind. He also took the exercise of my First Amendment rights very personally.

As he was trying to speed past, part of his vehicle was in the divider strip and the other half on the highway, so when he slammed on his brakes, he fishtailed until he regained control and then came up directly behind me. Smoke from his tires and dust from the divider strip flew into the air and blocked our view of each other.

I pulled clear across the freeway to the right-hand shoulder, and the trooper screeched to a stop directly behind me.

I could almost see the steam coming out of his ears as he leaped out of his car and charged towards us.

It took only an instant before he was at my window, white-knuckled and red-faced. He was standing in the ever-ready attack position, his body slightly turned, with his gun side away from me. I had barely time to get my window down.

He could not stand still. He was stuttering as he shouted commands. The blood veins in his neck were the size of a small garden hose. His color was that of an over-ripened tomato. Need I say he was pissed?

Let me clarify the scene just a little bit more. I have a pissed Nevada Highway Patrol Trooper just outside my window barking orders and a very angry wife sitting next to me in the car uttering something like, "You idiot, why did you do that?"

During the trooper's frenzied rant, he managed to ask for my driver's license, registration, and proof of insurance, which I produced along with my fire department identification. He promptly threw my FD ID back through the window and said, "That doesn't mean a G— damn thing up here."

Things were still rapidly deteriorating yet again.

I started to get out of the car, and he bellowed, "Stay in the car."

They like to maintain the aura of superiority; standing in an elevated position, while you're seated in front of them is part of their basic makeup.

He proceeded to tell me about all the terrible things he was going to cite me for, all the infractions I'd committed for which there was a violation. He even threw in some he had just made up on the spur of the moment. It was a complete laundry list. At one point he even threatened to take me to jail. His mind was the proverbial buzz saw of activity; he was thinking as fast as he could, and his lips were moving ever faster yelling the violations I had managed to rack up.

As soon as he paused to take a breath, I interjected, "You gotta be kidding me. You were driving like an asshole. You endangered me, my wife, and God knows who else by driving the way you were."

That got his attention. At least I think it did, or maybe he was just taking a deep breath and wetting his lips so he could continue on his harangue.

I seized upon his silence. "Get out your little pen and starting writing then hotshot. I'd love to get this in front of a judge."

You could see the instant change in him when I wasn't going to be intimidated. Since he had lost his upper hand, he started pondering his own conduct over the past few minutes. How could he defend his actions in a court of law?

It took several more minutes, as both of us were talking over the other, before any semblance of calm came and we started speaking in our normal voices.

He apologized for shouting at me, and said he was going to let me off with a warning.

Both of us had cooled down quite a bit, so I said, "I'm sorry I called you an asshole"—although I didn't mean it!—"I just didn't want you to get hurt driving the way you were."

He looked at me and said, "I wasn't driving dangerously."

Oh boy, that lit my fuse all over again, and we were back at the races, only this time I had Debbie pounding on my back, yelling, "You idiot, he said he was going to let you go!"

That's a real pisser. It was his inappropriate actions that brought us together, and he was going to *let me off* with a warning. It was amazing. Now, that's arrogance.

At this point, neither of us wanted to continue, so he again reiterated his feelings and returned to his car, and we were both quickly back on the road.

This was probably one of the few times his bullying tactics didn't work.

I might add, he was again swerving in and out of traffic, making up for lost time, I guess.

Debbie looked at me and said, "What just happened?" We were a little perplexed, and I truly wished I had gotten my point across to him. His actions were dangerous. After all, he was a cop, and he didn't listen to a thing I said.

⁚⁚⁚

Being above the law is so ingrained in the police culture it is going to take many years to correct. The problem was much bigger than the two of us could resolve out there on the roadway.

I wish I could say this is the end of the tale, and I was left with an interesting story to tell at cocktail parties, but it is not. Unfortunately, time and circumstances would prove me correct.

Within a few weeks, a Nevada Highway Patrol Trooper was killed in a tragic traffic accident only a few miles from where I had been stopped.

Accounts from the accident report have the trooper responding with red lights activated but with no siren, and entering a traffic signal-controlled intersection *against* the red light at seventy-five-plus miles per hour. A young father returning from his son's little league game struck the officers vehicle at the driver's side door, killing the trooper almost instantly.

The trooper was responding to assist at the scene of a reported bomb threat at a gas station, where the fire department and bomb squad had already secured the scene.

Teachable moments are uncommon, and I am sure this one went by the wayside. I seriously doubt the trooper who stopped me returned to his office that evening and shared with others how I viewed his driving.

The death of a peace officer is never a good time to say, "I told you so." However, despite the pain of that incident, drastic changes need to occur within their organization. Every detail should be examined so that tragedies such as this will never occur again.

I could not hold back my anger any longer and wrote to Jerald Hafen, director of the Department of Public Safety. The following is a brief excerpt from that letter.

"Several weeks ago, I had a chance encounter and a heated disagreement with one of your troopers on the highway regarding his inappropriate driving. It saddens me that I was not detained by your ill-fated trooper instead that day. Perhaps if I had, a little more caution would have been used while responding, and maybe, just maybe, the trooper would still be alive today. I share your grief for your fallen officer, and my thoughts and prayers go out to the family."

CHAPTER FORTY

TIMES THEY ARE A-CHANGIN'

In the early days of California the state's population and industrial base was flourishing. It had the reputation of offering endless opportunities for everyone. Los Angeles County also shared in that reputation.

Cities were growing. By 1920, thirty-five individual cities had incorporated. That number had swelled to sixty-eight by 1960. The infrastructure was struggling to keep pace.

The Los Angeles County Fire Department officially got its start in 1923 with the appointment of Stuart J. Flintham as the chief Forrester. The department was designated as the Los Angeles County Forestry Department and Los Angeles County Fire Protection Districts. Most of the county was open land, so the focus of fire protection was in the forested areas and the golden brush. Thirty small fire protection districts were established for community fire protection.

As the number of cities grew, so did the need for fire protection. To protect their citizens, the new cities created their own fire departments, most only having one fire station, and very few firefighters. The county protected the unincorporated areas.

To maintain cost effective city services, many municipalities elected to purchase fire protection from the county. The Los Angeles County Fire Department serves fifty-eight of the counties eighty-eight cities. Of the thirty-five original cities incorporated by 1920, almost two-thirds still maintain their own fire departments today.

The county has over ten and a half million residents, twenty-seven percent of the state's population. One million living in the unincorporated areas.

The history and background of the counties fire departments is unique.

The city of Vernon operates a four-station fire department with eighty-one career firefighters. What makes the department unique? The city population was 112 in the 2010 United States Census. The smallest of any incorporated city in the state. The cities of Sierra Madre and La Habra Heights are within a few miles of the county seat, and have a total combined population of sixteen thousand residents. They still serve their community with volunteer firefighters.

During the sixties, as I was starting my career, the department was still serving two masters. Two thirds of the county was still rural; the roots of rustic fire protection ran deep. Loyalties were divided between the forester and fire warden, which protected the wildland areas, and the consolidated fire protection district, which served the cities. It took many years to shed its image that the county fire department was nothing more than a *country* fire department.

The wheels of progress grind very slowly, so I was frustrated with the pace of progress. Perhaps the impatience of youth, however I had been a captain for a number of years and it seemed the department was stuck in neutral. Time was rapidly passing, but nothing seemed to change.

Change was slow as we emerged from the first half of the 1900's. The transformation of the department might have been inevitable, new and innovative ideas were on the horizon, but a catalyst was needed to put the wheels of progress into motion.

Conducting a national search for the fire chief was unheard of. It had never been done in Los Angeles County Fire Department history. The board of supervisors fully understood there was too much inbreeding within the ranks and it would take an outsider, with fresh new ideas to move the organization into the future.

P. Michael Freeman competed against fire department leaders from across the country. He became the department's eighth fire chief in 1989, the leader of one of the largest and most influential fire agencies in the world. The CEO of a four-thousand-person department, with an annual budget of more than nine hundred million dollars.

Mike Freeman was sort of a wunderkind in fire circles, which meant there was a certain amount of resentment toward him. For one thing, he was young. He was only forty-three when he was appointed by the County Board of Supervisors, and yet he had already been in the fire service for twenty-five years with the Dallas Texas Fire Department.

I think the scope and gravity of his new position was much larger than he first realized. The Dallas Fire Department is a quarter the size of the Los Angeles County Fire Department, and the land mass of the city of Dallas is one-twelfth the size.

The stress the chief must have been under during his first year is unimaginable. Everything was new; nothing was familiar. I am sure the strain was not limited to just him. His family most likely shared the anxiety and frustrations of his new job.

The honeymoon period was short, just long enough for him to become acquainted with both the formal and informal organizations. He recognized quickly, as with many large administrations, the informal organization is what makes the department tick. The undertow of the good old boys club, that had been in existence since the inception of the department, was timeworn, out of date, and needed to be changed.

Not only was he coming from a different fire department, he was also coming from different state. He was not unanimously welcome. The department was divided into several groups. Many embraced the status quo, and were intimidated by the inevitable change. The prevailing attitude was that if it works, don't fix it.

I had been frustrated by the lack of progress and change for many years, so I found a new look at old problems refreshing. I easily fell into the minority of thinking.

It was impressive the way the new boss promised to shake things up. His fresh innovative look at the department broke the cycle of archaic thinking.

It did not take long before changes became personal. Promotions and retirements are a subject of conversation throughout the department. Exams, at all levels are administered at two-year intervals. I had been through the testing process for battalion chief several times and never made the cut. I was never part of the inner circle, so I was at a big disadvantage. I finally came to grip with the fact that my upward mobility was nonexistent.

Shortly after the fire chief arrived, he offered his first battalion chiefs exam. After competing again, I finished higher in the process, but not high enough to be promoted in the first round. Actually, not even high enough to be promoted in the next four rounds. I sat on the list until it was almost terminated. At long last, the fire chief saw the potential in me and I was promoted. I owe a great deal of gratitude to him for giving me a chance.

He was a hands-on leader, a micromanager in the view of some of his chief officers. Within the chief officer's ranks, there was a wide divergent of opinions. The higher you went in the organization, the more opinionated chief officers became. At times, the tension at the top was palpable.

On one occasion, he described his own management style as "hellish." Supporting the fire chief comes with many hazards; not everyone saw him for his deeds, but rather for the way he treated his fellow chief officers.

I hold the fire chief in high esteem and cannot borrow any ill feelings from others. I can only analyze him through my eyes and my own personal interactions. The fire chief treated me with the utmost of respect and supported me at a time when I needed it the most.

Chief Freeman developed a mission statement, a set of core values, and a fire department vision that served as a road map for his administration.

The initial policy's he enacted were different from previous fire chiefs. He went back to the basics. His pride and work ethic were evident from the start. The first steps were small, seemingly unimportant at the time, but they had a tremendous impact on morale. At a quicker pace than most had expected, he swept out old guard attitudes and made improvements needed to ensure we remained a premier firefighting force.

The fire chief enacted a new policy that on all major emergencies, second alarms incidents and above, assistant chiefs and in many cases deputy chiefs were to respond. It was unusual if the fire chief didn't show up on major emergencies.

He loved the job, and he loved fire fighting. The premise was simple, he wanted the top staff to show support for all of the hard work the firefighters were doing. As simple as it was, it had not been done before.

During his two decades at the top, his accomplishments were numerous. Arguably, one of his leading contributions to the fire department, which eluded others, was putting the department in excellent financial shape. He preserved the funding for fire department services across the county, when he led the crusade to pass Proposition E, a special tax measure to prevent the closure of fire stations. Due to his efforts, the voters overwhelmingly approved the measure. The fire department has been on solid ground for more than two decades.

Under his stewardship, the department continued to grow. Eight additional cities joined the consolidated fire protection district. Twenty-four new fire stations were also constructed.

He instituted many new specialized response programs, including its internationally renowned Urban Search and Rescue, Swiftwater Rescue, and Canine Search programs. He upheld the department's reputation as the nation's leader in the use of air attack for wildland firefighting operations by introducing Super Scooper aircraft. It enabled increased water-dropping capability during the peak wild land fire season.

As the fire chief, he felt it was his obligation to inform the public of our accomplishments. He wanted the fire department to be well represented in the media, which was also something that had never been done before.

The board of supervisors, in order to honor his years of service, named the Fire Command and Control Facility after him. Quite an accomplishment and a heartwarming honor; most other facilities are named posthumously.

I would be remiss if I overlooked the contributions of the Los Angeles County Fire Department's union, Firefighters Local 1014. The relationship between the fire chief and the local has been contentious over the years, but the result was an excellent relationship between the two. Each has held the other in check, providing a middle ground, which was tenable for all. No one man can take credit for the all the accomplishments, it has been a mixture of efforts by many good individuals.

At the age of sixty-four, he announced his retirement after twenty-two years at the helm. Chief Freeman was the second-longest serving fire chief.

CHAPTER FORTY-ONE

GETTING OLDER IS BETTER THAN WHAT'S IN SECOND PLACE

Firefighting is extremely dangerous and labor intensive. It is a young man's job.

It started slowly at first, and then began to pick up steam, the way the younger firefighters would look at you. When I first became a battalion chief, I had a little grey hair starting at my temples, and some small wrinkles around my eyes. I'd look in the mirror and think, *Man, you are starting to look old.* That translated into pulling my stomach in, and running just as many laps as the younger firefighters during morning physical fitness.

It was inevitable. I was getting older. Getting up in the middle of the night for a response was becoming a pain in the ass, figuratively speaking, that is. I was starting to have more aches and pains than I ever remembered. Maybe it wasn't any more; I was just probably paying more attention to them than I used to.

As you grow older and get closer to retirement, your whole thought process changes. Routine becomes more palatable, and change more threatening. Each station you visit, the topic quickly turns toward retirement, and you begin to bore the younger firefighters with the same old calculations regarding pensions.

⁎

I was the second battalion chief on an industrial yard fire, and when I arrived, I reported to the command post. The incident commander was a friend of mine; we had many second-alarm fires under our belts together. He asked me to take a hot lap around the fire and report back. Pretty standard stuff.

The fire was burning in an outside yard of a waste reclamation business. There was about an acre of burning waste material, which was being sorted for aluminum cans, bottles, and cardboard before the remainder was taken to the dump.

I donned all of my safety gear and started working my way around the perimeter of the fire. It took several minutes to make my way along the outside perimeter of the business; finally, huffing and puffing, I made it to the rear of the property. To return to the command post, I needed to scale a six-foot block wall, something I had done many times before in my career. While I was preparing to leap the wall, two firefighters ran over and pulled several pallets up against the fence, and said, "There you go, Chief, that'll help."

It was a nice gesture, but the look on their faces said a lot more…"There, that will help the old bastard get over the wall."

I couldn't believe it. Their actions just validated what I had been thinking for some time: *this is a young man's job. How much longer will I be able to do it?* Smarter people than I had anticipated this issue long before I came along.

Within the family of Los Angeles county employment, all jobs are classified into four groups—sedentary, the least restrictive of the classes, to arduous, the most restrictive. Firefighters, police officers, lifeguards, and a few other professions are in the most restrictive class. Firefighting and rescue work is physically demanding, and requires long hours under severe conditions. Either you pass the requirements, or you are literally pushed out the door and forced to retire. There is no light duty for firefighters.

Until recently the mandatory retirement was sixty, and when retirement age approached, most had to be shown the door. Across the country the attitude toward their job is the same; firefighters love what they do. The fire service is part of their personality, and in most cases is inseparable from their core being. They love their work, their fellow firefighters, and in general love helping the people in their communities.

It is common for firefighters to set their retirement date several times, canceling each one before finally retiring. They loved the job and the people they worked with so dearly, it was difficult to retire.

Fire Chief P. Michael Freeman set his retirement date several times before turning the reins over to a younger man.

⁚’⁚

From its inception, the Los Angeles County Employee Retirement Association put requirements into place that protect the system and the employees. Benefits for safety members are skewed toward an earlier retirement, more so than for general employees. The cold hard fact is firefighters wear out their bodies and die sooner, so they can retire a few years earlier than the general county employees

In October 2000, I was injured, and never returned to work again. Over the next year, I visited doctors for evaluation and therapy, all to no avail. After years of emergency work, your body finally rebels and starts to weaken. I could not perform my job to the arduous requirements, so I was literally put out to pasture. I loved the fire service, and was too young to hang up my helmet, but I had no options left. I was forced to leave.

It was devastating to think I could no longer perform my duties.

I had looked forward to retirement for years; old guys speak of it often. Nevertheless, I found I was not prepared. The two families I fostered over the past thirty-plus years would soon be reduced to just one, or so I thought. I knew I was going to be saying good-bye to the friends and colleagues who had helped mentor me over the years. I felt as if I were going through a divorce, and leaving some family behind. It was a bittersweet event.

⁛

Growing up in the scouting program, one of the lessons I learned about camping was you always left your campsite better than when you arrived. I adopted this mantra and changed it a little to reflect my upcoming retirement. Speaking with a group of young firefighters, I would explain to them, "When I leave the fire department, it is going to be a better place." Somehow, it lost its meaning in the translation.

I changed my mind-set, reevaluated my position in life, and slowly slipped into retirement. To my surprise, I did not lose my second family. It just got smaller. The firefighters I grew to know and love have joined me in retirement. Not all that much has changed. Instead of sitting around the kitchen table at the firehouse and telling stories, we sit back at home, in our favorite chair, and telephone a close friend. We reflect upon old incidents, each time making it more exciting. Good recollections have now painted over most of the painful memories. I revisit the highs of my career because they cannot help but make you smile.

It is biblical: *"For everything there is a season, and a time for every matter under heaven."* I have had my time in the sun; I loved every minute of it, and have few regrets. As I get older, I am finding I had a unique and satisfying career. I can honestly say that if I had it to do over, I would not change a thing.

My thoughts mirror Teddy Roosevelt's in his Bull Moose speech of 1912, when he said, *"No man has had a happier life than I have led; a happier life in every way."*

CHAPTER FORTY-TWO

IT'S NOT EASY BEING MACHO

Never one to let a hot idea go up in smoke, Benjamin Franklin established a fire fighting club in Philadelphia called the Union Fire Company. He had started a relationship that would grow to inconceivable heights.

The concept was simple, members of the fire company pledged to help one another should fire break out or threaten one of their homes or businesses. Members of the newly formed company would meet once a month to discuss fire-fighting techniques, establish company policies, and, of course, socialize.

In the two hundred and seventy five plus years of fire department history, firefighting techniques, equipment, and building codes have changed dramatically. However, the love and respect for firefighters across the country is still the underlying theme, and it has grown with time.

Whether a volunteer or professional fire department, the community rallies around the fine men and women that are a part of this great institution. They take pride in their fire departments. There is a fellowship amongst firefighters, and it also exists between firefighters and the community they serve.

I attended the National Fire Academy in Emmitsburg, Maryland. Classes there were always motivating, but the real education was in the pub at night. The original planner of the academy had great insight about human nature, and opened a pub so firefighters from all corners of the country could share common experiences in a relaxed environment. It did not take long before you witnessed the solidarity that exists between firefighters—a special style of friendship unique to the fire service.

In the pages of this book, I have shared my accounts with other emergency organizations, most notably the police. Some might even call those narratives cheap shots, but they are not. Other organizations have camaraderie, but it is minuscule compared to what exists in the fire service.

Close relationships start the first day you enter the training tower, and continue to build over the years. I have been fortunate to have many such long-lasting friendships.

One of my closest friends is Roy Chapman. We did not meet until the middle of my career. Our friendship started with the competitive spirit when we were both studying for the battalion chief's exam.

Roy possessed a fierce competitiveness in whatever he did. He was a natural athlete, and a taskmaster with a superb work ethic. He played as hard as he worked. He was well respected member of the department.

As with everything he did, he prepared meticulously for the upcoming exam. Finally, after enduring months of the lengthy exam process, all of his hard work paid off; his final score was one of the highest. He received his promotion immediately.

I did not fare so well. I was one of the last on our list, a fact he would never let me forget. Roy and I bounced around in different positions before we came to rest in the same field division, headed by a long-term friend of both of ours, Skip Bennett.

The battalion chiefs in our divisions were some of the finest, Roy leading the group. It made the latter part of my career the most enjoyable time I spent in the fire service.

Roy was in top physical shape and always took care of himself, so it was a real shock when he was diagnosed with cancer. Cancer-causing agents surround firefighters on every incident. No one can say for sure why some are afflicted with the dreaded disease while others are not.

Shift after shift, Roy and I worked side by side. I could tell on many occasions he didn't feel well because of his cancer treatments. Nevertheless, he was always positive, not letting those around him know how miserable he was feeling.

He continued to work while he suffered through many years of medical treatments.

Roy and I were about the same age, so our retirement plans mirrored each other's. Neither of us was ready for retirement, but the county thought otherwise. Firefighting and rescue work is physically demanding, requiring long hours under severe conditions. Either you pass the arduous class work requirements, or you are shown the door and forced to retire. Both Roy and I left the department at the same time.

We stayed in touch and after I moved to Reno, each year during the Hot August Nights car show, a group of *old car guys* would come and stay with us. It was several days of reuniting and enjoying the friendship that was so prevalent during our working days.

The last year Roy came, he was completely bald from chemotherapy. He announced that after one final round of treatment, he'd finally be cancer-free. He was happy and was full of energy in spite of everything. He was excited he had only one more test left. Hopefully his treatments would be coming to an end.

I did not hear from him for the next month. I told myself I didn't want to trouble him with a phone call, but deep down I was afraid of what he had to say.

Roy wasn't doing well at all. After valiantly fighting cancer for many years, he was nearing the end. He had been admitted to the hospital a few days earlier, and Linda, Roy's wife, was at his side day and night.

She had left for only a few minutes when Roy turned on his cell phone to call her. He wanted to tell her to come back to the hospital because he knew he didn't have much longer to live.

Finally, I could stand it no longer. I had to find out how he was doing, so I called the cell phone he had just turned on. He quickly answered and sounded horrible. He was like a completely different person. I had trouble comprehending I was speaking to the same happy and healthy friend I had just seen a month earlier.

There was so much I wanted to say, but I couldn't find the words. I knew he needed to speak to his wife, so we cut our conversation short.

Years before when I was visiting my father, as I walked out of his hospital room, I looked back and said, "Good-bye, Dad," but I didn't say "I love you." He died that night, and I never had the comfort of knowing the last words I spoke to him were that I loved him.

As I was about to hang up the phone, I just said "Good-bye, Roy." You would have thought I had learned my lesson the last time I spoke with my father. I wanted to say, "I love you, Roy," but the words never came out. I said them many times in my head before I hung up, but I couldn't utter the words aloud. I'd repeated that unforgivable mistake once again.

Two days later, Roy died. I was never able to speak with him again. I regret to this day I didn't tell him how much he meant to me. For some reason, maybe because he'd shocked me so with his condition and the fact he needed to speak with his wife, I just didn't say what I wanted. It was that old macho mentality from my earlier firefighting days that prevented those words from being spoken. I'll never make that mistake again.

I still have Roy's cell phone number in my telephone; I just can't bring myself to delete it. It is a reminder how the good Lord allowed me to speak with him one last time.

Roy's retirement was cut short, very short, and so was the time I got to spend with my friend. I think of him every day. Some of the ethics I learned from him still live on, and hopefully I will be able to pass them on to others.

Over the years I have received comfort from the philosophy of my close friend, Timothy Joseph Murphy, a good Irish Catholic lad, and from my own wife, a good Mormon lady, regarding life and human tragedy. They both come from different religious perspectives and both have led me to the inescapable fact there is a higher being, *and he does look out after all his earthly children.*

CHAPTER FORTY-THREE

WE ARE GOING
TO BE JUST FINE

The protection of life and property is one of the basic needs of society. Satisfying that need is the cornerstone of a community. The fire service is a leader in public safety.

From the very beginning, there has been a group of civic-minded individuals, who at their core had a desire to help others. They want to make a difference with their lives. Those same qualities are still alive in today's firefighters.

The fire service has slowly moved forward. The struggles have included many setbacks, nonetheless the effort has been worth it. Improvements in working conditions and compensation came to fruition by the efforts of many good people. It has been a collective effort that has served both the community and firefighters.

There are 365,600 professional firefighters employed in the fire service across the country in just over 2,500 paid fire departments. The nation has 1.1 million firefighters who are volunteers, in two-thirds of all fire departments.

Professional firefighters and volunteer fire organizations protect their communities on a twenty-four hour a day basis. The two organizations have many differences, but at their core the values are the same; they get involved.

The 2010 report by the National Fire Protection Association estimates the services provided by volunteer firefighters save US taxpayers billions of dollars each year.

I'd say that's quite a bargain. However, economic statistics are misleading. They do not reflect the brave firefighters who have made the ultimate sacrifice. I became a firefighter in 1967, and since that time, fifty-one Los Angeles County Fire Department firefighters have selflessly given their lives assisting others. Their names are now enshrined on the departments Memorial Wall.

During the career of a firefighter, he will witness unspeakable tragedies. They befall those we serve, and touch the lives of our loved ones. I have had my faith tested many times, but I have never doubted the existence of our Creator. His plan does however sometimes escape me. I struggle with how God can allow terrible things to happen to good people. I know that is a rhetorical question asked by many, and I sincerely doubt if I will ever receive a satisfactory answer.

I might be disrespectful for doubting God's plan, but I can't help but think he has taken too many of my friends and fellow firefighters too soon. Their lives have been cut short for a reason I will never fully understand.

I still have a strong faith. It would be arrogant if I thought I was the only one in charge of my life. The good Lord has blessed my family and has answered my prayers, and left no doubt regarding his existence.

My prayer is others might share the peace, comfort, and success that I have been able to enjoy.

A year in a child's life is an eternity; thirty-four years to an old retired firefighter is a blink of the eye. Looking back, I cannot imagine doing anything else with my life. Most firefighters share that same thought.

Your life is a mosaic of memories and significant emotional events. They come together to shape you as a person. Some experiences change you for a moment; others alter you for a lifetime. My values are a mixture of lessons taught to me from variety of people that I have looked up to from inside and out of the fire department. I have been blessed to have them in my life.

Ronald Reagan said it best: *"We have every right to dream heroic dreams. Those who say that we're in a time when there are no heroes, they just don't know where to look."*[9]

I have been privileged to spend the majority of my life with the Los Angeles County Fire Department and the courageous people who make it so successful. I wouldn't hesitate to do it all over again.

Benjamin Franklin started the first organized fire department, so perhaps it is fitting I conclude with one of his witticisms: *"If you are not to be forgotten as soon as you are dead, either write something worth reading or do something worth writing."*

It has been an honor to work alongside true heroes and giants. They are a humble lot, and just do their jobs. They commonly refute any idea they did anything special. They have made a difference.

I was still in recruit training for the county, and Debbie was six months pregnant, when we arrived on the scene of a terrible car accident in Pasadena, literally moments after it happened.

An elderly couple turned left into the path of an oncoming car, and both were severely injured in the crash. The woman managed to get to the sidewalk before she collapsed, as several witnesses to the accident gathered around her.

She was badly injured, and someone else who arrived about the time we did brought over a blanket and tried to make her comfortable. Seconds later we heard sirens and knew help was close, so Debbie and I sat with her, waiting during those awful moments until additional aid arrived.

Just before the fire engine pulled up, the woman's eyes, which had been dazed and glassy to that point, briefly cleared as if in recognition of her situation. She looked up at me, her face a mask of fear and uncertainty, and she said what they always do, the people in peril. She asked me a question I would hear over the coming years. A question I would always answer the same way.

"Am I going to be all right?" she asked in a trembling voice.

"Yes," I answered. "You're going to be just fine."

Moments later she was being loaded into an ambulance, and Debbie and I were on our way again. We hadn't seen the accident and so were not needed as witnesses.

This was the first time Debbie had seen such a thing, and after we'd driven a few blocks in silence, she suddenly turned to me with a look of concern that nearly rivaled the elderly woman's.

"Was that true?"

"What?"

"Is she going to be all right?"

I took a deep breath.

"No. She's probably going to die," I answered, an assumption borne out in the next day's newspaper account of the incident.

Debbie didn't like that answer. I saw angry tears well up in her eyes.

"Why didn't you tell her?"

I thought carefully before I spoke. I was, after all, behind the wheel of a motor vehicle, and Debbie was, after all, six months pregnant. There was no point in getting anyone upset. Which, ironically, was the basis of my reasoning.

"She'd been through enough trauma. I thought it would be better to give her some hope."

To this day I'm not sure Debbie agrees with my decision. I guess maybe she feels like she'd want to know and therefore would extend the same kindness to someone else.

Kindness comes in many forms, and often it is a judgment call. As firefighters we usually try to ease the pain of people in whatever way we can. I've never witnessed a firefighter come out and tell someone she wasn't going to make it. Our job is to pull them back from harm's way. We pass the victims along to the doctors waiting to do their part. We all, every one of us, do what we can. In life it is what keeps our sanity; we tell ourselves what I told that elderly woman many years ago.

You're going to be just fine.

The fire service has the ability to attract as many good people today as it did at the beginning of my career. Each day is a fresh new beginning, and although times have changed and challenges are different, my beloved fire department will be just fine.

"We do all we can, and it has to be enough."

ENDNOTES

1   **Alice's Adventures in Wonderland**, shortened to Alice in Wonderland, is an 1865 novel written by English author Charles Lutwidge Dodgson under the pseudonym Lewis Carroll.

2   **Dustin Hoffman**, as Mr. Magorium, *Mr. Magorium's Wonder Emporium*. Directed by and written by Zach Helm. 2007, 20th Century Fox. Released on DVD March, 2008.

   At the end of his life, the titular character (played by Dustin Hoffman), tries to impart the lessons he learned over a very long life. His advice was very simple, and yet poignant admonition: "Your life is an occasion. Rise to it."

3   **Chris Farley** (February 15, 1964–December 18, 1997). *Tommy Boy*. Directed by Peter Segal. 1995, Paramount Pictures. Released on DVD November 1999 by Paramount Home Video.

   The late Chris Farley had a classic line in the movie Tommy Boy. He captured my feelings when he said, "Boy, that's going to leave a mark!" Firefighters suffer from a different kind of mark—not the physical ones that everyone sees, but the troubling ones that are hidden.

4   **Randolph Mantooth, Kevin Tighe, Robert Fuller, Julie London, and Bobby Troup.** *Emergency!* 1972-1977. Created by Robert A. Cinder, Harold Jack Bloom, and Jack Webb. Produced by Jack Webb and Mark VII Limited. Universal Studios Home Entertainment has released all six seasons of Emergency!, from 2015 to 2011.

   The television show Emergency! would eventually popularize and promote the new paramedic program, and made Los Angeles County Fire Department and paramedics into instant heroes.

5   **Jim Davis and Lang Jeffries**. Rescue 8. Directed by William Beaudine and Dan Cahn. Produced by Herbert B. Leonard. 1958,

Production company: Cinefilm, Wilbert Productions, and Screen Gems. Released on DVD.

The series portrays two rescue specialists with the Los Angeles County Fire Department, Fire Station 8, whose job it was to rescue people from a variety of dangerous and life-threatening situations. The show predates Emergency! by at least fifteen years.

6   **Michael J. Fox and Christopher Lloyd.** *Back to the Future.* Directed by Robert Zemeckis. Written by Robert Zemeckis and Bob Gale. 1985 Universal Pictures—Studio. Released on DVD December 2002.

Centered in the middle of town is the well-known Puente Hills Mall. Michael J. Fox and Christopher Lloyd blasted Back to the Future from the Puente Hills Mall parking lot.

7   **Andrew McCarthy and Jonathan Silverman, and Terry Kiser as Bernie Lomax.** *Weekend at Bernie's.* Directed by: Ted Kotcheff. Written by: Robert Klane. 1989 Studio, Gladden Entertainment, Distributed by 20th Century Fox. Released on DVD 1999.

I don't know if you've seen the movie Weekend at Bernie's, but if I ever meet the man who produced the film, I'm definitely going to buy him a drink. We got old Bernie, AKA dead gang member, into the back of the ambulance, and I asked one of the apprehensive-looking paramedics if he'd ever seen the movie. He knew what I meant immediately, and as that ambulance made its way through the crowd, I could see him sitting next to our victim waving the arm of our newly departed gang member, in a gesture of the living. That was just enough to calm the crowd.

8   **Arnold Schwarzenegger and Danny DeVito.** *Twins.* Directed by Ivan Reitman. 1988, Universal City Studios, Inc. May 26, 1998, Universal Pictures. Released on DVD December 2002.

9   **Ronald Reagan, 40th President of the United States.** First Inaugural Address, Tuesday, January 20, 1981

ABOUT THE AUTHOR

Douglas Ashby retired from the Los Angeles County Fire Department as Battalion Chief after 35 years in the fire service, beginning his career in 1967 and working his way through the ranks with assignments as diverse as fire prevention, and emergency communications. He earned his B.A. from Cal State Los Angeles and his Master's from Pepperdine University in Malibu. He believes firefighters are just ordinary men and women committed and trained for extraordinary circumstances, and hopes his story and the stories of the brave firefighters he has known reflects their service and sacrifice. He and his wife reside in the Reno-Tahoe area and try to keep up with their grandchildren.